D0295189

NO LONGER THE
PROPERTY OF
ELON UNIVERSITY LIBRARY

ARGENTINA
IN THE
POSTWAR ERA

ARGENTINA IN THE POSTWAR ERA

Politics and Economic Policy Making
in a Divided Society

Gary W. Wynia

UNIVERSITY OF NEW MEXICO PRESS

Albuquerque

781598

Library of Congress Cataloging in Publication Data

Wynia, Gary W   1942-
  Argentina in the postwar era.

  Bibliography: p. 277.
  Includes index.
  1. Argentine Republic—Economic policy—History.
2. Argentine Republic—Politics and government—
1943-   I. Title.
HC175.W87   330.9'82'06   78-55702
ISBN 0-8263-0481-8
ISBN 0-8263-0482-6 pbk.

© 1978 by the University of New Mexico Press. All rights
reserved. Manufactured in the United States of America.
Library of Congress Catalog Card No. 78-55702. International
Standard Book Number (clothbound) 0-8263-0481-8. International Standard
Book Number (paperback) 0-8263-0482-6. First edition.

To Mom and Dad

Contents

Acknowledgments

My interest in this project began in 1964 when I was privileged to spend a year in Buenos Aires and Córdoba with the support of a Fulbright-Hays fellowship. After studying development policy making in other parts of Latin America, where I developed and refined some of the concepts employed in this study, I returned to Argentina in 1971 under a grant from the Midwestern Universities Consortium for International Affairs and again in 1973 with the support of the University of Minnesota.

During both visits I interviewed many of the public officials responsible for the economic policies promulgated in Argentina between 1946 and 1973. I have used interview data, however, to guide my search for primary source materials rather than as an independent source of documentation. I have done so in order to permit others to verify my findings as well as to demonstrate the richness of the material now available to students of development policy in Latin American countries.

Nearly all of the sources listed in the footnotes and bibliography were found in the libraries of the Banco Central de la República Argentina, Banco Tornquist, Banco de Boston, Unión Industrial Argentina, Sociedad Rural Argentina, Confederación General Económica, Confederaciones Rurales de Buenos Aires y la Pampa, Federación Agraria Argentina, University of Minnesota, and the former public officials whom I interviewed. Needless to say, I am grateful for the access granted me by each of these institutions and individuals.

While preparing this book I have benefited from the criticism and advice of many colleagues. I owe a special debt to several Argentines who facilitated my work in Buenos Aires and shared their wisdom with me, most notably former ministers of economy Alfredo Gómez Morales and Roberto Alemann, and scholars Guillermo O'Donnell, Mario Brodeshon, Javier Villanueva, Juan Carlos de Pablo, Marcelo Diamand, and Alberto Belloni. I am also indebted to my American colleagues Peter Johnson, Frederick Turner, Lawrence Graham, Barry Ames, and

Jerry Weaver for their assistance, to Sue Brown who typed far too many drafts of the manuscript, and to Beth Gard of the University of New Mexico Press for expediting the project's completion. Naturally, I alone am responsible for the material in this book. None of those who assisted in the project should be held accountable for the views expressed here.

Finally, I want to thank Annie, Mario, and Paca for accompanying me throughout the entire journey.

1

Politics and Policy Management

This book is about Argentina, a country whose recent political and economic conduct has frustrated its citizens and confounded foreign observers. It is also a study of economic development policy, governmental processes, and the behavior of public officials charged with the formidable task of governing a conflict-ridden industrializing society.

Economic crises and intense conflict among private citizens competing for scarce resources have become commonplace in an increasing number of western nations in recent times. Political leaders in Europe, North America, and South America today seek not only solutions to their economic problems but also insights into the design of institutions that will facilitate the resolution of domestic conflicts over the production and distribution of economic goods. If the 1950s was the decade of recovery, and the 1960s of growth and development, then the 1970s appear to have been the decade of economic crisis, conflict, and deliberate efforts to impose order on unruly societies.

Although the causes of the current malaise may be economic, efforts to deal with them are explicitly political. They involve the deliberate reconciliation of labor and management, agriculture and industry, the state and the private sector. Increasingly, the "social contract" has come to replace the relatively free process of conflict resolution among private groups. As a result, eco-

1

nomic authorities have been forced to concern themselves not only with technical policy decisions but also with the selection of political and administrative techniques that will help them achieve their policy objectives. Politics, therefore, can no longer be regarded primarily as an unwanted intruder into the economy, one that too frequently undermines the best efforts of skilled economists to solve a nation's economic problems. For many it is *the* problem that must be solved in order to execute economic policy successfully. What policy makers require to guide their decisions is the kind of policy analysis that links political and economic considerations theoretically and prescriptively and contributes to an effective plan of action for dealing with public problems. One way to lay the foundation for such analysis is by extracting lessons from recent government experiences that help us identify the kinds of political choices available to policy makers, and to assess the consequences of each. A start can be made, I argue in this study, by examining ecomomic policy making as a process involving the creation of political organizations and programs that induce citizens to cooperate with officials as they try to achieve their policy objectives.

The Politics of Economic Policy Making

We can begin by viewing the economic policy maker as a public problem solver who brings to each problem he selects for resolution not only the economic policy instruments at his disposal but also his political authority and skills. In studying the behavior of the public problem solver we cannot stop once we have examined his policy choices, but must also ask what, if anything, he does to overcome the political obstacles that threaten his programs' design and execution. We want to know, for example, if he has an effective legislative strategy, if he can win over or neutralize his opponents, if he can resolve policy-related conflicts to his advantage, or if he ignores political problems entirely and tries to succeed on the merits of his economic measures alone. In other words, we seek to discover if he has a plan of political action and, if so, how it contributes to or detracts from the execution of his economic policies.[1]

A plan of political action may consist of nothing more than following conventional legislative and administrative procedures. It may also involve a major coalition-building effort to secure the passage of government proposals. Or, where existing institutions and processes are inadequate, it may even dictate the creation of new institutions aimed at resolving policy-related conflicts or mobilizing citizens in an all-out effort to see a program through to its conclusion. In his pathfinding study of the political economy of Franco's Spain, Charles Anderson convincingly demonstrated how the skillful adaptation of existing governmental processes to changing policy needs contributed to the success of economic liberalization in the 1950s. In so doing he illustrated how policy makers can deal with the problem of politics through the technique of institutional design, which allows them to reorganize governmental institutions and procedures in order to improve their chances of securing public cooperation with their efforts.[2] What is important in Anderson's findings are not the particular institutions used in Spain and the example they set but his description of economic authorities as leaders who can deliberately modify their policy-making processes in order to facilitate the design and execution of their programs.

In Latin America, a region long frustrated by the failure of policies aimed at economic development, there is increased concern with the creation of institutions that will maximize the chances of attaining particular development policy objectives.[3] Those who in the past argued that democratic institutions offered the most effective means for implementing the widest range of development policies now find themselves under attack from both the political right and left. Critics on the right, such as the current military leaders of Brazil and Chile, assert that centralized coercive government is required to maintain the kind of public order needed to promote the development of a capitalistic economy; those on the left, like the Cuban leadership, argue that authoritarian rule is essential to dismantle traditional power structures and to implement a radical program of property and income redistribution. Neither believes that the kind of development policy needed in Latin America, be it capitalist or socialist, can be executed through pluralistic, democratic politics where serious opposition is permitted and conflict tolerated. Unfortunately, the lack of well-developed theory linking governmental processes to development policy performance has greatly inhibited scholarly contributions to this critical debate. In order to fill this gap we must begin by identifying the fundamental components of the policy process and then proceed to the empirical analysis of the performance of different institutions and processes.

If we view the making of economic policy as a matter of adapting the capabilities of the state to the achievement of public purposes, then the tools or equipment used by political leaders to solve public problems become the principal objects of analysis. Government officials are not unlike entrepreneurs who must make risk-taking decisions and systematically organize the efforts needed to carry them out. But more than the private entrepreneur, the public official must respond to a wide array of political, social, and economic conditions and therefore requires more instruments in order to succeed. He can, for example, use conventional fiscal, monetary, and foreign-exchange incentives to induce certain economic behaviors. Where such instruments are inadequate, he can supplement them with regulations, controls, political bargaining, and even physical force. In the end it will be the wise use of this policy arsenal that determines his success.

Throughout this study I am concerned with economic policy management by presidents and their ministers. For the purposes of analysis, policy management is disaggregated into *policy formulation* and *policy implementation* activities. The first includes the recognition of policy problems, the generation of alternative courses of action, and the selection of policy objectives and instruments. The second refers to all activities aimed at securing public compliance with policy initiatives. Clearly these two sets of activities overlap somewhat, but to define policy management in this way does not assume that it involves a neat process of sequential decisions yielding optimal outcomes. How and in what sequence particular activities occur are questions that can be answered only by examining the real world of policy making where we are just as likely to find haphazard and unscheduled decision making as behaviors that conform to a rational model. But without some conceptualization of the policy management process to guide us, the systematic comparison of governments would be impossible.

Policy Formulation

Policy formulation has been aptly described as a kind of collective puzzlement on society's behalf, entailing both deciding and knowing. In addition to deciding which "wants" to accommodate and which "needs" to meet, policy makers must puzzle over societal problems and their solutions.[4] Their inquiries seldom resemble the comprehensive survey of ends and means outlined in textbooks on planning because the constraints of time, skill, ideology, and habit limit the search process. Instead, they are usually forced to choose from a limited set of economic policy objectives and then select from available fiscal, monetary, exchange, and regulatory instruments the ones which they believe to be the most appropriate to their objectives given prevailing bureaucratic capabilities.

Two of the advantages of studying policy making over an extended period of time are that it permits comparisons of the ways different presidents react to common problems, and it affords an opportunity to determine whether or not public officials learn from the mistakes of their predecessors. Many sources of learning are known to influence the ways officials design policy.[5] Economic theory with its assumptions, inferences, and prescriptions shape perceptions of problems and the identification of their solutions. Old economic ideas die slowly, especially when the survival of powerful vested interests depends on them. Nevertheless, they are frequently challenged by new theories and must either adapt to changing conditions or give way to innovation. Foreign example, through its provision of analogous problems and suggestive solutions, is another source of learning, although in using foreign experiences one always risks applying misunderstood examples to inappropriate circumstances. A third source of enlightenment, quite common in Latin America, is foreign advice, especially from advisors sent to the region by the United Nations and the International Monetary Fund. Foreign experts can be effective instructors in problem solving, but they are often hindered by their own orthodoxies and institutional interests and are no more immune to misapplied analogies than their hosts. Finally, and most important, one can learn from past experience. What governments lack in "institutional memories" may be made up by the knowledge gained by political leaders and economists who assume policy management roles after assessing the failures of their predecessors.

Anyone familiar with the apparent repetitiveness of economic and political crises in industrializing countries like Argentina is fascinated by the concept of policy learning for it forces us to ask what, if anything, a country's leaders learn from economic theory, other examples, foreign advisors, and their own past. Are the lessons they learn appropriate to their problems and, most critical, is the increasing sophistication of their economic knowledge matched by a greater understanding of the political problems created by their policy decisions? That is, do political leaders learn as much about the process of policy implementation as economists do about that of policy design? We will search for answers to these questions as we examine the conduct of Argentine presidents and their ministers between 1946 and 1978.

Policy Implementation

In industrializing capitalist economies the government may propose as much as it likes, but in the end it is the country's entrepreneurs and laborers, along with its foreign investors, who dispose, for it is they who must make the decisions on which the success or failure of the government's proposals depend. It is the policy manager's job to provide the incentives that secure the conformity of these groups and individuals with his plan of action.

In a utopian world, where policies can be designed to satisfy all private preferences simultaneously, policy implementation would be assured through the use of economic incentives alone. Unfortunately, economic policies aimed at industrialization, especially in primary-product export economies, will satisfy some interests more than others. In fact, what we often find in such societies is pervasive distrust among individuals and economic and social groups that prevents sustained cooperation among the owners of land, labor, and capital. Groups whose interrelationships were well defined in more traditional society, e.g., merchants, landowners, laborers, soldiers, and peasants, frequently discover a new divergence as economic growth and social change occur. They may come to disagree on the nature of economic growth, what causes it and what retards it, and the rules by which its increments should be divided. Except for ephemeral coalitions designed to meet special circumstances, citizens may cooperate very little with each other and thereby hinder further economic growth.[6] Economic development policies, in the short run at least, will become immersed in these conflicts because of their allocation of resources and frequent redistribution of income among economic sectors and social classes. And the more the income, privileges, and power of some citizens are endangered, then the more they will resist the implementation of the policies that threaten them. Moreover, even those who appear to benefit from economic development may be reluctant to cooperate because they do not want to change comfortable habits and practices.

This brings us to the need for a political strategy to guide policy implementation. If we assume that conflict and opposition will accompany economic development policies, we immediately become concerned about the means employed by authorities to secure the compliance of those affected by their policies. Their problem is one of generating understanding and cooperation, especially among the producers, investors, and laborers who make the decisions on which the success of their policies depends. If they cannot attain their cooperation through economic incentives alone, they will have to draw on their political resources and skills as well.

In theory the range of political strategies available to economic authorities is quite broad. The president and his ministers may, for example, take great pains to make their decisions understood through public pronouncements or direct discussions aimed at persuading citizens to invest more, limit wages, hold down prices, work harder, and so on. They may also bargain with citizens over the design and ratification of their policies, informally within the executive, formally through political party representatives in legislative institutions, or, as is increasingly common in industrialized capitalist countries, using quasi-governmental economic councils created specifically to encourage agreement among competing economic interests. The cooptation of interest group and political party leaders through their inclusion in cabinets or administrative bodies is another possibility. Of course, if unable to secure voluntary compliance, authorities may also resort to neutralizing the capacity of their opponents to obstruct them by using public authority and physical force to reduce their freedom to act. In sum, by skillfully adapting political institutions and policy-making practices to their purposes, they may be able to overcome the distrust and opposition provoked by their policy decisions. But therein lies the policy makers' primary dilemma.

Andrew Shonfield has observed in his study of postwar economic policy making in capitalist systems that when designing policies for complex economies the state will find itself "in the posture of bargainer—a powerful bargainer it is true, but one whose whole approach is influenced by the probability that at some stage it will have to enter into a compromise."[7] Yet, if authorities believe they have discovered the technical solution to their country's economic woes, they may not want to sacrifice it through bargaining with those who seek its modification. Unfortunately, there is no easy escape from this dilemma. Either they will have to take their chances through bargaining or risk alienating those whose support and cooperation they need by refusing to negotiate with them.

Ideally, one should employ a political strategy that reduces the possibility of the activation of conflict while increasing the probability of cooperation and compliance. Optimal strategies are, however, seldom feasible in a world where policy makers are not entirely free to create organizations and processes for the sole purpose of implementing economic policies. Still, within the limits imposed by existing legal and political structures, there is room for the adaptation of policy processes to the needs of particular economic programs. For example, elections, political parties, coalition governments, legislative processes, social-economic councils, informal bargaining, the cooptation of opponents, public exhortation, threats, intimidation, and physical repression were all available to Argentine presidents at various times during the postwar era. Their use of these and other devices and the effects of them on the attainment of their policy objectives will be assessed in the chapters that follow.

Finally, I recognize that my view of policy management may disturb some people because of its emphasis on the use of power and authority to secure the conformity of citizens with the wishes of their governors. For those who have traditionally concerned themselves with the abuse of power by public officials, the critical problem of institutional design is not one of encouraging conformity with the wishes of authorities but of limiting authority through various legal devices. While this is a valid concern, it does not change the fact that in most settings development policy making is a process that involves deliberate government attempts to reallocate scarce resources and alter traditional behaviors, often in the face of intense conflict within the country and between its leaders and foreigners who seek to dominate them. Under these conditions the development policy maker is concerned primarily with the creation and institutionalization of enough government authority to manage his nation's public affairs.[8] What should concern us, then, is not only the abuse of power—however we choose to define it—but also how its use by authorities affects the achievement of particular policy objectives. By focusing on political strategy, institutional adaptation, and economic management we can, at a minimum, supplement conventional economic analysis with the kind of policy analysis that is needed to understand development policy performance.

Argentina as an Extreme Case

Few nations offer a better opportunity to study competing strategies of policy management than Argentina, a country where for several decades politics appears to have frustrated the efficient use of ample human and physical resources. In many ways Argentina is an example of the extreme case where economic problems are severe, political conflicts persistent, and successful governmental economic programs scarce. If any country has challenged the ability of public officials to design and execute solutions to difficult development problems, it has been Argentina.

Even more than most of their neighbors, Argentine leaders have struggled since the late 1940s with periodic economic crises brought on in large part by foreign-exchange bottlenecks, the vulnerability of primary-product exports to unstable prices, and the high cost of industrialization.[9] They have also witnessed intense conflicts among political parties and energetic interest groups that process information quickly and respond to government decisions with amazing skill and rapidity. Not surprisingly, many observers of the Argentine scene are convinced that the country's economic performance and its political conflicts are closely related, though there is little consensus about exactly how they influence each other.

According to one currently popular interpretation of postwar Argentine politics, the primary cause of the intensification of political conflict during the past three decades was the country's failure to sustain its rapid economic growth after it had completed the first stage of import-substitution industrialization in the late 1940s. Initially, import substitution had made it possible to satisfy most entrepreneurs and laborers simultaneously. But once this stage came to an end, declining productivity, especially in the export sector, and the rising cost of raw-product and capital-good imports led to foreign exchange shortages, frequent recessions, and a decline in the economic payoffs available to Argentines of all social classes. To make matters worse, instead of accepting new limits on their appetites, propertied elites, the middle class, and workers intensified their competition for the country's increasingly scarce resources. That is, they responded to a zero-sum economic situation by struggling to prevent the gains of their competitors from coming at their own expense, frequently using political means to do what they could not do with economic resources alone. By the mid 1950s, it is argued, the conflicting parties had become polarized into two antagonistic coalitions, one composed of the propertied classes and most of the urban middle class and the other drawn from the labor union-led popular classes. It was the first group's belief that the appetites of the popular classes were excessive and harmful to the completion of the country's industrialization that led its members in the 1960s and 1970s to support authoritarian military presidents and the technocrats who advised them. The latter were convinced that they could increase capital accumulation and industrial investment if they made Argentina more attractive to multinational firms and international banks by repressing the popular classes and suspending competitive politics.[10]

Whether or not the Argentine economy actually took on the character of a zero-sum game, which caused an acceleration of political conflict, is still a matter of debate requiring more empirical investigation. Nevertheless, this interpretation of Argentine politics draws our attention to a critical relationship that deserves further analysis by students of development policy, namely the effects of economic conditions on political behavior and, conversely, the effects of the latter on the performance of the economy. But instead of accepting the popular contention that it is economic scarcity that causes growth-retarding political conflict in industrializing countries like Argentina, we must examine this relationship more closely and determine exactly how economic conditions and political behavior affect each other. It is also essential that we expand our investigation to include the analysis of public policy since it is through the execution of government policies that political and economic behaviors are most often linked. What should concern us is the process through which private economic groups and public officials design and implement economic policy and how that process has shaped Argentina's economic development since 1945.

One of the principal objects of our analysis is the conflicts that develop among private interests and between them and public officials. We already know that policy implementation is easier if there is little or no disagreement about its ends and means. If private economic interests believe that government policies will benefit them, they will behave differently than if they conclude that they will cause some to gain at the expense of others. For example, labor and management are usually more willing to discuss wages and working conditions, and farmers and industrialists to negotiate over taxes and tariffs, if they are convinced that they can gain something through such efforts. Conversely, if they are certain that the needs of others cannot be met without some sacrifices on their part, they will be more reluctant to cooperate with each other or the officials who offer policies that threaten their interests.

Similarly, if public officials believe that conflicts can be resolved without sacrificing the essential features of their policies, they are more likely to try to resolve such conflicts while formulating and ratifying their programs. But if they are convinced that conflicts among competing interests are irresolvable in the short run, or that to satisfy their opponents they must sacrifice vital parts of their programs, they will probably eschew conciliation in favor of the direct enforcement of unpopular policies. In practice, of course, officials in industrializing countries are not usually confronted by situations in which issues are either resolved without conflict or are completely irresolvable, but instead face combinations of the two that involve varying degrees of conflict. To achieve their policy objectives under these circumstances, authorities must either do all that they can to maximize those areas where agreement can be achieved or find alternative ways of securing compliance where agreement is unattainable.

Democrats, Authoritarians, and Peronists

Argentina also offers an excellent opportunity to compare the ways different types of political regimes have dealt with similar policy problems. During the past thirty years, the country has experimented with various democratic and authoritarian forms of political rule. We can therefore use its experience to test in a limited way some of the claims for democratic and authoritarian modes of policy making.

By democracy I mean a political system based on popular sovereignty in which public officials are selected through some form of competitive elections and where the participatory rights of all citizens are respected. Its most prominent policy-making attributes are said to be its consideration of diverse interests, its institutionalization of peaceful conflict resolution, and its pseudoexperimental way of applying trial-and-error methods to solving public problems. Its many weaknesses have also been noted. It can be slow and cumbersome, its decisions may be biased in favor of those who possess the most resources, its incrementalism may not allow for swift or radical problem solving, and its self-interest-motivated bargaining may obstruct society-wide goal setting. Moreover, as a conflict-resolution system it offers little guidance on how to deal with situations in which some groups refuse to compromise with others because of long-standing distrust and animosity. Unfortunately, this latter condition has arisen frequently in scarce-resource situations.

Political democracy has taken many different forms and we will examine one of the more imperfect varieties when we study the administrations of Arturo Frondizi (1958–62) and Arturo Illia (1963–66). Both presidents were handicapped from the outset by the fact that they were chosen in elections from which the party of the masses—the Peronist party—was excluded; naturally this led many Argentines to question their legitimacy throughout their tenures. They also differed from each other in subtle ways. Frondizi, who was elected by a bare majority of the popular vote, saw his electoral coalition disintegrate soon after his inauguration. He was forced by the military to relinquish control over his economic policies to cabinet officers not of his choosing and to suspend constitutionally guaranteed civil rights on several occasions. Illia, in contrast, was a minority president, elected by only 26 percent of the popular vote. Although he governed as a narrow partisan who eschewed coalition politics, he respected the rights of his opponents despite their persistent and harsh attacks on him. How policy was made and executed under these less than optimal conditions for democratic government will be the subject of Chapters 4 and 5.

Authoritarian government is political rule through the supreme authority of a person or group of persons who are not accountable to the people under their control and who cannot be removed short of forceful overthrow. It has become increasingly hard for leaders in low-income countries to resist the temptation to adopt authoritarian modes of political rule. In choosing authoritarianism they have often been encouraged by economic elites and technocrats who desire the elimination of private dispute and other apparent obstacles to economic development. The authoritarian mode of policy making claims an ability to maintain public order and facilitate a rational attack on development problems. It also purports to avoid the delays caused by unnecessary bargaining over policy issues and to contain a capacity for bold institutional reform. Yet, it too has weaknesses. We know, for example, that diversity and conflict cannot always be eliminated by repressing their most overt manifestations. Nor is the design of optimal development policy solutions assured by the inclusion of like-minded officials within a small decision-making elite. And by shunning incrementalism in favor of bold initiatives, the authoritarian invites large policy mistakes, which, when negative feedback is ignored or discouraged, go undetected until their costs become prohibitive.

Authoritarian regimes also take several forms.[11] One of the most common in Latin America has been the military regime,

TABLE 1.1
Postwar Argentine Administrations

	President	Mode of Selection
1946–55	General Juan Domingo Perón	Elected in 1946 and reelected in 1951
1955	General Eduardo Lonardi	Selected by military after leading coup that overthrew Perón
1955–58	General Pedro Aramburu	Selected by military after it removed Lonardi
1958–62	Arturo Frondizi	Candidate of Intransigent Radical party (UCRI) elected in 1958
1962–63	José María Guido	President of Senate selected by military after coup that overthrew Frondizi
1963–66	Arturo Illia	Candidate of People's Radical party (UCRP) elected in 1963
1966–70	General Juan Carlos Onganía	Selected by military after leading coup that overthrew Illia
1970–71	General Roberto M. Levingston	Selected by military after it removed Onganía
1971–73	General Alejandro Lanusse	Selected by military after it removed Levingston
1973	Hector Cámpora	Candidate of Peronist coalition elected in 1973
1973–74	Juan Domingo Perón	Elected in special election after Cámpora stepped down
1974–76	María Isabel Perón	Vice-president who succeeded her husband Juan Perón after his death in July 1974
1976–	General Jorge Videla	Selected by military after leading coup that removed Isabel Perón

which seeks to purge certain groups from the democratic process
or eliminate competitive politics altogether. In postwar Argentina military presidents have pursued each of these objectives.
The most notable attempt to do the first was made by General
Pedro Aramburu (1955–58). Aramburu accepted the formidable
assignment of purging public life of Peronism after the overthrow of Juan Perón in 1955 and then restoring some form of
constitutional rule to the country. He was a transitional leader
determined to use his authority to launch an experiment in circumscribed democratic government. General Juan Carlos Onganía (1966–70) did not share Aramburu's faith in democratic
politics; he was convinced that the country's malaise could not
be cured without authoritarian rule for an extended period. Encouraged by ambitious technocrats who welcomed the opportunity to impose the kind of firm order on the unruly Argentine

society that would help them attract foreign investors to finance the completion of the nation's industrialization, Onganía created one of the sternest autocratic regimes that Argentines had ever known. In Chapters 6 and 7 we will examine how each of these experiments in military ruled fared, paying particular attention to the strengths and weaknesses of authoritarian methods of policy management.

And then, of course, there are Argentina's two Peronist regimes, the first which governed between 1946 and 1955 and the second between 1973 and 1976, during a period that was marked by triumphal return of Juan Perón from Spain in 1973 and his death in 1974. If any governments defy conventional labels, they are the ones created by the Peronists. They have been called corporatist by some, populist democracies by others, and personalist autocracies by still others. Undeniably they enjoyed immense support throughout Argentina and were enthusiastically backed by the country's poor. In 1946 and again in 1973 the Peronists won honest elections and secured congressional majorities, claiming for themselves the mantle of democratic legitimacy. Yet once inaugurated, they used their power ruthlessly against opponents, intimidating, jailing, or exiling them when they challenged their rule. Perón also flirted with some of the techniques of corporatist rule in order to facilitiate his control over the industrial, agricultural, commercial, and labor sectors. During his first presidency his experiments in corporatism were largely symbolic and incomplete. During the second regime the device of the "social contract" was employed to induce economic interest group cooperation with the government's economic stabilization program. In neither case, however, were corporate institutions fully developed and employed; instead, the regime's rather elementary political organizations served as instruments of the very personalistic rule of its leader.

The description of the Peronist regimes requires more than the identification of the goals espoused and the organizations created. We must also study the Peronists' use of political power and their impact on Argentine society. The study of Peronist policy making will shed some light on these questions and contribute to the revision of conventional descriptions of Peronist government and its effects. It will also permit more explicit comparisons of Peronist approaches to the management of the

Argentine economy with those of the country's democratic and military authoritarian regimes.

In the chapters that follow we will learn several things about policy making in postwar Argentina. First, we will see how the substance of economic policy provoked intense conflicts among entrepreneurs, labor unions, and public officials. We will also see how discontent with the way policy was made generated sustained efforts to undermine policy implementation. Second, we will identify and compare some of the strengths and weaknesses of authoritarian and democratic approaches to policy management in a conflict-ridden, industrializing society. Third, and most important, we will discover that even though Argentine presidents differed from each other in many ways, they did have one significant policy-making trait in common, their refusal to play the role of mediator when faced with policy-related conflicts among the country's economic interest groups. Instead of negotiating with their adversaries, they relied on exhortation and compulsion to induce conformity with policies they hoped would eliminate the causes of the nation's social and political conflicts. What they lacked, and what few tried to create, were institutions and processes that facilitated cooperation between authorities and the citizens they governed.

What the study of Argentine policy making teaches us is that the solution of development policy problems faced by industrializing nations may depend not so much on the formal structure of the political regime or even on matters of economic strategy, as on the way leaders approach the problem of building support for whatever solutions they choose. In other words, as important as the content of policy decisions is the ability to devise methods that help authorities convince citizens that their decisions are worthy of support.

The evidence that supports this argument is presented in the remainder of this book. The method of presentation is a narrative one, organized around a set of questions asked of each postwar administration. With the exception of the chapter on the Aramburu presidency, which has been placed alongside that on Onganía to permit comparison of the two military autocrats, the postwar experience is presented chronologically. This has been done in order to facilitate the reader's comprehension of the continuities and discontinuities of Argentine politics and public policy and to provide the basis for assessing each government's ability to learn from the experiences of its predecessors and apply such lessons in its formulation and management of development policy.

The Comparative Analysis of Policy Management

Three questions will guide the analysis of each administration. First, what were the economic problems its leaders confronted, the policy options the president considered, and the objectives and instruments he selected? In each case we will focus primarily on production, balance of payments, employment, and income distribution objectives, and on the use of fiscal, monetary, exchange, and regulatory policy instruments.[12] Second, how did presidents perceive the problem of politics raised by their economic programs and what strategies and techniques did they employ to secure compliance with their policies? To organize the comparison of political strategies, I will focus on the specific techniques employed during each phase of the policy-making process; the phases examined are those of policy initiation, formulation, consultation, ratification, execution, and feedback.[13] Third, how did the choice of political techniques increase or reduce support for each economic program? My ultimate goal is an assessment of different political techniques and the generation of statements about their relative effectiveness.

Admittedly, the assessment of policy management is somewhat problematic. One is tempted to judge policy makers according to the fit between the intention and the outcome of their policies. As straightforward as this seems, it can be terribly misleading. Obviously the failure to achieve a policy objective cannot be blamed entirely on a faulty policy design or political strategy, for many unanticipated and unmanageable conditions may intervene to undermine the government's effort. Moreover, policy implementation is an ongoing process, a voyage of discovery, and therefore should not be judged entirely on assumptions of its predictability. Thus, rather than rank and compare Argentina's governments according to the proportion of their goals they accomplished, more indirect tests will be applied to their performance.

What interests me is not the wisdom of particular economic policies but the effectiveness of the political strategy used in their management. In other words, I want to know how the institutions and processes employed by Argentina's presidents to design and execute their policies helped or hindered their implementation. Accordingly, I will focus on two performance criteria when assessing each administration. First, since each president inherited serious policy problems from his predecessors, I will concentrate on his policy learning and how well he applied such lessons to the selection of economic and political strategies. I will be most concerned with the political problems raised by new economic knowledge and policy innovation, paying particular attention to the compatibility of political and economic strategies. Second, and most important, I will assess the effectiveness of the government's political strategy and institutional choices in securing the understanding and cooperation of entrepreneurs, laborers, traders, and financiers during the design and execution of its policies. The obstacles encountered by presidents will vary with the content of their programs, their prevailing political strengths and weaknesses, and the resources and will of their opponents. Their success in dealing with the last will in turn depend on their creative adaptation of political institutions and processes to these conditions. How well they did will be the central focus of this inquiry.

My analysis of Argentine policy making is not intended to yield precise measurements leading to a rank ordering of postwar governments on an effectiveness scale. It will, however, facilitate the identification of the relative strengths and weaknesses of different forms of political rule for making and executing development policy. Moreover, it will also help us discover the enduring features of Argentine policy management that have hindered the solution of the country's economic and political malaise.

PART ONE

The Peronists

2

Prelude to Perón

Many of Argentina's postwar development policy problems can be traced to the stubborn survival of institutions and attitudes that arose in the nineteenth century, were rescued and revised during the Great Depression, and then assaulted by the Peronists in the 1940s. It is essential, therefore, that we briefly review the political economy of prewar Argentina in order to comprehend both the Peronist attack on traditional institutions and their tenacious fight for survival thereafter. My purpose is not a comprehensive review of this much studied period. For detailed treatments of the era's personalities, political intrigues, and legislative debates the reader is advised to consult the works of Peter Smith, Rodolfo Puiggros, and other astute observers.[1] I will limit myself to a brief examination of prewar economic institutions and the measures adopted to preserve them by focusing on agricultural, industrial, and labor policies during the 1930s.

The Export Orthodoxy

We must begin with agriculture and its dominance within the Argentine economy before 1930. The dramatic increase in the country's prosperity at the turn of the century, and its rapid Europeanization thereafter, were due in large part to its bountiful production and export of beef, mutton, and grain. At the

21

same time, the cynical manipulation of its political processes by a small community of cattlemen, financiers, and exporters, its dependence on European markets and suppliers of manufactured goods, and its deep penetration by British capital were also products of the same rural economy. The importance of agricultural and livestock exports as both the historical promoters of economic growth and the stubborn obstacle to structural economic change has made Argentina's rural economy an object of public debate and official concern since 1930.

The development strategy that guided the growth of Argentina's export economy had its origins in the 1870s and 1880s when rural producers and political leaders discovered the comparative trade advantage made possible by the temperate climate and fertile grasslands of the country's pampas region. With Europeans demanding Argentine foodstuffs, it seemed only natural that the country's economy should become inextricably tied to the international trading system and that its leaders should design their policies in accordance with the system's dictates. Until World War I, the primary-product export strategy reigned supreme over Argentine life, lulling its designers into the complacent belief that they had unlocked the door to endless prosperity. Fortunes were made on beef and mutton exports and thousands of Spanish and Italian immigrants found new lives in Argentina as colonists and tenant farmers. Cities, especially the national capital, were transformed from muddy villages into modern metropolises whose architecture, transportation, and communication were replicas of European models.

The self-satisfaction of those who guided the country's development did appear justified, for their efforts had by 1914 created a thriving rural economy whose products were transported to market on efficient British-built railroads, processed and shipped by eager foreign packers and exporters, and carried swiftly to the markets of Europe where they were exchanged for the manufactured goods demanded by Argentine consumers. Nevertheless, Argentina's prosperity was not as secure as the country's leaders had assumed. It was not until the shock of the 1929 depression, however, that they were finally forced to acknowledge the vulnerability of the system they had created. But even then, when faced with the most devastating economic crisis the country had ever known, Argentine authorities refused to abandon their treasured economic beliefs. Instead, they tried desperately to adapt and revitalize them in order to preserve the way of life they had enjoyed for the past half century. To understand their obstinacy and its effects on the development of the Argentine economy, a brief look at the country's cattlemen and farmers and their political influence is necessary.

The Argentine Rural Society (SRA), organized by cattlemen in 1866, reigned supreme as the country's most influential domestic economic interest group until the 1930s. Despite the fact that its membership was limited to only 2,500 cattlemen, or just 10 percent of Argentina's stockmen in 1930, twelve of fourteen ministers of agriculture and 48 percent of all cabinet ministers between 1910 and 1943 held memberships in the Society.[2] The rural sector was not a monolith, however, and no matter how successful it was on rural policy matters, the small, elitist Rural Society could not legitimately claim to represent all farmers and cattlemen. In 1912 it was challenged by the less affluent immigrant and tenant farmers who organized the Agrarian Federation (FAA). Twenty years later cattle breeders launched their own campaign against the SRA cattlemen by creating the Confederation of Rural Associations of Buenos Aires and La Pampa (CARBAP). Although the preeminence of the Rural Society was not immediately threatened by either group, it could not avoid sharing a little of the rural stage with them.

The sudden appearance of the Agrarian Federation in 1912 gave Argentina's small farmers a vehicle for expressing their grievances against the rural elite. Most of those who joined the FAA were immigrants from Europe who had begun as colonists in newly opened territories north and northwest of the pampa or as sharecroppers and tenant farmers who raised grain on sections of large cattle ranches located on the pampas. Largely through their efforts, and those of stockmen who engaged in mixed farming, cultivated land increased by fifteen times (to 10 million acres) between 1872 and 1895 and cereals rose from a negligible share of exports in 1870 to 50 percent of export value by 1900.[3] As the Argentine grain trade became increasingly export oriented after the turn of the century, the practice of colonist farming, usually limited to units of about eighty acres, gave way to tenant farming of units up to five hundred acres. Not unexpectedly, the tenant farmers' dependence on cattlemen or absentee landlords for their livelihood gave rise to substantial resentment of the landowning class and eventually led to a concerted campaign to call government attention to the plight of the tenant farmer through the use of the FAA.[4]

Unlike the cattlemen, whose grievances against the packers and each other were limited primarily to pricing and marketing issues, the tenant farmer was also concerned with fundamental questions of property and income distribution, and demanded legislation that would facilitate the easy purchase of land. As might be expected, the FAA, which claimed 27,000 members and responsibility for the creation of over one thousand cooperatives by 1943, came to view the smaller but more powerful Rural Society as one of its principal antagonists, especially when the latter insisted on acting as guardian of the land-tenure status quo. Nevertheless, when it came to defending the rural sector from its urban critics, or to seeking protection aginst the vicissitudes of the international economy, the Agrarian Federation could set aside its differences with cattlemen in order to present a united defense of the rural economy, as it did frequently when the entire sector was threatened by Perón after 1945.

Disagreements between those who specialized in breeding cattle and others who used their large holdings of pampa grasslands to fatten cattle had long existed within the rural economy. But it was not until 1932 that the breeders formed CARBAP and joined with other regional breeder societies to limit the influence of fatteners and foreign meat packers over the level of cattle prices, which CARBAP spokesmen claimed were traditionally set through a fattener-packer conspiracy to squeeze breeders. By 1943, CARBAP had grown to a membership of 10,000, more than double the size of the Rural Society. With three other regional federations, it organized the Argentine Rural Confederation, which dwarfed the Rural Society in numbers if not in economic clout or social prestige. Its policy differences with the Rural Society appeared insignificant to anyone outside of the cattle sector. Yet, it never ceased campaigning for regulatory measures that would give its constituents market advantages over rival fatteners.[5]

The export of meat and grain brought prosperity to many Argentines, but it afforded them little protection against the vicissitudes of external markets or exploitation by foreign traders.

It was their acute sense of vulnerability, especially after trade was threatened by the outbreak of World War I, that led Argentine cattlemen and farmers to demand government support of minimum commodity prices and to insist on the regulation of monopolistic meat packers and shippers. But not until the Argentine economy and the way of life that it sustained were seriously threatened by world depression in the 1930s did they gain the kind of protection they wanted.

Cattlemen had always felt that they were disadvantaged by the commercial practices of the meat trade, but as long as trade was buoyant, inequalities in their business relations with foreign packers were tolerated. The decline in overseas markets after the First World War, however, intensified the producers' suspicion that packers had deliberately encouraged a crisis of overproduction in order to buy cheap and sell dear. Thereafter, all cattlemen rejected quietist proposals that promised more favorable prices once world markets had been revived. Instead they favored state regulation of the packing industry through the adoption of price controls along with the creation of a national meat company that would compete with the foreign packing firms. To the packers' surprise, Argentine cattlemen secured congressional approval of their regulatory proposals in September 1923, after seven months of intense debate. But the stockmen's apparent victory was short-lived, for on the day that price controls went into effect the meat-packing companies suspended the purchase of livestock and, after paralyzing the industry for twenty-two days, forced the government to rescind the new regulatory scheme. The reform effort did not end, however, with the loss of one battle. In the end it was the cattleman and not the packer who emerged victorious.[6]

As before, a collapse of foreign markets prompted new regulatory proposals, but this time, rather than bowing to the tactics of the foreign packers, government policy makers, backed by the cattlemen, held fast to their conviction that the rural economy could not survive without greater protection of producers against the debilitating effects of world depression and exploitation by meat packers. The 1923 measures were reintroduced in the legislature in June 1933 and became law in October. The law created a National Meat Board governed by nine directors charged with setting minimum and maximum liveweight prices.[7] Soon thereafter, the Board organized the long-sought government-subsidized but privately managed Corporation of Argentine Meat Producers (CAP), which it authorized to process up to 11 percent of the meat sent to the British market under the provisions of the Roca-Runciman bilateral trade agreement signed with the British government in 1932. As interesting as the legislation itself was the government's attempt to rationalize interventionist measures that obviously contradicted the traditional free-trade orthodoxy. Publicly, the scheme's defenders held that the free market was not endangered by their actions but rather had been saved from the monopolistic practices of foreign packers who had too long abused the rules of the market place; moreover, as they claimed with some pride, they had not only rescued the free market but Argentina's rural economy as well. Nevertheless, though it was not acknowledged at the time, the depression-induced reforms initiated important changes in the Argentine political economy by making available to public officials new instruments for exploiting as well as regulating the rural economy.

The need to rescue a private economic activity from debilitating market forces was even more obvious in the grain trade after the depression. Only 33 percent of the country's annual beef production was exported in the late 1920s while 70 percent of its wheat and 80 percent of its maize were sold abroad, making cereal production even more vulnerable to external conditions. If government intervention into the grain trade had depended entirely on the political clout of grain farmers, few reforms, if any, would have been enacted. But political power was not necessary this time since government ministers recognized that the vulnerability of one of the weakest and poorest groups in Argentine society posed a serious threat to the economy's postdepression recovery.

For two decades the Agrarian Federation and legislators representing cereal regions had campaigned for a program to stabilize the cereals trade by fixing grading standards, constructing grain elevators, and freeing farmers from their financial dependence on local storekeepers. But, as had occurred with the beef industry, it was only after the world crisis threatened to destroy cereal farmers that the champions of regulatory measures found an attentive audience in legislative chambers and executive councils. This time government ministers seized the initiative by decreeing the creation of a grain regulatory commission in November 1933 and assigning it both control over foreign sales and the authority to fix minimum prices for wheat, maize, and flax. Instead of raising prices by withholding supplies from the market, a practice employed in Canada and the United States but ruled out in Argentina because of the scarcity of storage facilities, the commission sought to cover the losses that would have been borne by producers by financing the margin between the official and world market prices out of government profits on recently established exchange control operations. Meanwhile, grain continued to be exported through the facilities of private exporters with the government paying them for the handling charges. Not to be left behind, the legislature finally ratified the scheme in September 1935.[8]

Argentine economic authorities had little choice but to rescue their rural economy during the 1930s, even at the cost of fundamentally altering the market rules that had fostered the country's economic growth so successfully for four decades. Clearly, if they had not acted, thousands of producers might have gone bankrupt, bringing down the export economy with them. Change was required and public officials acted swiftly and creatively. Were we to assess the policy-making process of the period in the rural arena alone, there is little doubt that it would score high, especially in creativity and adaptiveness. But farm policy was not the only issue that Argentina's economic authorities faced after the depression. Turning to the increasingly important matter of industrialization, we not only discover a less creative response to another depression-induced policy problem but also see how, in trying to preserve the export economy, the country's conservative leaders made their last stand against industrialization.

Uninvited Industrialization

Industrialization could not expect a warm welcome from those who directed the Argentine economy before 1929. According to the conventional economic wisdom of the time, internal commerce and domestic manufacturing were marginal activities that were best left to the immigrants who had taken advantage of the small opportunities opened by rising consumption after the turn of the century. It is not surprising, then, that the Argentine Industrial Union (UIA), created in 1886 by a few hundred small manufacturers, had little impact on government policy during its formative years. With its very measured requests for modest tariff protection falling on deaf ears, the Union's leadership reluctantly accepted the prevailing free-market orthodoxy of the rural elite and concentrated its efforts not on undermining the rural economy but on defending the vulnerable industrialization effort from the threat posed by the country's emerging labor movement. In fact, one cannot help but be impressed by how much the industrialists' fear of the labor movement, which led them to lobby in Congress against the eight-hour day, Sunday holidays, and the right to strike, distracted them from their obvious subservience to the dictates of the managers of the traditional export economy.[9]

The biggest boost to industrialization came unintentionally from the collapse of foreign trade in the early 1930s. While it did not immediately transform the export economy, the sudden loss of foreign suppliers did force Argentine authorities to adopt many stopgap measures that could not help but improve industry's chances. Among other things, the skillful economic team that designed the Agustín P. Justo administration's recovery program imposed exchange controls and dual exchange rates, improved tariff protection for industries believed essential to domestic consumption, and—aided by a plan prepared by England's Sir Otto Neimeyer—established a predominantly private-sector-managed Central Bank to coordinate monetary and credit policy.[10] As might be expected, tariff reform was the most controversial of the new policies and traditional free traders fought hard and often in Congress and before government ministers to limit the new tariff measures. On their side the free traders had a large and heterogeneous coalition: it included not only farmers and cattlemen but also spokesmen for Argentina's European trading partners and the small but vocal congressional wing of the Argentine Socialist party (which distrusted manufacturers and opposed their demands for special privileges). On the opposite side the industrialists, who had become more assertive in the defense of their cause after 1929, were joined by treasury officials, who viewed higher tariffs as a convenient source of public revenues, and publicists like Alejandro Bunge, whose nationalism demanded the use of industrialization to restore the national pride lost during Argentina's humiliating postdepression trade agreements with Great Britain.[11]

The measures demanded by the Industrial Union were summarized in its widely distributed pamphlet *Seis Leyes Económicas*, first published in 1935 and reedited three times during the following decade. In a bit of overstatement, the UIA claimed that it had been industry rather than agriculture that had rescued the country after the depression by overcoming a host of legal and economic obstacles to expand its operations and absorb 400,000 of those unemployed in 1931. It was only just and rational, therefore, that new legislation be enacted to facilitate even greater industrial expansion. Included on its list of legislative proposals were an antidumping law directed at cheap imported goods, a "drawback" measure permitting the deduction of import tariffs on components of goods elaborated nationally and exported, and a law giving priority to the creation of a customs and foreign trade commission that would manage the transformation of tariffs from strictly a source of government revenue to an instrument of industrial policy.[12] Gratification was not immediate, however, since the combined legislative opposition balked at most of the proposals. Even after the adoption of some of them, such as the selective application of the drawback arrangement, they went unenforced. To add to the industrialists' woes, the government, over UIA objections, promulgated some long delayed, though admittedly minimal, labor legislation designed to assure a six-hour work day for minors and to guarantee some financial compensation for dismissed workers.[13]

Despite this relatively hostile environment, Argentine manufacturers, stimulated more by the demands of the Argentine consumer and a reduced supply of imports than by government policy, expanded the value of their production in constant pesos by 54 percent between 1935 and 1945.[14] To be sure, virtually none of this expansion involved heavy industrialization, but it did include machinery, chemicals, and fuels as well as the traditionally dominant food and textile industries. With such dynamic growth the ostrichlike posture of the antiindustrial forces became less and less tenable and the self-confidence of industrialists stronger. Yet, before they would succeed, the industrialists had to fight and lose one more legislative battle.

The last successful campaign of industrialization's opponents was carried out within the Argentine Congress against Minister of Finance Federico Pinedo's Plan of Economic Reactivation in 1940. Pinedo, a free trader who had modified his stand in the face of the depression and had led the government in designing the interventionist rural policy reforms of the mid 1930s, offered his Reactivation Plan in response to the outbreak of World War II and the fear that the depression experience might be repeated as a result of the cutting of shipping lanes to Europe. His proposal deliberately included something for almost everyone in the hope of building a legislative coalition broad enough to secure passage of what was essentially a proindustrialization, moderately Keynesian policy scheme. For agriculture he included the obligatory government purchase of all production that could not be placed on the foreign or domestic market. For the middle-income urban consumer, represented at that time by the Radical party in Congress, there was a new public works program and special credits to finance private as well as public construction. And finally, for industry he offered credit supplied by a proposed government-owned industrial bank, increased tariff protection, and the long sought enforcement of drawback and antidumping statutes.[15] Contrary to opposition propaganda, Pinedo, the pragmatic free trader, did not advocate the supremacy of industrialization within the Argentine economy; on the contrary, his principal objective, he argued, was the preservation of the traditional export economy, a goal that could be achieved only through some industrial expansion to lessen the country's external vulnerability. Failure to act in 1940, he warned, would lead to more rapid and less manageable industrialization in the near future.[16]

The adoption of Pinedo's program depended largely on acceptance by rural producers and their legislative spokesmen of his assertion that industrialization was essential to their own self-preservation. Starting with the anticipated enthusiastic support of the Industrial Union and the initial acquiescence of the Rural Society, Pinedo secured the program's passage by the Senate, then controlled by the government's conservative coalition, only to be halted by an aroused opposition in the Chamber of

Deputies. The opposition was led by CARBAP, the breeders
society that had risen a decade before to challenge the Rural
Society; its resistance to industrialization came from its suspicion
of Pinedo's motives and fear that the cattle breeder's economic
standing would be endangered if industrialization succeeded. Its
lobbying campaign would have come to naught were it not for
the opposition Radical party which, instead of supporting industrialization as one might have expected from an urban, middle-
class political party, voted against it, claiming that a protected
domestic industrial sector would exploit the consumer through
its artificially high prices. In the end, CARBAP and the Radicals
were joined by the Rural Society as well, making the conservative alliance of the rural sector with the party of the urban middle class just as potent an obstructionist force as it had been
during the 1920s.[17]

Pinedo failed but the shift toward industrialization could not
be halted. The turning point came, as it often does, in the wake
of a wholesale change in government administration, this time
following the military coup of June 1943. Significantly, it was
also in 1943 that Argentine industrial production surpassed rural
output in total volume, having already exceeded it in value in
1936. The military government soon made it clear that, for the
first time, Argentina's political executive would encourage rather
than obstruct the country's industrialization. Although it proposed
no comprehensive development scheme, it did sanction the creation
of an Industrial Credit Bank, much like that proposed by Pinedo in
1940, built several new military factories to produce armaments and
other materiel, and later boasted with some exaggeration that under
their leadership 25,000 new industrial establishments had been
started between 1943 and 1946.[18]

The Unwelcome Working Class

The rise of organized labor in Argentina can be conveniently
divided into four phases, each shaped primarily by the strategies
adopted by the labor movement itself, the rate of commercial
and industrial growth at the time, and public policy toward labor
organization. During the 1880–1900 period, the Argentine labor
movement was established under the influence of European
ideologies and the leadership of European immigrants. Between

1900 and 1930 the movement grew, reaching a peak of unity and militancy in 1920, only to weaken under the strain of internal conflicts thereafter. It went into decline in the postdepression 1930–43 period as a result of government repression and the difficulty of reorganization under adverse political and economic conditions. And finally, after 1943 organized labor was transformed by populist political leaders into a potent political force and given many of the labor reforms that it had consistently failed to achieve on its own.

The Argentine labor movement arose under the leadership of a small, European-born proletariat during the last decades of the nineteenth century. Foreign-born outnumbered Argentine-born urban workers between 1895 and 1914, bringing with them the socialist, anarchist, and syndicalist doctrines that had already taken root in many parts of Europe.[19] Gradually their activism grew as strikes, which had averaged only three a year between 1887 and 1893, increased eightfold in the mid 1890s and rose to over one hundred per year after the turn of the century.[20] At about the same time the organization of the first national confederations began to meet with some success, although continual battles between socialists and anarchists greatly reduced their stability and longevity. Labor protests, led primarily by the anarchist Argentine Regional Workers Federation (FORA), continued to rise, reaching a peak in 1920 when over 3.7 million work days were lost in strikes, a record that was not broken until the late 1940s.[21] (See Table No. 2.1.) Nevertheless, the labor movement did not succeed in forcing industrialists or the conservative governments before 1916, or the Radical party governments thereafter, to sanction collective bargaining and regular wage contracts. To be sure, after brutally repressing strikes as they did during the infamous *semana trágica* of early January 1919, the Radicals did promulgate some palliative but weakly enforced legislation fixing employer responsibility for on-the-job accidents, sanctioning the eight-hour day and the forty-eight-hour week, and creating a public employee pension program. On other issues like collective bargaining, however, the Radicals proved more responsive to the demands of the Industrial Union and its affiliate, the notorious Asociación del Trabajo, which fought to deter labor organizations through its strikebreaking Liga Patriótica, than to those of the labor movement.[22]

TABLE 2.1
Average Annual Workdays Lost in Strikes*, 1911–45

1911–15	350,154
1916–20	2,296,481
1921–25	278,739
1926–30	404,390
1931–35	966,640
1936–40	511,301
1941–45	303,727

*Strikes are recorded only for the Federal Capital

Source: República Argentina, Dirección Nacional de Investigación Estadística y Censos, *Síntesis estadística mensual de la República*, Año I, no. 1, enero de 1947, p. 7.

Economic depression and increased government repression reduced the labor movement to its lowest ebb since the turn of the century after the Radicals were driven from office by the military and its conservative supporters in 1930. FORA was immediately banned and its leaders jailed or exiled. In its place the General Confederation of Labor (CGT) was created in September 1930. Though similar to FORA in structure, and led by a coalition of socialists, communists, and syndicalists long active in the labor movement, it shunned FORA's militancy under the constant threat of government intervention. The CGT's compliant posture toward public authority and its industrialist foes is not surprising given not only the ever present threat of physical repression but also the economic deterioration that had begun in 1930. As jobs grew scarce in the immediate aftermath of the depression, workers were forced to accept lower real wages and longer working hours and to shun union activities.

Not until the middle of the decade, when industrial activity was again on the rise and union membership increasing, was the CGT able to assert itself with the militancy that had characterized its predecessors.[23] By the time of its first national convention in 1936, it claimed a membership of 262,630 workers, a total which increased to 330,681, or 75 percent of the country's organized workers, in 1941. Of even greater significance for the future of organized labor was the fact that nearly 80 percent of the CGT membership still came from the traditionally well-organized, nonindustrial work force, while only 5 percent were employed in the newer textile, metalurgical, and chemical industries.[24] (See Table No. 2.2.) This left a large and expanding pool of workers for mobilization by a new generation of political leaders, who in the decade ahead, would make conservative industrialists and their allies pay dearly for their neglect of the working class.

TABLE 2.2
Distribution of General Labor Confederation
Membership by Economic Sector, 1941
(Six largest components)

Transportation	118,000
Construction	73,500
Commerce	45,000
Food Processing	24,550
Government	17,000
Textiles	10,000

Source: Rubén Rotondaro, *Realidad y cambio en el sindicalismo* (Buenos Aires: Pleamar, 1971), p. 145.

Governing by Exclusion

After a decade of combating the effects of the depression, Argentina's conservative leaders could take some pride in their performance. Their task had not been easy, and their decisions had not endeared them to many of their fellow citizens, but their rule had been marked by some innovative and productive responses to very grave economic conditions. The ministers who served the Justo regime after 1931 clearly perceived the dangers of inaction in the face of the world economic crisis and can be credited with overcoming some of their free-market prejudices in order to reorganize commodity, export, and exchange markets as well as to impose greater central control over monetary and credit policy. As a result of their leadership, Argentina managed a gradual but steady economic recovery and relative price stability after 1934. To be sure, their policy responses included many controversial measures, such as reductions in public expenditures between 1930 and 1934 and the granting of humiliating concessions to traditional trading partners like Great Britain in order to revive foreign commerce. Yet, it was under the same conservative regime that public expenditures were increased by 86 percent and the number of government employees per 100,000 inhabitants enlarged by 26 percent between 1935 and 1942, clearly reflecting a deliberate expansion of government activity.[25]

But what about the policy process through which these recovery measures were designed and implemented? Certainly one could argue that heavy-handed, military-backed conservative rule offered many advantages to economic authorities determined to impose a recovery program that demanded economic sacrifices from many quarters. Nevertheless, that which they gained in short-term expediency and policy-making efficiency must be weighed against the very high long-term costs of further discrediting the Argentine political system through the abuse of constitutional procedures and the exclusion and repression of political competitors representing a majority of the Argentine people.

The Radical party governments that ruled Argentina between 1916 and 1930, for all of their faults—and they were many—had tried to govern according to constitutional norms and competitive electoral practices. Their conservative successors, in contrast, not only ignored constitutional rules with great frequency, but cynically manipulated them with no apparent concern for the damage they were doing to the country's fragile democratic institutions. The manipulation of electoral laws, which began after the 1930 coup that overthrew the Radicals, was continued during subsequent elections. Fearing Radical party victories in 1931, the military government prohibited the candidacy of several party leaders, provoking the abstention of the party's largest faction from the election. With its principal opponent out of the way, the government coalition of conservatives, antipersonalist Radicals, and Independent Socialists, calling itself the Concordancia, easily placed General Agustín Justo in the presidency and captured 63 percent of the seats in the Chamber of Deputies and 87 percent of those in the Senate.[26] Faced by increasing opposition, the Concordancia again used manipulated elections to retain the presidency and its congressional majority in 1937, thereby assuring conservative rule through the end of the decade. Against such determined leadership the congressional opposition, led by the small farmer-oriented Progressive Democrats and urban consumer supported Socialists, had few opportunities to influence government policy and had to be satisfied with public denunciations of fiscal austerity, trade concessions, and political repression.

The most notable contribution of the Concordancia to Argentine policy making was its renewal of the traditional practice of excluding one's opponents from the initiation, formulation, and implementation of government policy. Before 1900, exclusive rule by public officials representing the agroexporter elite had been managed with great effect and little serious opposition. In contrast, the Radicals who replaced them in 1916, though prone to narrow partisanship and patronage, openly bargained with opposition parties in the legislature and encouraged the influence attempts of a variety of private sector groups. With the return of the conservatives in 1930, and their determination to save their depression-ravaged economy, came the restoration of the old practice of exclusion.

To the conservative's surprise, the tactics which they had employed to good effect during the late nineteenth century, when newly arrived immigrants were too preoccupied with their economic survival to challenge them, provoked bitter and sustained opposition when tried again after 1930. Organized labor, for example, would not conform willingly to official policy but had to be repressed, often violently. Traditionally quiescent industrialists, now more sophisticated and in possession of expanding economic resources, were less tolerant of public officials who refused to amend their export orthodoxy with tariff and credit concessions to domestic manufacturers. And political parties, like the personalist Radicals, having once enjoyed the experience of political rule between 1916 and 1930 only to have it denied them arbitrarily, refused to lend their support to the government's abuse of national institutions. Yet despite the obvious long-term threat posed by this disenchanted and heterogeneous opposition, Presidents Justo, Ortiz, and Castillo held fast to their divide-and-conquer political tactics, ignoring their critics and the emerging social and economic problems that their complaints reflected until it was too late to save the Concordancia from its nationalist opponents in the military.

In sum, despite its initial success in managing short-term economic recovery, the conservative regime that governed Argentina for thirteen years after 1930 gradually sowed the seeds of its own demise through its refusal to respond to any but the most traditional economic and political interests. By reconfirming Argentina's subservience to the dictates of its trading partners and those who guided its primary-product export economy, it provoked a nationalistic reaction that would eventually mature into a concerted campaign to liberate the country from foreign domination. By the mid 1930s the critics of conservative rule, who included political parties like the Progressive Democrats and the personalist wing of the Radical party, had added many nationalistic and ambitious junior army officers to their ranks. By denying these groups and the emerging forces they represented an opportunity to influence the way the country's resources were used and distributed, Argentina's postdepression leaders undermined their own effort to preserve the institutions of the export economy. For once denied the means to influence the content of government decisions, those who were excluded eventually came to reject the process by which those decisions were made and turned from attacking policy to attacking the system itself. Most critical in the long term, by reinforcing the notion that Argentine policy-making was a kind of game in which those who made policy were the obvious winners and those who did not were the equally obvious victims, Argentine conservatives set political precedents that could not help but influence the practices of their successors. After all, rule by exclusion did offer some obvious short-term advantages for dealing with groups who posed immediate threats to one's policies. For those who would eventually displace the conservatives, the temptation to turn the tables and use some of their own exclusionary tactics against them would be hard to resist.

Policy Problems Unsolved

By 1943 Argentina had changed significantly from the country governed by the Radicals in the 1920s. As we have seen, responsibility for most of those changes belonged to the economic forces set in motion by the changing world economy and Argentina's involuntary adjustment to them. Before concluding this chapter we must consider the development policy implications of depression-induced economic change and conservative responses to it, by focusing on the policy problems the conservatives left behind for their successors to contend with after 1943. Of the many that would confront postwar leaders, those involving the management of the vulnerable export economy, the challenge of accelerating industrialization, and the welfare demands and political power of the working-class consumer were the most critical.

Despite the official contention that interventionist measures had not significantly altered the laissez-faire rural economy, the depression had set in motion lasting changes in the country's political economy if only because it shifted the main arena of economic competition and conflict among farmers, breeders, fatteners, packers, and consumers from the marketplace to the chambers of public commissions and government ministries. During the 1930s the Argentine government had assumed responsibility for the protection of 450,000 farmers and cattlemen by intervening in the economic processes that threatened them. Moreover, in so doing they unintentionally provided the means that their not-so-conservative successors could use after 1943 to control the price and volume of exports and domestic food products, often to the disadvantage of rural producers.

It is not surprising that farm policy issues continued to dominate the public agenda long after industrial production had surpassed that of the rural sector in the early 1940s. Despite repeated efforts to liberate the country from its dependence on commodity exports, after 1943 it was to the rural producer that economic authorities frequently turned to supply the foreign exchange needed to finance industrial growth. This gave the rural elite the weapons it needed to fight long and hard throughout the postwar period to resist policies that sought to redistribute its earnings to urban activites and reduce its hold over the economy. Farm policy confronted policy makers with some of their most formidable problems after 1943, involving the rationing of short commodity supplies between foreign and domestic consumers and the distribution of scarce financial resources between rural and industrial producers. Failure to deal with them satisfactorily would make rural policy the Achilles' heel of Argentine development policy in the years ahead.

Typical of the newly politicized problems that economic authorities would face repeatedly after the war was the phenomenon known as the "beef cycle." The beef cycle involves the fluctuations in beef production that commonly result from the inverse relationship between beef prices and the slaughter of cattle. Other things being equal, the slaughter of cattle tends to decline when wholesale beef prices rise because cattlemen will take advantage of higher prices to increase their herds while enjoying the same level of income from the slaughter of fewer cattle. Such behavior is largely due to the fact that the cattleman's product, the cow, is also his capital good and, therefore, when opportunity strikes in the form of higher prices, he will increse the size of his herd in order to take advantage of higher prices at a later date with more marketable stock. But because cattlemen will retain cows and bulls in response to higher prices, the immediate supply of animals for slaughter will decline and, as a result, prices will continue to rise. Finally, when grazing limits are reached, a condition common in Argentina because of its dependence on natural pastures, cattlemen will be forced to increase their shipments to market, producing a drop in prices and a likely increase in new shipments as competitors rush to compensate for declining prices. When shortages are again reached, prices will rise and the cycle will be repeated, as it was several times in Argentina after 1945.

To manage the beef cycle and its effects on domestic and foreign consumers, the policy maker needs well-timed, countercyclical tax, credit, and price measures. Not only does he require the technical tools and data needed to forecast the peaks, troughs, and lengths of such cycles, but he must struggle to remain free of policy and constituent commitments that might hinder his use of the right instruments at the right time. His problem is further complicated by the fact that any solution to the beef cycle involves the trade-off not only between production and slaughter but also that between domestic consumption and exports. In the face of rapidly expanding domestic beef consumption, he would be forced to decide whether to satisfy relatively inelastic domestic demand or limit it in favor of exporting more beef in order to provide desperately needed foreign exchange. While the former would be popular with the mass of Argentine consumers, the latter would from time to time be demanded by a critical foreign-exchange shortage. Unfortunately, conflicts like this one, between economic necessity and political popularity, were to become familiar ones to postwar Argentine presidents.

There were also the issues raised by accelerating industrialization. By 1941, Argentine industry, though greatly enlarged, was still dominated by the traditional food-processing and textile firms. Chemical, metal, machinery, and fuel industries accounted for only 23.8 percent of the industrial work force and for 22.8 percent of the production of firms employing more than five workers. Moreover, the industrial sector continued to be characterized by the prevalence of small firms; only 56 of approximately 60,000 firms employed more than 1,000 workers while 43,523 of them employed 5 or less. (See Tables 2.3 and 2.4.) Any government determined to implement long-term industrialization, therefore, would have to decide upon the policy incentives required to stimulate the growth of selective industries. Decisions would also have to be made on the role of foreign capital and its regulation, and on whether or not the state should move from the use of conventional fiscal, tariff, monetary, and credit incentives to the subsidization and management of industrial enterprises. As we shall see, it was Argentina's misfortune that no consensus emerged to resolve any of these issues during the postwar era.

TABLE 2.3
Relative Importance of Principal Industries in 1943
(Percent of total)

	Workers Employed	Value of Production
1. Food, Beverages, and Tobacco	22.6	37.1
2. Textiles	17.9	18.4
3. Machinery and Vehicles	10.5	6.6
4. Forestry Products	9.7	4.6
5. Metals and Metal Manufacturers (excluding machinery)	8.8	7.3
6. Stone, Sand, Glass, and Ceramics	4.7	3.2
7. Leather and Leather Goods	4.4	4.1
8. Chemicals, Pharmaceuticals, Paints	3.9	5.8
9. Printing and Publishing	3.4	3.2
10. Paper and Cardboard	2.0	2.1
11. Petroleum, Coal, and Derivatives	0.6	3.1
12. Rubber and Rubber Manufacturers	0.5	0.7
13. Other	11.0	3.8
Total	100.0	100.0

Source: United Nations, Economic Commission for Latin America, *Economic Survey of Latin America 1949*, p. 174, Table 48.

Finally, someone had to answer the question of the future role of the working class in Argentina's changing political economy. Industrialization had increased the number of industrial and commercial workers quite rapidly as thousands of laborers from

TABLE 2.4
Industrial Establishments in 1941

Size	Number of Firms	Number of Workers
1. Without workers	13,184	—
2. Up to five workers	28,296	70,087
3. 6 to 10	6,914	52,295
4. 11 to 50	7,236	159,023
5. 51 to 100	1,197	83,800
6. 101 to 200	644	89,779
7. 201 to 500	340	102,698
8. 501 to 1,000	90	60,855
9. More than 1,000	56	113,460
Total	57,957	731,997

Source: Juan Carlos Pereira Pinto, *Aspectos de la historia económica de la República Argentina durante los últimos setenta años 1900–1971* (Buenos Aires: Editorial El Coloquio, 1973), p. 189.

the country's interior hastened to join those already in Buenos Aires. If there was one matter on which industrialists and Argentina's conservative leaders were agreed, it was the necessity of preventing the growth of militant unionism by refusing to grant economic concessions to the emerging urban proletariat. Industrialists were guided not only by their traditional fear of labor militants but also by their conviction that working-class demands, if not checked early, would eventually undermine capital formation by transferring their profits to their employees. Their strategy for preventing the workers' mobilization rested heavily on one essential assumption, namely that the state would contribute directly to the antilabor campaign or, at worst, remain neutral as the managers of industry dominated their employees. Should the state, as it did after 1943, take up the cause of industrial workers, either out of a sense of social justice or more likely because of a desire for working-class political support, the industrialists' strategy would fail and a host of new policy issues would be unleashed. Then, rather than asking how long labor could be held back in order to stimulate the growth of capital, one would be forced to determine which of labor's demands could be met without undermining industry. Similarly, by granting labor the right to strike and bargain collectively, public officials would have to take upon themselves the task of regulating and resolving labor conflicts.

The legitimization of organized labor and collective bargaining was also accompanied by new incomes policy issues, ranging from the increased probability of inflationary wage-price spirals to the design of comprehensive measures directed at dealing with them. Questions of equity, technical feasibility, and political acceptability would take on a new importance in the design of economic policy, and the government's answers to them would become critical in charting the course of the nation's development. As a result, the policy maker's task, already complicated by the necessity of managing the recently intervened rural economy and of coping with increasing industrialization, would become even more formidable as Argentina entered the postwar era of labor activism.

3

Perón and the New Political Economy

Few Latin American leaders have influenced their nations' politics for as long a period as Juan Perón, the soldier-turned-politician who shaped political events in Argentina for nearly thirty years before his death in 1974. In 1946 he rose from obscurity to erect a government that defied conventional labels. In fact, whether it was authoritarian, democratic, corporatist, populist, liberal, or conservative is still a matter of dispute. What we do know is that he began his political career while serving as labor secretary in the military government that succeeded the Concordancia after a coup in June 1943. Three years later he won a presidential election and then launched a campaign to build a modern, mass-consuming society using the authority of the state to promote rapid industrialization, national economic independence, and the redistribution of wealth to the laboring masses. To attain these ends he ruled in a belligerent and occasionally autocratic manner, frequently making it impossible for his critics to remain in the country. In 1951 he was reelected. Four years later, in September 1955, he was overthrown by his military colleagues and forced to flee into exile from where he continued to influence Argentine politics until he returned from Spain in 1973 to serve as president for one year before his death. For three decades Perón was a master performer on the political stage, but one whose promises were seldom matched by his achievements. Nevertheless, he altered his

country's political and economic life more than any of his predecessors. For that reason alone his performance merits close
scrutiny.

The Road to Mass Consumption

The rise of a little known army colonel from the minor
bureaucratic post to which he had been assigned after a military
coup in June 1943 to the presidency of Argentina three years
later has already been chronicled by many observers and needs
no lengthy repetition here.[1] What does interest us about his
political origins is how the commitments he made in gaining the
presidency affected the policies he implemented after taking office.

Perón began with the conquest of the Argentine working
class through the adroit enforcement of new labor laws which
strengthened unions that joined his emerging political movement
and punished those that did not. In this he was not too different
from other ambitious Latin American leaders in the 1930s and
1940s who used public authority and policy rewards to mold
previously ignored or repressed labor movements to their personal political needs. What makes Perón's campaign stand out
from the others is the swiftness and thoroughness with which he
transformed the Argentine labor movement into a loyal instrument of his rule. Beginning from his post in the obscure labor
department, which he elevated to a secretariat of labor and social welfare in November 1943, Perón gained control over the
General Confederation of Labor (CGT) by adding thousands of
previously unorganized industrial laborers to its membership and
by handpicking new leaders for the reorganized unions. His
principal instrument was a 1943 military decree creating the
Regulation of Professional Associations—later amplified into the
Professional Association Law of 1945—that made government the
patron of the labor movement by granting it the responsibility
for recognizing one industrywide union as each industry's only
bargaining agent, and by guaranteeing unions the right of organized political activity, a right long denied them by previous
governments.[2]

The reorganization of the labor movement did not come without some resistance from the older unions, such as the railway workers' La Fraternidad, which fought vigorously against Perón's campaign to take over the CGT. In fact, Perón's victory was not secured until, in one of its most historic decisions, the CGT Central Committee voted 21 to 19 on October 16, 1945, to call a "revolutionary strike" to secure Perón's release from jail, where he had been placed by military colleagues opposed to his presidential candidacy. With his dramatic release by the military the next day, in response to the CGT protest, the marriage between the political leader and his working-class followers was consummated.[3] Where generations of labor leaders and Socialist party legislators had failed in their attempts to mobilize Argentine workers into a powerful political force, Perón succeeded by adroitly using state authority to create new unions and to provide benefits previously denied workers, such as government tribunals to arbitrate labor disputes, obligatory paid vacations, and guaranteed social security benefits for CGT members. Most important, he also transformed the traditional relationship among employers, workers, and government by making the government labor's principal ally in its struggle for social justice rather than its enemy.

Perón's labor reforms, though crucial to his conquest of public office, were only one component of a larger scheme of industrial development. After assessing the humiliation suffered by Argentina during and after the depression, he and his advisors reasoned that Argentina's economic development would always be unnecessarily constrained as long as domestic consumption responded to the dictates of the export economy and the traders who exploited Argentina's dependence on foreign markets by purchasing its agricultural exports at the lowest possible price and selling Argentina manufactured goods at the highest. These constraints could be removed, they reasoned, by turning the tables and letting national consumption and production, rather than external demand, determine the pace and form of national development.

Using the industrial nations on which they had become so dependent as their models, they began by asking what it was that had brought them their economic prosperity. They concluded, to no one's surprise, that industrialization and mass consumption were primarily responsible for economic development of Western Europe and North America. But the industrial countries too had suffered from the worldwide depression and therefore were hardly compelling models to be emulated during the 1930s and early 1940s. Once more their record was examined, albeit superficially, and again inspiration and guidance were found, this time in the economic programs the industrialized countries had adopted during their postdepression recoveries. If "pump priming" and deficit spending could help restore economic prosperity by increasing consumption and restoring idle industrial capacity to full production, they concluded, the same instruments could be used by Argentina's economic authorities to create an industrial capacity where there has been little or none before. Just as the industrial economies had been lifted from the depths of the depression, so would Argentina escape economic dependency through industrialization and mass consumption.

No one would have been more surprised by this reasoning than the recently converted Keynesians of the industrial nations, who had not directed their measures at creating new industries where few existed but at smoothing the business cycle in their already industrialized economies. Yet, the Argentines' twisting of Keynes to serve their own needs is not all that surprising. Argentines, like many Latin Americans, frequently had turned in the past to European and English theorists in search of solutions to their own problems, often revising and adapting them, and making them almost unrecognizable to their authors.

With their assessment of the country's economic development problem completed, the Peronists next turned to the design of an appropriate strategy to solve it. To free their countrymen from excessive reliance on imported goods, they proposed the rapid expansion of the domestic consumer-goods industry using high tariffs and an overvalued exchange rate to protect it from foreign competition. To induce industrial growth they turned to the Argentine consumer, whose demand for goods they promised to increase through higher wages and easier credit. Thus, rather than limit consumption in accordance with the country's import capacity, as had been done in the past, they planned to stimulate it in order to ignite higher industrial production.[4]

Critical to the success of the Peronist plan was its controversial redistribution of income and power from rural producers to urban consumers and industrialists through tax, price, wage, and credit measures. Perón did not hide his intention to improve the condition of those who had been least favored by the traditional export strategy by transferring wealth from the rural rich to urban entrepreneurs and laborers. Nor did he ignore the obvious fact that the implementation of so sudden a shift in income would be resisted by the cattlemen, farmers, exporters, and trading partners who stood to lose in the short run. He was convinced, however, that by expanding the power of the state and using public authority to regulate private-sector responses to his redistributive measures, all resistance could be overcome.

The Peronists at Work

Doubts about the seriousness of Perón's intentions were laid to rest even before his inauguration when, at his urging, lame-duck President Edelmiro Farrell shocked the Argentine rural and financial elite to its foundations. On March 25, 1946, Farrell nationalized the Central Bank, transferring it from the hands of private bankers to a board of public officials, asserted state control over all private bank deposits, and, most disturbing to rural interests, created a state trading organization that extended the government's authority to control all import and export commodity trading.[5] Against a history of economic domination by cattlemen, meat packers, exporters, and private banks, these measures were viewed by some, especially those most threatened by them, as the beginning of a revolutionary campaign to dislodge the private sector from its management of the Argentine economy. Yet, in retrospect, it is clear that they also marked the limits of institutional reform beyond which the Peronists had no intention of going.

During the remainder of 1946 and throughout 1947, it became quite evident that Perón did not intend to replace Argentine capitalism with some nativist form of socialism, but wanted only to transform it by using state institutions to transfer resources, rights, and obligations among its members. No special insight was required to recognize how, until 1943, economic allocations within Argentina had been determined principally by those who managed and financed its export trade. Though domestic industries had sprung up in the wake of depression and war, their

growth was circumscribed by financial, market, and supply constraints imposed by the larger export-directed economic system.
Consequently, Perón concluded in 1945 that rapid industrialization required more than the creation of a new industrial bank,
higher tariff barriers, and special tax incentives; it was also essential that the state increase its control over the allocation and
distribution of financial resources, and in nationalizing private
savings and foreign trade, he believed he had gained access to
the instruments he needed to redirect Argentina's capitalistic
economy.

To reduce the foreign hold on the economy, the Peronists
drew on the extensive gold reserves accumulated during the war
to purchase several foreign-owned properties (like the much
criticized British-owned railways). Controversy still surrounds
Argentina's nationalization of the inefficient and deficit-plagued
railways, for which many believed Perón had paid an exhorbitant
price.[6] But at the time the purchase was made, it was regarded
by Peronists as a major step toward the country's liberation from
British imperialism. By 1949 they had not only gained control
over most of the nation's foreign owned utilities, but were already well along with a program of infrastructure development.
Guided by a loosely conceived five-year investment plan, they
constructed hydroelectric facilities, expanded the exploitation of
the country's coal reserves, increased the operations of the state
petroleum company, built a merchant fleet, organized a national
airline, and supported existing military plans for the construction
of a major iron and steel complex. In so doing Perón also
launched the Argentine public sector along an irreversible journey that would eventually overtax the country's fiscal resources
and severely limit the economic policy options of his successors.

Of all the institutional reforms none provoked more opposition
than the state monopoly over commodity trading. The Peronist
government had inherited a sophisticated network of agricultural
policies and institutions, designed largely by rural interests during the 1930s to protect them against economic uncertainties
resulting from their vulnerability to international prices and
markets. But the grain and meat boards of the 1930s, governed
as they were primarily by cattlemen and farmers, were inadequate for Perón's purposes. Where his predecessors had
sought to protect and encourage Argentine farmers, he was de-

termined to exploit them for the benefit of industrialists, workers, and state enterprise. To succeed he needed to assert more public authority over the agricultural economy than ever before. Export agriculture, along with the substantial gold reserves accumulated during the war years, was expected to finance Argentina's economic development after 1945 through government exploitation of high prices in the markets of war-torn Europe, Argentine participation in the American Marshall Plan, and, in the event of an outbreak of hostilities between the United States and the Soviet Union, Argentina's advantageous position as a nonparticipant in such a conflict.[7] In retrospect such inflated expectations may appear foolhardy, but in 1946 and 1947 world events seemed to confirm the Peronist belief that the opportunity for Argentina's national liberation had finally arrived.

The principal instrument of Peronist agricultural policy was the controversial Argentine Trade Promotion Institute (IAPI), an organization created by a March 1946 preinaugural decree. The Institute, which the government's National and Industrial Credit Banks served as financial agents, was designed to reap and reinvest agricultural profits by purchasing commodites at low official prices and selling them bilaterally or on the world market at high prices and keeping most of the profit for allocation by the national government. In principle, IAPI was also to be the protector of the rural sector by providing price supports in times of world or domestic price decline. But in 1946, this possibility appeared remote to the Argentine farmer, who saw IAPI blocking his access to high profits on the hungry world market. Soon after IAPI's creation, the grain and meat boards were reorganized to exclude direct producer participation and were placed under IAPI's supervision. Similarly, CAP, the semipublic packing and marketing enterprise, which the cattlemen had fought so hard to create a decade before, was taken over by the government. Yet, the foreign meat packers, objects of nationalist rage since the 1920s, were left untouched. Moreover, when packer profit margins declined due to IAPI's maximum price restrictions, forcing the packers to reduce their volume of production in the early 1950s, none other than IAPI came to their rescue with subsidies to keep them in the business of supplying meat to Argentine and foreign consumers.[8]

Despite the pleas of some of Perón's reformist supporters, the

new program did not include agrarian reform among its primary
objectives. Very soon after his inauguration, in fact, Perón retreated from campaign pledges to reform land tenure and even
assured Rural Society cattlemen that there would be no legislation to redistribute property through wholesale expropriations.[9]
He turned instead to more indirect methods to help poor farmers. One was to support tenant farmers in their struggle with
landowners. As early as 1943 the military government had decreed a 20-percent reduction in land rents. Then in 1948 the
Peronists promulgated tenancy legislation extending tenant contracts from five to eight years; they simultaneously froze rents in
an effort to encourage landowners caught between frozen rents
and rising costs to sell land to tenants. The tenants, in turn, were
offered National Bank credits covering the full purchase price.[10]

Once the institutional infrastructure had been created and
greater government control over economic allocations asserted,
the Peronists turned to the implementation of the expansionary
economic policy for which they have been both cursed and
cheered to this day. Their principal objectives, as we have seen,
were the redistribution of income in favor of wage earners, the
creation of full employment through the absorption of surplus
agricultural labor into urban activites, and industrialization. In
adopting a policy designed to achieve a rapid expansion of internal demand, they believed they could pursue all three objectives
simultaneously, and that the three would become reinforcing.
The policy of industrialization, which was begun tentatively by
the military government in 1943, was strengthened through
monetary and credit expansion, high tariffs, exchange controls,
and an overvalued exchange rate that subsidized the importation
of raw materials, fuels, intermediate products, and capital goods.
Moreover, through the Industrial Bank, created in 1944, new
loans were channelled to handicraft, food-processing, textile, and
clothing firms. Between 1946 and 1949 the Bank's share of industrial loans within Argentina increased from 22 to 78 percent.[11] During the same time, relative prices were shifted to aid
industry as the prices of agricultural commodities declined in re-
lation to those of industrial products by 27 percent.[12]

The most attractive feature of the program to its multitude of
supporters was, of course, its redistribution of income in favor of
wage earners. Government authorities secured wage settle-

TABLE 3.1
Peronist Economic Policy 1946

Objectives	1. Full employment
	2. Progressive income redistribution
	3. Industrialization
	4. Economic independence
Instruments	
Fiscal	1. Increase investment
	2. Increase transfers
	3. Increase current expenditures
	4. Raise revenues through commodity sales
Money and Credit	1. State control over banking deposits
	2. Expand money and credit supply
Exchange	1. Maintain overvalued exchange rate
Controls	1. Price controls
Income Redistribution	1. Major shifts from rural producers to urban consumers and industrial producers
	2. Foreign investors to government and domestic investors

ments favorable to loyal CGT unions and nominal wages were raised considerably, exceeding the rise in sectoral prices and thereby contributing to a significant improvement in real wages—42 percent in 1947 and 1948 alone. But collective bargaining, though important, was not the only means used to improve working-class income. Between 1946 and 1949 over one-half of the increase in the proportion of national income claimed by wages was due to the expansion of urban activities and to the improvement in their relative prices; that is, the shift of wage earners to urban activities was sufficient to raise wage income, thus benefiting wage-earning groups as a whole because of the movement of part of the labor force to more remunerative activities. Though it was expected that industrial and construction activities would absorb most of this new labor force, transport and government services actually took a greater share as the limitations of industrial absorption were compensated for by a burgeoning bureaucracy and its public enterprises.[13] In sum, the period from 1946 to 1949 was truly the golden age of Peronism and its expansionary, nationalistic economic strategy. A new group of national leaders had in only three years established their firm control over public institutions and reorganized the country's financial and trading systems to their liking. Not only had they improved the welfare of the urban working class, but despite their opponents' predictions of immediate economic disaster, they had helped raise the country's GNP by 25 percent.[14]

Perón as Policy Manager

Any program that proposes as many changes in traditional economic relations as did Perón's in 1946 immediately raises questions about how the feat was to be managed. Could he, for example, merely by presidential decree confiscate the annual profits of an agrarian sector accustomed to getting its way within the Argentine economic system? Could he settle wage disputes in labor's favor, nationalize bank deposits, and spend most of the country's gold reserves without angering industrialists and the foreign and domestic financial communities? It is quite plausible that Perón asked himself these questions in 1946; but the mere fact that he went ahead with his policies indicates that he had some confidence in his ability to succeed. If, as is likely, some adverse reaction was inevitable, we must ask how he prepared his regime for the task of overcoming such resistance. In particular, what kind of political strategy and institutional reforms did he employ to assure the compliance of producers, traders, and laborers with his policy objectives?

Before turning to the political strategy used by Perón to execute his program, a brief discussion of the problems raised by his economic policies is in order. Critical to the fate of the Peronist program was the economic response of rural producers and exporters to the controls imposed by IAPI. The Peronists gambled that they could redistribute income away from rural producers while simultaneously maintaining a high enough level of commodity exports to assure a steady flow of foreign exchange to pay for the imports required by industrialization and rising mass consumption. The likelihood of success depended on the accuracy of three assumptions: first, that cattlemen and farmers would not reduce production after commodity controls had been imposed; second, that high world commodity prices would continue for four or five years; and third, that import substitution would in only a few years reduce the economy's dependence on commodity exports. Should farmer confidence and rural production decline, world prices fall, or domestic consumption take a much larger share of commodity foodstuffs than anticipated, then the Peronists' gamble might not pay off. Moreover, there was the question not only of the accuracy of their assumptions, but also of Perón's ability to persuade rural producers that their short-term sacrifices were for a just cause and should be made willingly without any thought of sabotaging the government effort. This was, needless to say, a difficult assignment at best.

The same was true of the other sectors. The nationalization of bank deposits, for example, assumed that private banks would tolerate the new regulations, viewing them not as a form of confiscation but merely as the government's way of channelling investments into areas given priority within its development plan. At the same time, Perón also needed a vigorous effort by industrial investors in response to the new tariff and credit incentives. While the government's program offered obvious advantages for entrepreneurs, it should be recalled that many of Argentina's industrialists, especially those in the Industrial Union, were anti-Peronist and initially viewed the Peronists' expansion of state activity with great concern. They were especially disturbed by Perón's labor reforms and the working-class militancy they encouraged. To succeed with his industrial program, then, it was essential that Perón alleviate industrialist fears and persuade entrepreneurs to respond energetically to his initiatives.

In combination these problems confronted Perón with an intriguing dilemma. On the one hand, the execution of policy would have benefited from his program's acceptance by all major economic interests; this in turn might have been achieved through the involvement of the affected parties in the design and administration of the government's new policies. On the other hand, given the probable opposition of cattlemen, farmers, and industrial entrepreneurs to his methods, their participation in the policy-making process invited their obstruction of the reform effort. What Perón needed was a political strategy that could secure the compliance of his potential opponents without sacrificing the content of his program. He found it, he belived, in a plan directed at expanding presidential control over the nation's political process.

At first glance, Perón's political strategy appears quite simple: he merely adapted the institutions of the twentieth-century corporate state to Argentine conditions and used them to regulate economic and political behavior.[15] The evidence usually offered to support this view includes the fact that his government often operated in an authoritarian manner, especially in the treatment of its political opponents, that it created a mass organization (though one whose class origins distinguished it from similar European organizations), that it sought to glorify the Argentine state and nation as well as its strong leader, and that its founders did not hide their sympathies for the wartime leaders of Germany, Italy, and Spain.[16] All in all, the initial form of the Peronist government convinced many observers that it was simply a new variant of the conventional authoritarian corporate state whose peculiar working-class base of political support could be explained by the country's level of social and economic underdevelopment.

Appearances are deceiving, however, and nowhere is this more true than in Peronist Argentina. First of all, Perón never created a corporatist state in Argentina. On closer analysis, in fact, the structure and behavior of the Peronist government conform more closely to those of a regime whose popularly elected leadership cleverly manipulated its huge electoral and legislative majorities in order to maintain its political control than to one that ruled using corporatist institutions. This is not to claim that Perón held fast to the canons of democratic government, for he did not, but only to argue that the organization of his administration departed in several ways from the model of the corporate state.

Much of the confusion over the character of the Peronist regime results from misplaced emphasis on Perón's vaguely stated corporatist objectives rather than on his actual behavior and substantive accomplishments. Before we can distinguish between the two, corporatism must be defined. The term refers to a political system in which groups representing the owners of land, labor, and capital are directed by the state through some form of hierarchical structure rather than allowed to compete freely for economic gain and political influence. It usually arises from a desire by authorities for greater control over the capitalist economy and the subjugation of the popular classes, and is supported by the belief that national economic goals can be achieved through a cooperative effort directed by the state rather than through private competition. While most property is privately owned in the corporatist system, its use is guided by the state through its control over functional associations that represent the various economic sectors.[17]

Clearly Perón sought to redirect the Argentine economy by asserting greater state control over investment decisions, domestic and foreign trade, and the setting of prices and wages. There is also evidence indicating that the creation of some form of corporate organization was among his plans before taking office. José Figuerola, one of his closest advisors and the architect of his Postwar Economic Council, was a recognized authority on Spanish corporatist law.[18] The Council, a personal vehicle employed by Perón to formulate his economic program in 1945, was thought by some to be the precursor of a corporatist organization that would be created after his inauguration. To the Council he brought the dissident industrialists, cattlemen, bureaucrats, and military officers who took him and his bold economic vision seriously. Among this group of ambitious malcontents was tin-plate manufacturer Miguel Miranda, a man who withdrew from the conservative Industrial Union after leading a pro-Perón slate of candidates to defeat in the Union's 1946 elections and was later rewarded with the directorship of Perón's reorganized Central Bank. There was also Juan Picazo Elorde, the first Peronist minister of agriculture, a member of the economic elite who turned his back on his conservative upperclass rural family in order to join Perón. There were also many young, nationalistic economists like Dr. Ramon Cereijo, aged 34, an honors graduate from the University of Buenos Aires who rose from obscurity to become the first economist named minister of finance.[19] What they lacked in common background or coherent economic philosophy this disparate group made up in determination, fostered by Perón himself, to use their authority to promote the creation of an industrialized welfare state.

The Postwar Economic Council might have been intended to serve as the first stage of a crusade to impose corporatist rule on

Argentina as many observers believed at the time. But if it was, it marked the beginning of a political transformation that was never completed; although Perón announced many plans for the reorganization of the Argentine state, few of them were actually carried out.

In order to build a corporate regime Perón had to gain control over the country's entrepreneurs much as he had done with the labor movement in 1944 and 1945. But since most entrepreneurs opposed his rule, their subjugation was much more difficult than that of the labor movement had been. Nevertheless, Perón did try to bend them to his will, though his attempt, it turned out, was a rather feeble one. It involved two separate but complementary efforts: one that attempted to coopt economic interest group leaders by involving them on social-economic councils attached to the presidency, and one that sought to drive entrepreneurs and merchants into a new government-sponsored national organization.

Social-economic councils, which bring representatives of a country's economic sectors together with public officials to make and execute national policy, play a central role in most corporatist systems. Undoubtedly, Perón recognized this when he organized his government in May 1946. Nevertheless, he stopped far short of creating the kind of institution found in other corporatist regimes. Here again he was content with the form rather than the substance of corporatist policy management.

Perón began in July 1946 with the creation of the Economic and Social Council, which, in addition to the president as its chairman, included all cabinet officers, four government bank directors, and management and labor representatives from arable and pastoral farming, mining, manufacturing, construction, commerce, transport, light and power, entertainment, catering, hygiene and sanitary services. But after its much publicized inauguration, the Council was seldom called into session.[20] Perón tried once more in August 1949 when he launched the National Economic Consultative Commission and gave it a membership similar to that of the Council.[21] But this second effort fared little better than the first since the president persistently refused to convene the Commission. When asked at a press conference on February 7, 1950, why he had not fulfilled his pledge to use the council mechanism, Perón confessed that he had been too busy to bother with such time-consuming activities.[22] Yet, undaunted, he inaugurated a new body—called the Economic Commission— in 1952, simultaneous with the initiation of his second five-year development plan. But, alas, this third try also withered soon thereafter due to presidential neglect. In fact, there is no evidence that any of these so-called consultative bodies served any purpose other than to satisfy Perón's desire for symbolic gestures aimed at placating those who complained of their exclusion from his policy-making process. One cannot help but wonder why, given his general disregard for the opinions of most entrepreneurs, he bothered to create any councils at all.

One explanation was given several years later by Dr. Alfredo Gómez Morales, minister of economy between 1949 and 1955. Echoing Perón's remarks to the press in 1950, he claimed that while Perón had frequently suggested that it might be useful to develop and institutionalize private-sector collaboration with the government, he was in too much of a hurry to complete his economic reforms to expend the effort needed to build such collaboration. Instead, he preferred either to speak directly with individual cattlemen or industrialists when help was needed or, more often, just to ignore them and trust in the ability of his subordinates to get the job done.[23] Gómez Morales might also have added that by refusing open consultation with angry private sector delegates Perón also preserved, in the short run at least, his decision-making autonomy. Not averse to playing his enemies off against each other, he could in this way make secret promises and threats to competing entrepreneurs and thereby sow enough distrust among them to prevent the formation of opposition coalitions, a tactic that served him well, especially during his first three years in office.

The Peronists seem to have taken the creation of a national organization of entrepreneurs and merchants more seriously from the outset than they had their social-economic councils. Yet, here again they stopped short of the fulfillment of their announced objectives. As a result, they never did gain as much control over the nation's producers as they desired.

Perón's campaign against the organizations that traditionally had represented the interests of the economic elite began immediately after his inauguration in May 1946 when he intervened the Industrial Union, ostensibly for having contributed illegally to his opponent's electoral campaign. Actually, he had been at odds with the Union's leadership since early 1945 when some of its members expressed strong opposition to the military government's interventionist policies. Divisions within the UIA over the new government's program emerged in 1945, and opposing factions clashed in April 1946 during the UIA's internal elections. A group of "collaborationists," led by Perón's ally, industrialist Miguel Miranda, challenged the antigovernment faction of long-time conservative UIA leaders Luis Colombo and Raul Lamuraglia. The latter won the skirmish for control over the UIA but lost the larger battle when on May 17, 1946, Perón closed the UIA and appointed Miguel Miranda to the presidency of the Central Bank.[24] The message contained in the closure of the UIA was clear to other economic groups, and soon thereafter the Rural Society replaced its hardline anti-Peronist leadership with a slate of officers who, if not supportive of the government, were at least more restrained in their criticism.[25]

The government's attempt to merge all entrepreneurial groups into one official organization began in late 1946 with the creation of the Association of Production, Industry, and Commerce (AAIPIC), an official entity which joined representatives of an estimated 30,600 firms, including some that had previously belonged to the UIA. In 1949 the AAIPIC was reorganized as the Argentine Economic Confederation. The function of the latter, however, was never made clear and seldom did it do anything more than lead cheers for the government's program when called on by authorities to do so.[26]

At about the same time a group of small businessmen in northwestern Argentina launched their own association to attract government support for the industrialization of Argentina's interior provinces, until then largely neglected by the industrial surge concentrated in and around Buenos Aires. Driven by the hope that the antiestablishment leaders of the new government would be receptive to their pleas for easier credit and a decentralization of economic infrastructure investments, they championed the government's economic policies throughout the country's interior, gaining not only eventual government recognition but also official support for the merger of their burgeoning organization with that of the aforementioned Argentine Economic Confederation, an action taken in 1952 that resulted in the creation of the General Economic Confederation (CGE).[27] With the launching of the CGE the stage appeared finally set for the conversion of the system into a corporatist one in which the government directed the economy through the use of the CGE and the already loyal General Confederation of Labor. But again Perón hesitated. Not until early 1955 did he finally bring the two organizations together, and then it was only to participate in a brief national productivity congress designed to increase public support for government policies.[28] By then it was too late; a few months later the Peronist experiment was halted by a military coup.

Perón's treatment of rural economic groups was marked by even more hesitation and ambivalence than his campaign to gain political control over urban entrepreneurs. In the first place, despite his antipathy toward the rural elite, he never closed or seriously harassed the elitist Rural Society. Even more revealing of his apparent lack of interest in rural sector politics was his failure to mobilize the country's less affluent farmers into a base of organized support. Among the largely immigrant tenant farmers of the Agrarian Federation there existed a potential source of enthusiastic support for any reformist government. By exploiting the small farmer's displeasure with the rural status quo, he might have manipulated rural-sector cleavages between rich and poor and thereby lessened concerted sectorwide opposition to his policies. Instead, though he acceded to tenant-farmer demands by freezing land rents, Perón undertook no campaign to formalize ties between them and his government. As a result, he could not avert their frequent joining with the Rural Society to denounce commodity price controls and other government policies. Perón's lack of interest may have been due to a conviction that the solution to the plight of some tenant farmers rested with their absorption into the urban work force, a belief no doubt reinforced by the massive rural-to-urban migration stimulated by the government's economic and social policies. At the same time, it also reflects the Peronists' preoccupation with urban over rural welfare, a preference made manifest in the government's determination to keep food prices low for the urban consumer, even at the cost of alienating the tenant farmer.

By now it should be apparent that several factors contributed to Perón's failure to complete the creation of a corporatist system of government. First, he was a very impatient and ambitious leader, and one who jealously guarded his authority from the business and industrial leaders who sought to limit it. The creation of corporatist institutions would have slowed him down and invited attempts to reduce his room for maneuver. Second, his campaign to reorganize economic interest groups proceeded very slowly, taking nearly ten years before it neared completion. Yet, even in 1955 there remained substantial opposition to him among cattlemen, farmers, bankers, and the more traditional industrialists, making it all but impossible to gain the cooperation of those sectors through the use of compulsory membership in official organizations. And third, his confidence in his ability to govern without the help of rural and urban entrepreneurs was constantly reinforced by expressions of popular support, especially at the time of his reelection in 1951. Thus, it was not hard for him to convince himself that he could govern without the assistance of a complex system of corporatist organizations.

Perón had needed enough authority to implement a program of nationalistic economic reform and had secured it by amassing electoral victories in 1946 with 56 percent of the vote and 1951 with 63 percent, and persuading his military associates to respect this massive demonstration of popular support. Moreover, the legislative majority gained by his Peronist party in 1946 and expanded, with the help of a new electoral law and some strong-arm tactics, to over 80 percent of all legislative seats in 1951, assured him a virtual blank check for making economic policy. What is important from a policy-making point of view is not the purity of his democracy but his ability to use (or misuse) its institutions to generate a highly visible and vocal base of support to defend his programs. That his cynical manipulation of democratic authority would help to undermine Argentines' already weak faith in the democratic process would become evident later, but in the late 1940s the way seemed clear to perpetual Peronist rule.

In sum, Perón used political strategy to free himself from rather than tie himself to the industrial, agricultural, and financial leaders who, he was convinced, were determined to sabotage his programs. Buoyed by a strong electoral mandate, a legislative majority, and the inclusion of organized labor within his regime, he acted as a man convinced that his programs were impermeable to the protests of those victimized by them. His repression of the Industrial Union was the exception rather than the rule in his treatment of economic interest groups, for he found it just as effective to ignore as to repress his most outspoken critics. Consequently most rural producers were left free to affect the outcome of the government's program through the use of their economic if not their political power, as were industrialists, despite the loss of their association and the rise of a new government-sanctioned one in its place. The true test of his centralized, executive-dominant, insulated policy-making process would not come, however, until he discovered how vulnerable his programs were to the economic reprisals of the traders and producers who opposed them. Only then would he learn how their exclusion from the policy-making process, which he believed essential to the formulation of bold policy initiatives, might deny him the private-sector cooperation on which the success of his economic policy depended.

TABLE 3.2
The Peronist Policy-Making Process

Phases	Political Institutions and Techniques
Initiation	Perón's Postwar Council and its Plan of Economic Reconstruction
Formulation	A small group of Perón's personal advisors and cabinet ministers
Consultation	Symbolic use of socioeconomic councils but little consultation outside inner circle
Ratification	Peronist-controlled Congress
Execution	Heavy reliance on administrative controls, intimidation, and public exhortation
	Limited use of economic incentives
Feedback	Few direct channels from interest groups to government
	Peronal contacts with officials or group petitions and public protests

Coping with Crisis

Not until 1948 and 1949 could anyone begin to answer the question of how the Peronist program would affect the Argentine economy. Of major concern was not merely the rate or form of economic growth that the expansionary measures induced, but more critically, the ways in which Argentina's producers and trading partners responded to the regulation of the market place and the redistribution of income. That Perón succeeded in real-locating income is apparent from the data presented in Table 3.3. Real wages increased and their claim on national income grew with the expansion of the industrial work force. Equally impressive was the decline in relative commodity prices and the real income of beef producers. He had gambled that neither labor's sudden gains nor the rural producers' losses would endanger Argentine development, convinced that both would contribute to a more equitable and productive national economy. His hopes proved ill-founded, it turned out, for even before the celebration had ended, the cracks in his economic edifice had begun to appear.

TABLE 3.3
The Income Effects of Peronist Policy, 1946–49

	Salary Income as % of National Income[a]	Real Salaries of Industrial Workers (Percent Change)[b]	Relative Agricultural Prices* (Base 1960 = 100)[b]	Beef Production Real Income (Percent Change)[c]
1946	38.7	− 6.3	116.22	− 13
1947	37.3	+ 8.5	102.38	+ 13
1948	40.5	+ 34.1	96.00	− 5
1949	45.7	− 7.0	85.94	− 14

*Ag total product
_____
Nonag National product

Sources: [a] United Nations, Economic Commission for Latin America, *Economic Development and Income Distribution in Argentina* (New York: United Nations, 1969), p. 170, Table 39.
[b] Lorenzo Juan Sigaut, *Acerca de la distribución y niveles de ingreso en la Argentina* (Buenos Aires: Ediciones Macchi, 1972), p. 49, cuadro 13; p. 66, cuadro 21.
[c] Banco Ganadero Argentino, *Temas de economía argentina: mercados y precios de ganado vacuno* (Buenos Aires: Banco Ganadero, 1966), p. 45.

Perón's opponents had warned repeatedly that the new regulatory and income measures would undermine entrepreneurial confidence and lead to economic ruin. No doubt these dire forecasts came as no surprise to Perón who knew that Argentina's farmers and businessmen chronically complained of their abuse by public officials. There was a danger in taking these warnings lightly, however; even more so if policy makers welcomed them as evidence that their programs had succeeded in taking from the rich and giving to the poor. It was equally plausible that such complaints signaled serious discontent, which might indeed undermine investment and production if ignored. What the government required then was a means for distinguishing between idle threats aimed at securing more favorable treatment and real threats leading to changes in entrepreneurial behavior that endangered policy implementation. How well the Peronists did in making such distinctions can be best seen through their responses to rural critics after 1946.

Most rural producers had never forgiven Perón for his plan to redistribute profits from commodity sales abroad to the urban industrial economy. The fact that by 1946 they had come to expect increased government regulation did not alter their displeasure with the form it finally took. The transformation of the price support and marketing regulations adopted in the early 1930s into tough new state controls actually began soon after the military coup of June 1943. Ignoring rural sector objections, the new military government confiscated the one-billion peso exchange margin fund, created in 1933 to finance price supports in lean years, and committed it to nonagricultural government projects. Soon thereafter military officials announced their intention to monopolize the grain trade, ostensibly to keep inflation-inducing, postwar profits out of the farmers' hands. Under the proposal an agricultural products control board was to purchase wheat, linseed, and maize at a price 10 percent above cost, using its profits from sales as a reserve fund for future commodity price supports, much as had been done with the ill-fated exchange margin fund created in 1933. Needless to say, Argentine farmers, fresh from the government's expropriation of the original exchange fund, saw little advantage in the new proposal and protested accordingly. Their opposition succeeded in forestalling the program's adoption only temporarily, for in early 1945 the military took over the wheat trade, paving the way for the state control over all commodity trading in April 1946, just prior to Perón's inauguration.[29]

Perón's rural policy relied on both the carrot and the stick, blending threats of confiscatory measures with promises of improved prices and state protection against the world economy.

Undoubtedly Perón was aware that a productive rural sector was essential to his program's success, since he counted upon the profits from foreign commodity sales to finance much of the industrial development program. In fact, the recognition of his short-term dependence on those whom he sought to exploit may have contributed to the abandonment of an agrarian reform program that would have divided large rural estates and temporarily interrupted production.[30] Yet, with the exception of the postponing of agrarian reform, he held fast to his income-redistributing, commodity-marketing scheme, apparently convinced that farmers and cattlemen would have little choice but to continue to sow grain and raise cattle even when facing declining returns on their investments.

The leaders of the rural sector, as anticipated, were among the first to denounce Peronist policy publicly. The attack was led initially by the cattlemen of the Rural Society and CARBAP, who resented their sudden eviction from the agricultural policy-making process as well as the income lost through controlled prices. In contrast, the tenant farmers of the Agrarian Federation took some consolation from their successful campaign in 1948 to secure legislation which extended the rent controls adopted by the military government in 1943 for another five years, with a three-year option thereafter. To the displeasure of landowners, this meant that, in effect, anyone who had leased a plot in 1937 expecting its return by 1942 under the conventional five-year contract, might not have it returned, thanks to the 1943 and 1948 control extensions, until 1955.[31] Obviously these reforms did little to endear the government to large landowners; yet, it is also notable that, although they were well received by tenant farmers, they were not sufficient to prevent the outspoken opposition of the Agrarian Federation to the commodity price control measures, which penalized small as well as large farmers, especially after 1948.

The Rural Society began its antigovernment campaign cautiously by testifying against administration bills in Congress, but once the futility of trying to influence the Peronist legislative majority became apparent, they turned to the executive branch to demand a relaxation of marketing controls and an increase in maximum commodity prices. By 1947 their mode of protest and the government's response to it settled into a fixed pattern from which neither party deviated until Perón was overthrown in 1955. For its part, the Rural Society devoted its energies to the organization of special congresses where they were frequently joined by representatives from CARBAP and the Agrarian Federation in issuing joint antigovernment manifestos demanding more favorable price policies. And the once festive Palermo stock show, an annual event used by cattlemen since 1933 to reconfirm publicly their support for government farm policy, degenerated into a ritual of bitter denunciations of the government, that were more often than not totally ignored by the Ministry of Agriculture officials in attendance.[32]

The government controls might not have been so disturbing to rural leaders were it not for the process by which they were adopted and implemented. Accustomed to influencing the formulation of farm policy, especially between 1933 and 1943, the country's cattlemen and farmers especially resented the way in which the Peronists rudely turned them aside when deciding the fate of the rural economy. Typical of the insults borne by rural interests was Perón's treatment of the meat and grain boards created in 1933 and manned until 1946 primarily by rural leaders. Rather than continue with the boards in their original form, Perón created new ones and staffed them entirely with government officials, a step which he justified as necessary to regulate an increasingly complex and problem-ridden rural economy. The original meat board, he pointed out, had been designed during a time of large exportable surpluses and was expected to foster domestic consumption and regulate exports to assure producers adequate markets and prices. The Peronist meat board, in contrast, was created because rising internal consumption, which the government had intentionally encouraged, threatened to absorb the entire exportable surplus. In order to protect cattlemen from the loss of export markets, the government had to impose greater restrictions on the domestic meat trade. As convincing as they seem, these rationalizations for the expansion of state authority hardly satisfied the cattlemen, who never tired of asking why such measures, if they were designed to protect cattlemen, were formulated without their advice and consent.

Needless to say, such questions went unanswered.[33] In fact, the cattlemen's protests, as well as those of grain farmers, induced no significant modifications in farm policy during 1947 and

1948. Despite the cattlemen and farmers' outspoken criticism, Perón seemed convinced that they could be converted to his cause by Miguel Miranda, the supersalesman of Peronist trade policy whom he sent frequently to lecture rural leaders about the blessings of a program that would take their profits in good years and return them in lean ones. Likewise the minister of agriculture, in the face of bitter criticism at the annual Palermo show, continued to sing the virtures of the government's effort as if convinced that repetition alone would finally win over his rural critics. But rural spokesmen saw only insensitivity and maliciousness in the government's hollow promises and rosy forecasts, and did not abandon their opposition until Perón was removed in 1955.

The seriousness of the cattlemen's warnings did not become apparent until mid 1948 when the production of export crops began to falter. The well-known rural decline under Peronism is documented in Table No. 3.4. After coming off slumps in 1945 and 1946 with impressive growth in 1947, the production of beef declined in 1948; grain dropped in 1949 and 1950, due in part to a severe drought, which also contributed to a slight increase in

TABLE 3.4
Annual Growth Rate of Export Commodity Production,
1947–50

	1947	1948	1949	1950
Beef Production (tons slaughtered)	20.3	− 3.2	2.3	2.0
Wheat and Corn Production (tons)	61.0	2.4	− 26.1	− 31.0
Total Rural Production (tons)	8.6	− 4.2	− 8.8	0.7
Beef Exports (tons)	45.2	− 26.7	− 1.0	− 8.0
Wheat and Corn Exports (tons)	29.6	1.2	− 38.2	22.4
Total Export Value	39.1	1.1	− 36.0	12.9

Source: Computed from: Centro Internacional de Información Económica, *La economía argentina: treinta años en cifras*, (Buenos Aires: CIDIE, 1971), pp. 24, 30, 44.
———, *La economía argentina: comercio exterior 1940–1971* (Buenos Aires: CIDIE, 1971), p. 14, cuaderno 4.
Organización Techint, *Boletín Informativo no. 188* (octubre-diciembre 1972), p. 20.

beef production as cattlemen liquidated stock because of the loss of pastures. The plight of the cattlemen during this period is revealed in the fact that their real income, which had grown by 13 percent in 1947, declined by an estimated 23 percent between 1948 and 1950. (See Table No. 3.3.) Similarly, the farmer's gross income per hectare of wheat declined by 27 percent in 1949 and 14 percent in 1950, and as a result, the area sowed to cereals with fixed prices declined by 50 percent, while that devoted to the few crops not subjected to controls increased by 43 percent.[34] Had the economic warning signs been limited only to the rural sector, they might not have upset public officials, who were at first prepared to tolerate some rural malaise. But problems in the rural economy were part of a much more general process of economic deterioration in 1948 and 1949. For example, one only had to look at industrial production in 1948 to discover that Argentina's industrial revolution had also turned sluggish. (See Table No. 3.5.) After initial spurts in 1946 and 1947, industrial production fell in 1948 and 1949 and grew at low rates thereafter.

TABLE 3.5
Industrial Product Growth Rates, 1947–50
(Percent)

	1947	1948	1949	1950
Food, Drink, and Tobacco	8.9	– 11.9	0.6	– 1.1
Textiles, Leather, and Clothing	– 0.7	13.0	– 6.6	7.3
Metals, Metal Products, Machinery, Vehicles, Electrical Goods	46.9	– 8.6	– 15.5	– 28.1
Chemical, Rubber, and Petroleum Products	17.5	4.2	– 4.3	2.3
Total Industrial Production (not summed)	16.3	– 2.8	– 7.0	2.4

Source: Computed from: Organización Techint, *Boletín Informativo no. 188* (octubre-noviembre 1972), p. 26, Cuadro 5.

In 1946 and 1947, Perón tried to rebut his critics by pointing to a 10-percent annual rate of growth in gross national product, but by late 1948 it was the dire predictions of his critics rather than his own rosy assessments that most accurately described the country's condition. On the international side, his ambitious debt-repatriation and railway-nationalization schemes had reduced the country's gold holdings by 89 percent (from 4,099.5 million pesos in 1945 to only 433.9 million in 1948) and the bulk of the country's foreign currency, which had been in the form of freely convertible currencies after the war, was by 1947 composed primarily of inconvertible pounds sterling.[35] The exhaustion of gold and foreign currency would not have been so damaging had it not been followed by a rapid decline in the country's export earnings after 1948. As we have learned, Perón's export policy had assumed that the rural sector would hold to past production levels despite government controls and that Argentina's export earnings would rise rapidly through adroit bargaining in commodity-scarce world markets. Given a more tolerant rural sector and the continuation of a sellers market abroad, the scheme might have succeeded, but as European production recovered and North American commodity surpluses edged Argentina out of the Marshall Plan, the assumptions on which his dictation of commodity prices depended were completely undermined. To make matters worse, these external problems were accompanied by internal ones, the most prominent of which was a rise in demand-induced inflation caused by the rising incomes, which the government's wage, monetary, and credit policies had encouraged.[36]

The allocation of responsibility for Argentina's economic problems after 1947 is still much debated by Perón's followers and opponents, but the conditions themselves are obvious and well documented. What is not so well known, and what interests us here, is how his policy-making process shaped responses to the crisis after 1948.

Initially, Perón refused to admit publicly that the Argentine economy was in any danger. But privately he expressed grave concern about the exclusion of Argentina from the Marshall Plan because of an American decision to send its own surplus grain to Europe as well as the British curtailment of triangular trade with the United States by their declaration of the sterling's inconvertibility in 1947. These concerns led in late 1948 to his request for a confidential study of the Argentine economy by his closest aides. The report, received in late January 1949, focused its attention on the deterioration of Argentina's external position, which, it was claimed, had been caused by forces beyond the government's control. It went on to warn that unless imports were curtailed, an external crisis would undermine the government's development program. At the same time, the government economists rejected any major policy changes in favor of a stopgap approach, recommending controls over nonessential imports rather than an embarrassing devaluation.[37]

Perón reacted swiftly, first by firing the outspoken Miguel Miranda, who was no longer needed to preach the virtues of the government's faltering trade policy, and then by appointing Alfredo Gómez Morales and Roberto Ares, the young economists who had written the confidential report, to direct the economy. Simultaneously, he placed new limits on imports, tightened credit to the private sector, curtailed several public-works projects, and, to the delight of workers, asked employers to cover rising wages from their profits rather than with increased prices. Publicly, he still refused to concede that there was any cause for alarm. In May 1949, in his annual address to Congress, he argued that his original program was still operative and that public attention should focus on the new Peronist Constitution of 1949 and not on these minor adjustments in economic policy.[38]

The patchwork measures of 1949 were not sufficient, it turned out. Argentina's external position worsened, especially after droughts in 1950 and 1951 further curtailed the production of export commodities. But officials still refused to admit their plight openly; in fact, if the Central Bank report for 1948 is taken as an indicator, it seems they were intent on concealing the severity of the crisis. Until 1948 the Central Bank reports had detailed the economy's performance by providing data that permitted comparisons with previous years. The 1948 report, in contrast, was published nearly a year late—in January 1950—and conspicuously omitted most of the data required to assess the economy's performance.[39] Nevertheless, there was no lack of commentary on Argentina's deteriorating situation during 1949 and 1950, for what the Argentine government refused to do, many Argentine and foreign reporters did for them, with *The Economist* of London and the Argentine *Bolsa Report* leading the way.[40] Characteristically, Perón, who was preoccupied with preparations for his reelection bid in 1951, denounced such reports as fabrications by enemies at home and abroad who were determined to undermine his controversial industrialization effort.

Although his reelection was never in doubt, given the government's ability to intimidate opponents and mobilize its supporters, Perón waited until after the returns were in before asking his economists for another confidential evaluation of the country's economic plight. This second study, like the one of 1949, was circulated only within the presidential office. Government officials still refused to involve the Argentine Congress or the country's entrepreneurs in the formulation of embarrassing emergency measures.[41] In so doing, they reconfirmed a style of policy making that would last well into the 1970s. It involved a centralized and secretive process that responded to crises only after substantial prodding and extensive economic deterioration. The usual sequence of events went as follows: first entrepreneurs would warn of impending doom and clamor for swift government action only to be ignored by officials who denied the existence of a crisis. Nevertheless, rumors of a drastic change in policy would persist, contributing to increased financial speculation, until finally, amid much fanfare, authorities suddenly announced a host of measures, conceived in secrecy, which they promised would cure the country's ills.

Thus it was that on February 18, 1952, a somber president, in a nationwide radio broadcast that resembled a general's charge to his troops before a major battle, announced what became known as the emergency Economic Plan of 1952. In it he promised to attain a short-term trade balance and restore relative price stability through the application of controls on the internal consumption of exportables, notably beef and wheat, raise prices and provide easier credit for rural producers, reduce public expenditures, and impose a two-year freeze on wages. As significant as the measures taken was the style of the speech itself. He began by denouncing Argentina's foreign imperialists, whom he blamed for the country's plight, and assured the Argentine people that his new measures represented only a temporary setback in their march toward industrialization. From industrialists he asked patience while the government restored the country's capacity to import fuels and raw products; from his supporters in the working class he demanded higher productivity and a reduction in consumption, drawing on the reservoir of loyalty that had been fostered by his labor reforms and wage policies in the mid 1940s. But rather than concede to the rural sector that their warnings had proven correct, he announced that higher commodity prices would not be accompanied by an abandonment of the state's monopoly over foreign trade as rural leaders demanded, for now more than ever IAPI was needed to deal with sagging commodity markets.[42]

After 1952 Perón turned to price, credit, and tax measures to boost rural production and to his control over the labor movement to hold down wages and prices. Although he did not cure most of the economy's ills after 1952, he did secure a modest recovery during 1953 and 1954. The external situation was quickly stabilized using government controls and cuts in public expenditures, along with a stringent monetary and credit policy that suppressed the level of internal demand. Critical to the success of stabilization was the response of the rural sector and the continued cooperation of workers. To secure the former Perón improved relative agricultural prices at a time when world prices for Argentine exports were declining. He did so not by resorting to a humiliating devaluation of the peso, but through IAPI acceptance of heavy losses, which it covered with new currency issues. The irony of IAPI's rescue operation, of course, was not lost on the country's farmers and cattlemen. Beef production did not rise immediately with improved prices, because, as might be expected, cattlemen responded to high prices by retaining stock and expanding their herds. Grain production, on the other hand, delighted officials with a 170-percent increase in 1953 alone.

Equally pleasing was the quiescence of organized labor. Officials had hoped to freeze wages for two years while avoiding a loss in real working class income by also freezing prices after some initial adjustments. But the real income of industrial workers, which had declined by 8.8 percent during the previous two years, fell by 10.7 percent in 1952 alone. Yet, as we can see from Table No. 3.6, the "volume" of working-class protests through strikes did not rise significantly during 1952 or 1953. In fact, the average annual volume was much less during this period than it had been during the golden years of Peronism, when the government had occasionally encouraged strikes in order to force a rise in wages and thereby reward its supporters.

TABLE 3.6
Labor Protests and Wage Responses, 1950–54

	1950	1951	1952	1953	1954	Annual Average 1950–54	Annual Average 1947–49
Strikes							
1. Frequency	.0059	.0045	.0027	.0080	.0035	.0049	.0140
2. Duration	20.9	9.3	19.8	10.8	12.1	14.58	11.75
3. Size (thousands)	3.2	.7	1.1	.1	6.7	2.4	7.7
4. Volume	398.91	29.76	60.41	11.92	281.63	156.53	706.93
Wage Response							
1. Change in Monetary Income of Industrial Worker (percent)	22.6	27.9	23.3	9.8	15.0		
2. Change in Real Income of Industrial Worker (percent)	− 2.0	− 6.8	− 10.7	5.3	11.0		

Sources: *Strikes* computed from, República Argentina, Secretaría de Estado de Trabajo, *Conflictos del trabajo*, junio de 1970, cuadro 25. Strike data are available only for the Federal Capital where approximately 40 percent of the country's organized workers are employed. *Wages* are taken from, Lorenzo Juan Sigaut, *Acerca de la distribución y niveles de ingreso en la Argentina* (Buenos Aires: Ediciones Macchi, 1972), p. 57, cuadro 16.
    Frequency: Strikes per 1,000 civilian wage and salary workers.
    Duration: Mandays lost per striker.
    Size: Strikers per strike.
    Volume: Frequency*Duration*Size.

In return for its support, labor was given, as Perón had promised, real income increases in 1953 and 1954 after the government's success in temporarily halting inflation made possible its renewed stimulation of economic activity.

At the beginning of 1955 Perón boasted that he had won most of his battles against those who sought to undermine his development scheme. A positive payments balance had been restored in 1953 and 1954 after large deficits during the preceding two years, and the gross national product rose by 6.8 percent in 1953 after a decline of 6.7 percent in 1952. Moreover, the rate of inflation, which had reached 38.1 percent in 1952, descended to an annual average of only 3.9 percent in 1953 and 1954.[43]

But these successes, no matter how impressive, could not hide some of the deeper problems that continued to haunt the Argentine economy. These included the accelerating decapitalization of the private sector, the declining quality of economic infrastructure, and faltering entrepreneurial confidence, especially in the rural and financial sectors. In addition, the responsiveness of rural producers to the financial incentives contained in the 1952 stabilization program was more apparent than real, for the production of exportable grains in 1953 and 1954 seemed large only when contrasted to the drought years of 1951 and 1952; in fact, although production had risen impressively, it still lagged behind that of the war years by as much as 50 percent.[44]

Perón did not get another chance to deal with these problems. Instead, he was forced to flee the country by a military insurrection in September 1955. Since 1950 he had been struggling to stem the rising tide of opposition to his increasingly defensive and abusive rule, retreating step by step into the kind of authoritarianism that only further undermined his authority, especially over the church and the military. The military's attempt to drive him from office in June 1955 failed, but their next effort, which was supported not only by Argentine conservatives, but nearly all non-Peronist political parties as well, forced him into exile, from where he would spend the next eighteen years campaigning for his successful return to the presidency in 1973.

The Peronist Performance

The Peronists have been maligned for the damage they did to the Argentine economy as well as for their cynical abuse of

democratic institutions. But it is not my purpose here to
evaluate the technical errors of Peronist economic policy or to
stand in judgment of their political ethics; rather I will limit myself to their use of political and economic strategy to execute
their development program.

We have seen that Perón stopped short of creating a corporatist regime in Argentina and instead was content to concentrate power in his very personalistic presidency and to use it to
create an industrialized welfare state. He was, of course, not the
first Argentine leader to rule through a powerful presidency.
With few exceptions, Argentina's government had been dominated by strong executives throughout the country's modern history. Nor was he departing from past practices when he ignored
and abused his critics. He simply turned the tables on the conservatives who had ruled Argentina in the 1930s by using their
own heavy-handed methods against them. This time it was they
rather than nationalists and labor leaders who were excluded
from the inner presidential circle. Actually, one is struck by how
little the Peronists changed traditional policy-making practices.
To be sure, they mobilized the working class for the first time
and brought a new vigor to the intimidation of opponents, but
on the whole they behaved in a manner not unfamiliar to their
countrymen. Peronist political institutions and processes were
never as radical or as innovative as the movement's leaders and
enemies proclaimed. No doubt Perón had studied the achievements of the corporatist regimes of Spain, Italy, and Germany
and assessed the shortcomings of liberal regimes throughout
Latin America. Nevertheless, his search for models appropriate
to Argentina's postwar needs yielded little more than a few
skeletal organizations and a colorful but superficial political
philosophy, which he used to clothe a rather simple populist authoritarian regime.

Similarly, his policy learning took more from Argentina's immediate past than it did from foreign models. The Peronists did
study the recovery of industrial capitalism from the Great Depression and tried in a crude way to emulate its fiscal and
monetary practices. But it was to Argentina's experimentation
with the regulation of financial, exchange, and commodity markets in the 1930s, the Pinedo Plan that Congress rejected in
1940, and the expansion of state power by the military in 1943,
that Perón looked for guidance in his search for solutions to the

country's problems. Rather than begin anew with an alien set of institutions and policies, he merely adapted the instruments employed by his predecessors to his revised policy objectives. The regulation of wages was used to increase rather than contain working-class income; commodity-marketing and pricing mechanisms were transformed from means of promoting rural wealth to ways of transferring it to other sectors; and instead of denying tariff protection in order to satisfy trading partners, it was used to stimulate domestic industry.

If anyone gained in the long run from Peronist development policy it was not the Argentine working class (who would later pay a high price for the first-round rewards of Peronism) but the Argentine state, whose public enterprises and regulatory powers took on a new and lasting importance under the Peronists. The transformation of the state from the promotional bystander of the predepression era to the involved manager of economic growth, which had begun cautiously under the Concordancia, was completed by Perón. With it came a politicization of economic policy making that would never again allow authorities to withdraw from their deep involvement in the regulation of the nation's economy.

Most striking about Perón was his apparent lack of concern for the congruity of his political and economic strategies. Certainly it was a matter that deserved his attention. After all, his farm policy violated conventional norms through its punitive confiscation of farm income and provoked a hostile rural reaction; and his industrial, financial, and commercial policies, while they were for a time rewarding to those who cooperated with them, also became a divisive influence within those sectors. In fact, only his labor and wage policies could expect to elicit clientele support on their own. Nevertheless, the Peronists saw no need to adopt a political strategy aimed at reducing the uncertainty and resistance provoked by their economic policies. On the contrary, through his inflammatory populist rhetoric and personalistic policy-management style, Perón aggravated conflict by increasing the suspicion and distrust of the farmers, bankers, and industrialists already opposed to his programs.

To some extent Perón's choice of a combative rather than a conciliatory political strategy was influenced by his campaign to win and hold working-class support, for it was through his attacks on the oligarchy that he had built a working-class following between 1943 and 1946. But even after 1949, when he was assured of labor allegiance, he refused to tone down his rhetoric or open his policy-making process to the producers and traders who demanded greater involvement in the management of the economy. Instead, he held fast to the habits that he had developed during his campaign for public office and the preparation of his controversial program in 1945, ignoring the increasing alienation that they fostered and the damage they did to the implementation of his development program.

In Perón's defense one might argue that he did rather well, despite his unwillingness to lessen tensions through a more open and conciliatory dialogue with his opponents, for he did accelerate the country's economic growth in 1946 and 1947 and execute a successful stabilization program in 1952. Moreover, the latter, due to Perón's control over Argentine workers and his adroit use of financial incentives, led to a modest recovery in 1953 and 1954. But such claims ignore not only the long term economic costs of his initial policy errors, but also the demoralization of private producers and financiers, who learned between 1946 and 1955 to distrust economic authorities more than ever before and to survive by defying regulations and cynically manipulating economic conditions for narrow, short-term gains. This legacy, combined with the expansion of state responsibility for economic management, left his successors with the near impossible task of fulfilling the state's expanded role by seeking the cooperation of citizens who distrusted their motives and were determined to avoid the enforcement of their policies.

Perón's preference for "going it alone" in the implementation of his programs may have been due not so much to his fear of his policies being captured by his rural, industrial, commercial, and financial opponents as to an overconfidence in his ability to regulate their behaviors through the use of economic instruments alone. Heady with electoral victory and the ease with which their first reforms were executed in 1946, the Peronists were easily able to convince themselves that they could succeed without dealing directly with those who managed private economic institutions. But in doing so, they fell victim to a very naive view of what was required to manage a complex, industrializing economy. Neither the industrial nations from whom the Peronists had taken their inspiration, nor the European corporatist regimes from whom they derived their view of political leadership had been as unresponsive to their nation's entrepreneurs as had the Peronists. On the contrary, in the industrial nations postdepression and postwar policies were directed at promoting the recovery of farmers and industrialists, while the leaders of corporatist regimes worked closely with industrialists and landowners to sustain the domination of capital over labor. Perón, on the other hand, chose to be the champion of labor over capital and, even though his favoritism of labor lessened rapidly after 1949, he never opened his inner circle to those whom he had excluded initially from the policy-making process.

Perón had wanted to propel Argentina into the elite of the world's affluent industrial nations so that it would no longer serve the whims of foreign consumers and creditors and its laboring masses would no longer be exploited by the country's economic elite. Economic dependence was to give way to national autonomy and the agrarian export economy to industrial self-sufficiency. Within a decade Argentina was to take its place among the world's prosperous nations, a fate that many Argentines believed they more than any of their neighbors deserved. But prosperity, national autonomy, and social justice eluded the Peronists. By 1955, Argentina, the land destined for greatness, had become the sorry paradox, a country that appeared to enjoy the resources necessary for sustained economic growth but somehow failed to use them efficiently.

Depression, War, and Peronism: Lessons and Legacies

In the twenty-five years that followed the 1929 depression, Argentines sowed the seeds of the policy disputes that rage to this day. First conservatives and then Peronists attempted to impose their solutions on the country's vulnerable economy. The failure of either to prevail has left Argentina divided and in a state of sustained conflict over fundamental economic issues.

One cannot help but be struck by the contrast between the intense conflicts that accompanied the responses of Argentine leaders to the depression and the war and the policy consensus which grew out of the postdepression and postwar recoveries of the Anglo-American, Scandinavian, and Western European nations. Whereas many of the economic policy successes of the more industrialized capitalist nations were due largely to agreements among political and economic elites on what was needed to rescue capitalism from depression and war, Argentina's difficulties appear to be due in no small measure to her leaders' failure to secure a similar agreement on how they should respond to these two monumental events. We have seen, for example, how, after 1930, most rural spokesmen, financial leaders, and conservative industrialists accepted the trade concessions demanded by the British under the Roca-Runciman pact, the repression of the working class, and the belt-tightening measures adopted by the Justo administration as policies not only demanded by the country's temporary condition but also appropriate for dealing with similar externally induced problems after the war. More nationalistic Argentines like Juan Perón, on the other hand, resented the humiliation suffered by the country at the hands of its trading partners and the sacrifices that harsh recovery measures demanded from the country's urban consumers, and dedicated themselves to the design of development strategies that would make the country more economically independent. The essential point is that while the leaders of some capitalistic countries were agreeing on how to revitalize their economies, Argentines were disagreeing on whether or not they should try to reorient theirs.

Of course the Argentines' task was in many ways a more formidable one than that of the industrialized capitalistic nations. Where the latter had to concern themselves, after 1929, primarily with putting unused industrial capacity into production and, after 1945, with reconstructing an industrial economy on a talent base that was reduced but not destroyed by war, the Argentines were still debating the merits of changing their economy from a predominantly foreign-financed, export-oriented one to a more autonomous industrial one. Nearly all sectors of society stood to gain from the restoration of industrial production in Western Europe, but the reorientation of the Argentine economy directly threatened many members of the economic elite. To make matters worse, the transition to industrialization in vulnerable, export-dependent countries like Argentina is seldom smooth. Regardless of the measures employed, industrialization must be financed either by the sale of the country's raw-product exports or by heavy doses of foreign investment. The latter, however, makes the country more rather than less dependent on foreigners in the short run, while the sale of commodities on the world market, because of fluctuating prices, often makes stable economic growth impossible and industrialization more costly than originally anticipated. And the more difficult and expensive that industrialization becomes, the easier it is for its conservative opponents to defend their claim that it is too costly a process for countries like Argentina to pursue.

The intensity that has characterized Argentina's postwar policy conflicts is also a product of the way policy was formulated by Argentine officials during the 1930s and 1940s, largely in isolation from those threatened by it. Labor leaders never accepted the legitimacy of the conservative governments who ignored and repressed them after the depression. Similarly, the rural elite never forgave Perón for evicting their representatives from the inner circles of the executive branch where rural policy was determined. Peronist policy was not especially radical; industrialization was already well under way by the time Perón had arrived and the state have been expanding its authority over the economy for at least a decade. The Peronists did redistribute some income, but they did not redistribute much property. Consequently, what appeared to disturb those who had directed the economy before 1943 the most was not the change in policy but their systematic exclusion from the central decision-making process and their repeated abuse by inexperienced but belligerent Peronist officials.

The governance problem that Perón faced at the outset was similar to the one that has traditionally plagued reformist governments in pluralistic societies elsewhere. Perón wanted to secure changes in the country's political economy that appeared to threaten well-entrenched producer groups who, if not held in check, could block the government's reform effort. What he had to do was prevent opponents who were accustomed to a government that had served their interests in the 1930s from forcing him into a retreat midway through the implementation of his program. When faced with this dilemma, democratic reformers have tended to blend state authority with legislative and interest-group bargaining in the hope of reaching policy compromises conducive to the achievement of most of their policy objectives. But Perón, operating as he did against the legacy of a conservative monopoly over economic policy making, had no desire to bargain with the country's powerful economic elite. He chose to be combative rather than conciliatory. He deprived them of their positions on official boards and commissions, dictated policy to them, and ignored their warnings and complaints.

But Perón only went half way. Like many reformist politicians who face a well-entrenched elite, he antagonized the economic elite but he did not destroy it. To some extent he had no other choice given his rather moderate economic strategy, which relied on their contributions to industrial and agricultural growth. But by excluding and antagonizing them, while at the same time remaining dependent upon them, he allowed them the means they needed to undermine his economic program and eventually bring his regime to an abrupt halt.

Finally, a word about the political legacies that Perón left to frustrate his successors is in order. Most consequential was his expansion of the political process through the mobilization of the working class into active participation. All future policy decisions, whatever their purpose, would have to take the expectations and political strength of organized labor into account. No problem preoccupied post-1955 policy makers more than the threat posed to their rule by an antagonistic labor movement. As a result, much of their time has been devoted to devising techniques for coping with working-class responses to government policy. Second, as a result of Peronist reforms, the state would never again be able to withdraw from its deep involvement in the management of the Argentine economy. Not only did a generation of laborers and entrepreneurs come to rely on their protection by the state, but economic affairs had become too complex to be left to the rules of the market place and some occasional prodding by economic authorities. Moreover, Perón had made income distribution a central issue of public policy, obligating future presidents to address it whether they wanted to or not. And third, Perón did little to disabuse Argentines of the notion that economic policy making was a very partisan activity that one had to control in order to influence. There was no intermediate means for influencing policy, it seemed. Perón, like his conservative predecessors, had made it clear that economic policy making was the job of central decision makers working without interference from private groups not already within the governing coalition. Thus, he reinforced the notion that there was little room for compromise in the governing of the nation. The effects of these legacies on post-Peronist governments will be explored in the examination of democratic regimes in Part 2 and military regimes in Part 3.

PART TWO

The Constitutional Democrats

4

Frondizi and the Politics of Survival

Policy making in constitutional democracies is not hard to characterize. One usually finds presidents or prime ministers initiating programs that are ratified or rejected by legislatures in which political parties are represented and interest groups consulted. Policies are then implemented by a bureaucracy that seeks the compliance of appropriate clienteles, some of whom may have already been involved at various points in the formulation and ratification of the government's program. Although the power distributions and policy outcomes of democratic systems vary, they do share a process in which aggrieved citizens may apply their resources at multiple points to influence policy decisions. The task of the chief executive in such systems is one of channeling influence attempts in a direction that supports his policy objectives and maximizes his or his party's chances of reelection. Within the context of Latin American democracies, Albert Hirschman's "reformmonger" comes immediately to mind. Motivated by a progressive spirit, yet practical in his politics, he is the consummate policy maker who works within constraints, imposed by his imperfect democratic institutions, by bargaining and logrolling his way to satisfying policy outcomes. He knows when to invite particular partisans to join him in the formulation of his policies and when and how to secure their ratification. And even though he will not win on all issues, he will succeed with many important ones by skillfully maximizing his resources through the use of coalitions and appropriate bargaining strategies.[1]

But how appropriate are such chracterizations to democratic policy making in Argentina after 1955? Admittedly, constitutional government was no stranger to Argentina when it was restored in 1958. For nearly a century before the adoption of the Peronist constitution in 1949 the country had been governed under the same constitution since 1853. In form it differed little from the presidential systems created throughout the Western Hemisphere in the late eighteenth and early nineteenth centuries.

If we focus on political practice rather than legal forms, however, we quickly discover that constitutional norms were often ignored in Argentina, starting with elitist rule in the late nineteenth century and extending through the Concordancia's persecution of opponents in the 1930s. Nor did Perón's cynical use of the 1949 constitution for his own political advantage do much to increase public confidence in constitutional rule. In fact, only the Radical governments of the 1920s could legitimately claim to have made a serious attempt to abide by constitutional rules, but their brief tenure could hardly compensate for the abuses that came before and after them. Consequently, when the military took on the assignment of returning the reigns of government to civilians in 1958, they were not restoring a system already well-founded in the Argentine experience, but one whose legitimacy had never been fully established.

Unfortunately, a legacy of political abuse and cynicism was not the only difference between Argentine democracy and the idealized model. There was also the problem created by the military's determination in 1958 to exclude what they termed antidemocratic groups like the Peronists from the political process. Although they would justify their actions by claiming that they were necessary in order to protect democratic institutions from further abuse, the practical effect of excluding the Peronists was to handicap the newly elected president by raising serious questions about the legitimacy of his election. Argentina was also plagued by relatively weak and narrowly based political parties. Traditionally, the country's parties had not performed well as aggregators of diverse economic interests, for they either lacked ties to economic interest groups altogether or, like the Peronists with their CGT and the Progressive Democrats and their small farmers, they were linked to only one organized constituency. Especially after the decline of the conservative parties in the 1940s, most rural, industrial, and financial interests found themselves isolated from the prevailing political parties whose pursuit of Argentina's urban electorate had led them to bypass traditional interest group intermediaries. To make and implement economic policy, then, Argentina's democratic presidents had to deal with two separate constituencies. First, there were the political parties represented in the legislature with whom they would have to negotiate in order to gain formal ratification of their programs; at the same time they also faced a variety of economic groups whose cooperation had to be secured through nonlegislative means. But while there existed constitutional institutions and processes to manage the first, the liberal democratic model adopted in Argentina in 1958 offered no formal means for accomplishing the second. That task would be left, it turned out, to the political skills and inventiveness of the presidents themselves. We will examine how it was managed by Arturo Frondizi (1958–62) in this chapter and Arturo Illia (1963–66) in the next.

A Policy Dilemma: Development vs. Stabilization

How does a president who was elected with the support of a multiparty coalition that collapsed after his inauguration retain enough authority to implement harsh economic stabilization measures? Moreover, how does he do it under the watchful eye of a military that has forced the resignation of his closest advisors and replaced them with economic policy makers of their own choosing? This unfortunate scenario was the one that faced Arturo Frondizi soon after his inauguration in May 1958. What Argentina appeared to require in 1958 was strong leadership that could bring together diverse political forces in an attack on the country's post-Peronist economic problems. But what it got was a president who was deprived of much of his authority by the early loss of his coalition partners and the constant meddling of the military in presidential politics. Frondizi, who began his presidency as a skilled political tactician, ended it by watching his constitutional regime torn down by military officers who had lost faith in his ability to deal with the resurgence of Peronism. To understand how this unlikely transformation came about we must go back to 1958 and Frondizi's ambitious plans for his divided country.

Arturo Frondizi desperately wanted to bring his Radical party and Argentina into the modern industrial era. A nationalist, he had shared Perón's concern with the country's excessive reliance on a strategy of export-induced economic growth. But he also recognized that his party had contributed few innovations to Argentina's economic policy arsenal during its fourteen-year rule under Irigoyen and Alvear between 1916 and 1930, and had added little to its policy debates since 1930. Instead, it had been forced to play the role of the loyal opposition for over twenty-five years, first denouncing the Concordancia for its political repression and economic internationalism and then attacking Perón's autocratic and corrupt enforcement of his simplistic industrialization scheme. The Radicals emerged from the events of 1955 determined to recapture the presidency that had been taken from them by a military coup in 1930. Their opportunity came when the military officers who had deposed Perón prohibited the participation of the Peronist party in the 1958 elections. Most Radical party leaders were convinced that through the use of their grassroots urban and small-town organizations and well-worn platform of moderate, nationalistic programs, they could easily defeat the remaining opposition, which came largely from small parties on the right and extreme left. For Frondizi, however, old formulas were not sufficient to deal with the problems of post-Peronist Argentina; so, in addition to his candidacy, he offered his party and Argentine voters an ambitious new development strategy.

Frondizi recognized that innovative economic policies as well as electoral opportunism were needed to solve the problems left behind by Perón. Aided by advisor Rogelio Frigerio, an ambitious and politically astute entrepreneur, and guided by the structuralist critique of export dependent development popularized by the United Nations Economic Commission for Latin America (ECLA) in the early 1950s, he prepared a comprehensive program aimed at promoting sustainable economic growth. He began with the observation that Perón's industrialization scheme, which had depended almost entirely on the stimulus of increased demand and public financing, had failed because it had treated the symptoms rather than the underlying structural causes of the country's underdevelopment. Perón had erred, Frondizi argued, by failing to understand that a rapidly enlarged consumer demand could not be satisfied using Argentine resources alone, for neither the private sector nor the government could generate the capital required to establish the heavy industrial base on which a consumer-goods industry would depend. Instead, under Perón's naive approach to industrialization, inflation was accelerated by the overstimulation of consumer demand and balance-of-payments deficits increased by the importation of expensive capital goods and raw products. If Argentina was to be saved from its excessive dependence on meat and grain exports, it could not be done using the Peronist method, because it failed to deal with the economy's structural deficiencies.[2]

As Frondizi and Frigerio saw it, the principal question was how to industrialize a country that suffered from an acute capital shortage. The answer, it turned out, was not hard to find. Abandoning his ardent nationalism, Frondizi announced that Argentina would be industrialized through the use of foreign capital to finance the construction of essential industries and a modern economic infrastructure. When the Peronists criticized Frondizi's proposal as nothing more than a poorly disguised capitulation to economic imperialism, he defended himself by pointing out that the use of foreign capital to industrialize was qualitatively different from traditional dependence on foreign markets. Whereas the latter is a form of dependence to which all other economic activities must be subordinated, the former is only a temporary expedient leading to eventual national economic independence. The critical variable is not the foreign or domestic origin of the capital but its use in reducing the country's heavy reliance on foreign exchange producing raw product exports. Similarly, it is not the temporary transfer of income to investors that matters, but the creation of sufficient productive capacity to satisfy increased demand over the long haul at relatively stable prices, an objective that could be realized only if the economy were built on the secure foundation of heavy industry and sound infrastructure.

The expansion of production and the maintenance of price stability were to be the primary short-term objectives of this strategy. To achieve them, consumers would have to yield income to the investor, especially foreign ones, as rates of return were raised to attract foreign capital. Agricultural income, meanwhile, would be sustained until the economy's dependence on raw product exports had been reduced. But once the strategy succeeded, a larger proportion of rural production would be sent to domestic markets to satisfy the demand of urban consumers, since the country would no longer be as dependent on the export of basic commodities for its livelihood.

Where Perón's industrialization scheme had represented a short-term gamble, Frondizi's was a long-term one that sought gradual industrial development through the efficient use of foreign capital. But given existing high consumption levels, as well as the nationalism of small business in Argentina, his call for short-term consumer sacrifices and greater reliance on foreign investors invited opposition from those who had gained economically under Peronism. Only if he could convince nationalists and urban consumers, as well as doubting rural producers, that the strategy would serve their long-term interests could he expect the patience and support that its implementation required.

We shall never know if Frondizi's scheme would have succeeded for he was never given an opportunity to implement it as planned. As frequently happens with the best laid plans, an economic crisis intervened just before his inauguration and forced substantial modifications in his ambitious proposals. Again it was the recurring problem of a deteriorating balance of payments that forced the new administration to turn from long-term development planning to solving the problems of the moment.

Frondizi began by asking the International Monetary Fund (IMF) for emergency stand-by credits to help him deal with his foreign exchange shortage. In their preloan review in July 1958, the IMF economists advised that import restrictions were not enough to solve Argentina's payments problem. Instead, it was essential that Frondizi also reduce domestic demand sharply by cutting public expenditures, curtailing credit, keeping salaries in line with productivity, and reducing public investments below the levels anticipated in his development plan.[3] Given his desire to get on with the expansion of the nation's economic infrastructure and basic industries, Frondizi was naturally reluctant to implement the IMF proposals, even though they were consistent with the diagnosis of the more pessimistic members of his own staff. Gradually, however, he too came to recognize that his policy options were few; it required little tutoring in economics to understand that inaction in the face of the payments crisis would be disastrous for the entire economy, negating whatever development programs he might choose to sponsor. Moreover, few foreign investors would be attracted to a country that had been condemned as financially irresponsible by the International Monetary Fund. Nevertheless, not until the last obstacle to the adoption of the IMF measures had faded away, namely Frondizi's hopes of retaining working-class political support, did he finally commit himself to the belt-tightening measures.

In the wake of his election, Frondizi found himself torn between the tenuous electoral alliance that he had established with partyless Peronists on the one hand and the demands of anti-Peronists in the military, industrial, financial, and rural sectors on the other.[4] Immediately after his inauguration in May 1958, he had rewarded wage earners with a 60-percent pay increase in the hope of retaining working-class support, but then came the deteriorating payments situation and the IMF report, followed by increasing strains in the president's relations with labor. Finally, in November 1958, with his tenuous alliance with organized labor on the verge of collapse, he gave the go-ahead to those who would formulate IMF-sponsored policy measures that he would announce a month later. His final break with labor came when most Peronist unions, ignoring the president's plea for restraint, supported a strike against the state petroleum company. After some hesitation, and several failures at compromise, he declared a state of siege to supress the strike and in so doing hastened the end of his coalition with organized labor.

With his path cleared, Frondizi addressed the nation on December 29, 1958, to announce the most drastic economic stabilization program in Argentine history. In addition to an attack on the fiscal deficit through public service rate increases and layoffs of public employees, and an expected tightening of the monetary supply, the new program included increased reliance on foreign investment, a sharp devaluation, the elimination of all price controls and most subsidies, and wage guidelines to be enforced by a denial of credit to enterprises exceeding wage ceilings.[5] (See Table No. 4.1.) In short, it represented an all-out effort to achieve the elusive goals of price and balance of payments stability by freeing the private sector from heavyhanded state regulation and redistributing financial resources from consumers to entrepreneurs.

TABLE 4.1
Frondizi's Economic Policy, 1959

Objectives	1. Improve balance of payments 2. Price stability 3. Industrial growth
Instruments	
Fiscal	1. Reduce deficit 2. Increase prices of government services
Money and Credit	1. Very tight money and credit
Exchange	1. Devaluation 2. Export earning retentions
Controls	1. Free-market pricing and wage setting
Income Redistribution	1. Major shifts from consumers to rural producers 2. From domestic to foreign investors

The government's harsh new program was still not enough to satisfy some of Frondizi's critics, especially those in the miltary who feared a sudden restoration of the president's alliance with the Peronists, which might force his abandonment of the IMF program. The military took no chances; to prevent such a change in course, they forced Frondizi to dismiss his entire economic team and replace them with one headed by Alvaro Alsogaray, a former air force officer and well-known free-market ideologue, in June 1959. With Alsogaray came a group of officials not devoted to the president's politics or his industrialization plan but to Alsogaray's execution of the IMF stabilization program.[6] At last, it appeared, the laissez-faire ideologues and free traders, along with the monetarists from the IMF, had triumphed.

Despite the immense constraints imposed on him by the IMF program and the arrival of Alsogaray and his team, Frondizi

struggled to retain as many projects from his original development scheme as possible. Leading the list was the attainment of
self-sufficiency in petroleum production. In 1922 the Radical
government had created a state monopoly over the exploration
and exploitation of petroleum, excepting a few concessions previously granted and an officially sanctioned retail cartel managed
by Shell and Esso. But as energy needs increased during the
1930s and 1940s, state petroleum production failed to keep pace,
and by 1957 Argentina was consuming twice as much petroleum
as it could produce at a cost of over $173 million annually in
scarce foreign currency.[7] Finding such costs intolerable in the
face of almost depleted foreign exchange reserves in 1958,
Frondizi, in one of his first presidential acts, reversed his well-
established nationalistic stance on the petroleum issue and authorized the state petroleum company to contract foreign firms
to extract Argentine oil for domestic consumption.[8]

The petroleum program was an overwhelming success: domestic production was trebled and met 90 percent of domestic needs
by 1963. Nevertheless, Frondizi was never forgiven by Peronists
as well as nationalists within the Radical party for what they took
to be his "sell-out" of the national interest.[9] While the controversy raged, Frondizi managed some achievements in other
areas as well. For example, with the aid of the record $369 mil-
lion in foreign capital that he attracted to Argentina between
1959 and 1961, he completed the country's first integrated steel
complex in 1960 (a project begun by the military over a decade
before), increased the number of automobiles produced domestically from 3,715 in 1958 to 78,667 in 1962, greatly expanded the
production of chemicals and pharmaceuticals, and improved
many public facilities.[10]

Like Perón in 1952, Frondizi was also forced by a foreign-
exchange crisis to rely more than he had anticipated on the producers of commodity exports to rescue the Argentine economy.
His initial development program had proposed a gradual increase in rural production through accelerated mechanization,
using equipment manufactured in Argentina. But with the
economic crisis he was forced to rely on exchange and price incentives to stimulate rural production. He abolished exchange
controls completely for the first time since 1930 and, in pursuit
of a freer market, abandoned most of the remaining price con-

trols and freed the wheat trade, the only cereal whose marketing was still controlled. At the same time, exchange retentions were imposed (20 percent for cereals and 10 percent for beef and mutton), ostensibly to prevent excessive liquidity as a consequence of exchange windfalls, but also to boost sagging government revenues.[11] Whether or not Argentine farmers would trust the new government and respond enthusiastically to its measures as expected was one of many unanswered questions confronting Frondizi in 1959.

Finally, organized labor would also play a critical role in the implementation of the government's rescue operation. Frondizi had hoped for its acceptance of a policy of wage restraint during the initial phases of his original program. But, as we have seen, his tenuous alliance with the Peronists, which would have enjoyed only a low probability of survival under normal conditions, was doomed by his repression of the petroleum workers and the promulgation of stabilization measures, which, if they did not freeze wages, did remove price controls and weaken working-class purchasing power. Thus, the government's ability to withstand the effects of likely labor protests became another critical factor in stabilization's chances for success, and one made especially interesting by Frondizi's determination to use collective bargaining rather than governmental controls and wage freezes to set wage rates.

Implementing Policy Under Siege

Frondizi's presidency was handicapped from its inception by three adverse conditions. First, he won an election from which the Peronists, who represented at least one-third of the electorate, had been excluded. This left him haunted by the question of the legitimacy of his own mandate and the temptation—one to which he succumbed to his regret in 1962—to reopen the electoral process to the previously excluded Peronist party in the hope of defeating it and gaining the popular legitimacy that had eluded him in 1958. Second, he had lost the support of nearly half of his own Radical party when it split over his candidacy at its 1956 convention. The division was caused by the opposition of Ricardo Balbin, the party's presidential candidate in 1951, and his Unionist faction, to Frondizi's plan to pursue Peronist votes through an "integrationist" campaign strategy in 1958. In protest of Frondizi's nomination, the Unionists walked out and formed their own committee in February 1957, taking with them most of the delegates from the provinces of Córdoba, Santiago del Estero, Buenos Aires, and the Federal Capital. Soon thereafter they renamed themselves the People's Radicals (Unión Cívica Radical del Pueblo—UCRP) and nominated Ricardo Balbin to oppose Frondizi and his Intransigent Radicals (Unión Cívica Radical Intransigente—UCRI) in the 1958 election.

What he lost from the Radical party split, Frondizi made up with the votes of Peronists and won the 1958 election with 52 percent of the popular vote, defeating Balbin and the People's Radicals, who polled 33 percent. In 1963 the latter would get their revenge when they finally won the presidency for Arturo Illia and immediately reversed several of Frondizi's policies. But in 1958 it was the tenuous coalition of one-half of the old Radical party and the supporters of exiled President Juan Perón, who had earned the right to govern the country.[12]

The president's very narrow base of hard-core political support, especially after his abandonment by the Peronists six months after his inauguration, contributed to his third problem, his vulnerability to the demands of the Argentine military, which placed him and the constitutional system on trial throughout his tenure. Although most of the high command had supported the restoration of the constitutional process in 1958, fears of the Peronists' return to power, either directly through electoral victory or indirectly through their influence on the president they helped elect in 1958, kept the military deeply immersed in presidential politics thereafter. Rumors of military coups became the norm rather than the exception during Frondizi's four years, with more than a few attempts progressing beyond the rumor stage and being thwarted by officers loyal to the president, or called off after the president had yielded to military demands for policy or cabinet changes. In a very special sense, it was the military that became Frondizi's coalition partner after 1959, but instead of lending the government popular support, as might have occurred with the addition of a civilian partner, it merely set the policy limits beyond which he dared not venture if he wished to remain in the presidency. Coalition formation, which

under more normal conditions might lead to a greater probability of legislative success and continued rule, was for Frondizi no
more than a means of political survival.

A high price had to be paid for the regime's vulnerability to
military demands when in June 1959 the president was forced by
anti-Peronist officers to replace his cabinet with one of their
choosing. He had begun his administration with cabinet ministers drawn from UCRI party stalwarts or close campaign advisors
like Rogelio Frigerio. Only thirteen months later Frigerio and
the rest of the cabinet were forced to resign in order to placate
the leaders of a military revolt against the president. The leaders
of the revolt, many of whom had opposed Frondizi's election,
accused the president of conspiring with the exiled Perón and
paving the way for his movement's political resurrection, of mis-
using the military by demanding that it mobilize labor unions in
order to halt strikes, and, finally, of dragging his feet on the
enforcement of economic stabilization, especially with regard to
budget cuts and administrative reforms. Nothing less than the
replacement of his cabinet with one less sympathetic to his integrationist political strategy and more supportive of stabilization
would satisfy the revolting officers, and in early June, as we saw
above, Frondizi saved his presidency by appointing a new
cabinet led by Alvaro Alsogaray.[13]

TABLE 4.2
Frondizi's Policy-Making Process

Phases	Political Institutions and Techniques
Initiation	International Monetary Fund advisors and cabinet ministers
Formulation	Inner circle of presidential advisors
Consultation	Within executive With UCRI party leaders
Ratification	Congress indirectly through budgetary process
Execution	Heavy reliance on market incentives Selective use of force against labor protests
Feedback	Informal access to cabinet ministers Public protests

Although Alsogaray was blamed by the critics of stabilization
for the execution of many unpopular policies in 1959 and 1960,
he actually did little more than implement the program an-

nounced by Frondizi in December 1958. But if the substance of economic policy was not changed by the military revolt of mid 1959, the form of its management certainly was. In contrast to Frondizi and Frigerio, the clever and opportunistic political tacticians, Alsogaray was a man of conviction, a simple-minded ideologue, who thrived in the role of the tough enforcer of drastic measures believed essential to save the Argentine economy. He was at his best not when bargaining with critical interest group leaders, which he seldom did, but when lecturing his countrymen on radio or television about the blessings of the free-enterprise system, often using elaborate charts and graphs to convince his audience of the need for personal sacrifice and hard work. Ironically, the closest thing to the Alsogaray phenomenon that Argentines had seen was Miguel Miranda, the equally enthusiastic salesman of economic policy who had labored so hard in the mid 1940s to gain followers for Perón's new trade policies. But where Miranda had preached the virtues of state intervention, Alsogaray offered the doctrine of the "social economy of the market" and the model of Ludwig Erhard's postwar German recovery to inspire Argentina's skeptical producers and consumers.[14]

What we must now ask is how a president who had campaigned on a platform of political integration and foreign-financed industrial development, only to be forced by adverse economic conditions to adopt a harsh stabilization program and by political opponents to appoint a new cabinet to implement it, adapted his original political strategy to the requirements of economic stabilization. That is, once he had committed himself to the IMF program and accepted the constraints imposed on its execution by the military, how did Frondizi use the political instruments that remained to mobilize support for his fight against inflation, lagging rural production, and capital shortages?

Although his choices were narrowed by the loss of cabinet officers loyal to him and by the military's opposition to a coalition with the Peronists, his UCRI party still held a narrow majority in Congress. Also, the country's economic interest groups, many of them revitalized after 1955, presented opportunities for the creation of a prostabilization coalition which might facilitate policy implementation. And, of course, Frondizi, despite his weakened status, was still president and could make some use of

his office in leading the recovery effort. But if the opportunity
for bold, innovative leadership was present, he did not take advantage of it.

Despite his reputation as the supreme negotiator and back-
room wheeler-dealer, a reputation he gained during the 1958
campaign rather than as president, Frondizi did very little to
adapt his political strategy to the requirements of stabilization
policy. Instead of looking for new leadership opportunities in his
unfortunate condition, he accepted the constraints imposed upon
him by the arrival of Alsogaray and his economic team and withdrew into his presidency to watch the unwanted intruder struggle with the implementation of the new measures. Although the
president could not completely escape association with them, he
was willing to let Alsogaray take the responsibility and, quite
often, the blame for the harsh stabilization policies. If he had a
political strategy at all, it was to disassociate himself as much as
possible from the day-to-day implementation of stabilization so
that once it was completed he could divest himself of the minister responsible for it and, he hoped, pick up where he had left
off in 1959 with his campaign for political integration and industrial development.

Frondizi's reluctance to involve economic interest group leaders directly in the design and administration of economic stabilization is most apparent in the ways he dealt with entrepreneurs,
the legislature, and his new planning agency. He had promised
in his campaign not only to recognize the rights of those
economic interest groups that already existed in 1958 but also to
restore the rights of Peronist organizations that had been closed
by the military in 1955. In fulfilling those pledges he not only
increased the number of active groups, but also gave new life to
conflicts among them, and significantly complicated the task of
securing their collaboration in the execution of policy.

Just after his inauguration the new president earned the en-
mity of both the Rural Society and the Industrial Union when he
repealed the anti-CGT legislation promulgated by the military in
1956 and restored the legal status of the General Economic Confederation, the national entrepreneurs' association that had been
closed by the military in 1955 because of its close collaboration
with the Peronists.[15] This unleashed a bitter rivalry between the
two industrial groups that continued until the early 1970s. The

CGE, which included nearly 60 percent of the country's industrial firms, opposed the IMF stabilization measures and championed the cause of easier credit and higher tariff protection. The UIA, which claimed that the larger firms that composed its membership accounted for 80 percent of the country's industrial sales, continued to denounce the CGE as an authoritarian organization that naively advocated the ruinous subsidization of inefficient domestic industries.[16] Rather then stand by idly and watch the resurgence of the CGE the UIA joined with the Rural Society and the Argentine Chamber of Commerce in 1960 to form the Action of Free Enterprise Institutions (ACIEL), an anti-Peronist coalition that campaigned vigorously against government acceptance of CGE and CGT policy demands during the 1960s.[17]

By the time Frondizi had announced his stabilization program, this enlarged system of rival groups was in full swing. To make matters worse, his sudden shift in policy, rather than bringing him a host of new supporters, reinforced widespread distrust of the country's unpredictable new president. CGE and CGT leaders who had supported Frondizi's election as the lesser of many evils saw the president abandoning their cause, while the more conservative leaders of the Industrial Union, Rural Society, and CARBAP, on the other hand, discovered that the candidate they had opposed and whose political ambitions they still distrusted now offered them policies that, in principle, they supported. Still, they were not certain about how to interpret the sudden change of course, and Frondizi offered them little help in making up their minds. Instead of trying to work closely with labor and entrepreneurial group leaders, Frondizi held back, keeping interest groups at arms length and leaving the task of winning their support to the public exhortations of Economy Minister Alsogaray.

Frondizi had planned to use his congressional majority to build a solid legislative program guided by his original development strategy, but with the sudden switch to stabilization, those hopes quickly faded. Occasionally he did ask Congress to ratify his economic policy decisions, though with the exception of its annual approval of the budget, it was usually consulted only after the fact. This was the case when Alsogaray testified in defense of the stabilization program in August 1959, eight months after its promulgation. In fact, Alsogaray's subjection to bitter and often petty attacks by the UCRP minority legislators for "selling out" to the International Monetary Fund led Frondizi to bypass Congress on economic matters as much as possible thereafter. The People's Radicals used every opportunity after December 1958 to embarrass the president over his conversion from a nationalistic critic of foreign investment in Argentina a few years before to a defender of IMF stabilization measures in 1959. But if anything, such criticism only encouraged the president to retreat from the legislative process.[18]

A third opportunity to mobilize private interests by involving them in the policy-making process came with the creation of a national planning agency (later called CONADE) in 1961, in compliance with one of the requirements for Argentine participation in the Alliance for Progress. Frondizi might have followed the popular French model of national planning with its reliance on the inclusion of the representatives of economic and social groups in discussions of plan design and implementation. Demands for this kind of involvement were frequently heard, especially from the small businessmen's General Economic Confederation. Nevertheless, Frondizi did not invite interest groups to join him in the design of long-range development programs. Instead, he continued to try to establish a posture of independence from partisan concerns, while at the same time frequently resorting to covert negotiations, especially with labor leaders whenever they threatened to sabotage his policies. But in doing the latter he only reinforced private-sector suspicions that he was secretly favoring some interests over others, and thereby earned their continued distrust.

Argentina's restored constitutional regime could hardly have been subjected to a more severe test than it was after 1958. In Frondizi, the country had a president whose ligitimacy was continually called into question, whose economic polices had been turned over to ministers chosen by his military opponents, whose working-class allies had abandoned him, and whose attempts to legalize once prohibited political groups had intensified political conflict. How policy was executed under these difficult circumstances is the question to which we must now turn.

ELON COLLEGE LIBRARY

The Fate of Stabilization

The International Monetary Fund had prescribed a shock treatment for Argentina's ills and that is exactly what Frondizi and Alsogaray gave their countrymen. The liberation of domestic markets quickly redistributed income in favor of commodity producers and exporters as stabilization's designers had intended. As we can see from Table No. 4.3, real working-class income dropped sharply, the share of national income claimed by salaries declined to one of its lowest points of the postwar era, and rural income, especially from beef production, rose impressively. Frondizi had, it was believed at the time, boldly completed the economic reconstruction begun so cautiously by the military in 1955, making it possible for the forces of the marketplace to carry on the efficient allocation of development resources with only limited help from the state. At long last rural producers would receive a fair return on their investments, workers the wage justified by their productivity, and investors an optimum climate in which to finance the country's industrial development.

TABLE 4.3
The Income Effects of Stabilization and Liberalization, 1958–61

	Salary Income as a Percent of National Income[a]	Real Income of Industrial Worker (Percent Change)[b]	Relative Agricultural Prices (Base 1960 = 100)[b]	Beef Production Real Income (Percent Change)[c]
1958	43.3	+ 4.9	92.39	+ 6
1959	37.8	− 25.8	103.63	+ 97
1960	38.4	+ 6.4	100.00	− 10
1961	39.9	+ 11.6	96.09	− 29

Source: [a]United Nations, Economic Commission for Latin America, *Economic Development and Income Distribution in Argentina* (New York: United Nations, 1969), p. 170, Table 39.
[b]Lorenzo Juan Sigaut, *Acerca de la distribución y niveles de ingreso en la Argentina* (Buenos Aires: Ediciones Macchi, 1972), p. 66, cuadro 21, and p. 57, cuadro 16.
[c]Banco Ganadero Argentino, *Temas de economía argentina: mercados y precios del ganado vacuno* (Buenos Aires: Banco Ganadero Argentino, 1966), p. 45.

Frondizi had no illusions about the likelihood of labor support for stabilization. Nevertheless, he agonized throughout his presidency over the choice of tactics for coping with working-class opposition. As a democrat and a reluctant convert to the free market, he preferred to solve labor conflicts through peaceful, government-regulated collective bargaining. But as an insecure president faced with military demands for an orderly but stern enforcement of stabilization, he was compelled to use physical repression to keep recalcitrant unions in line. Initially, he tried to win Peronist support with higher wages and the restoration of Perón's collective bargaining law. But once the honeymoon with labor had ended, he retreated from his conciliatory posture, refusing to keep his promise to lift the state intervention of the General Confederation of Labor, and then authorizing the military to execute its Contines Plan, a scheme which included a campaign of repression against union militants.[19]

Though divided and harassed, the labor movement, through its individual federations, managed to carry out general strikes to protest government economic policies in April, May, and September 1959. Simultaneously, new attemps to reunite the labor movement were made, though each lasted only long enough to denounce the government before internal disputes led to renewed disunity. In August 1959, for example, Peronist and Communist unions invited independent ones to join them in creating the United Workers Movement (MOU), which, before it collapsed six months later, issued a "Declaration of Principles" that not only denounced the International Monetary Fund for the policy demands it had "imposed" on the Argentine government in 1958, but also called for the enactment of thirteen measures (including the fixing of maximum prices by a commission on which labor would be represented, the cessation of worker dismissals in both the public and private sectors, an end to the privitization of public enterprises, and the return of the CGT to its constitutents).[20] The only dissenters from the labor manifesto were a small group of "independent" unions, composed primarily of white collar workers who had traditionally opposed Perón and, as they were to do again under Illia and Onganía, collaborated openly in government efforts to prevent the reunification of the CGT under Peronist control. Again, in October 1960, Peronists inititated a campaign to unify the labor movement, this time forming the Commission of 20 and on November 7 implementing one of the country's most inclusive general strikes. The strike ended with Frondizi promising to restore the CGT's full legal status by March 1, 1961, a pledge that he he did not keep.

Throughout 1961 the Commission continued its protests, first with twenty-four general strikes in July and October and then with a seventy-two-hour work stoppage on November 7, 8, and 9, in support of the striking railway workers.[21]

The railway strike marked a major defeat for the president and one from which, in the eyes of the military at least, he would not quickly recover. The deficit-plagued and union-dominated state railways were a major drain on the government budget, accounting for over half of the deficit in some years, and were therefore a primary target of government economizers. As expected, the railway unions struck in protest against a government austerity plan on November 2. Frondizi initially held firm, but after failing in his attempts to divide the strikers by negotiating with some while ignoring others, he finally backed down, permitting the settlement of the strike in labor's favor under the good offices of the Catholic Church while he was conveniently out of the country.[22]

The shock treatment of stablization, with its accompanying 25.8-percent decline in the real income of industrial workers, produced a record volume of working-class protests in 1959, as one would expect. But as we can see from Table No. 4.4, the volume of strikes declined thereafter. Moreover, as the fight against inflation took effect in 1960 and 1961, the real income of industrial workers increased once again, though the gains of those two years fell short of full compensation for the losses incurred in 1959. As a result, the rank and file, constantly reminded of their losses by union leaders, never forgave Frondizi for the events of 1959. When he sought their votes in the March 1962 congressional elections they repaid him with a humiliating defeat that provoked a military coup that ended his presidency.

Frondizi's loss to the Peronists at the polls contained bitter lessons for those who had shared his faith in the restoration of democratic politics through an integrationist strategy. He had hoped that with a return to collective bargaining and the limited use of force against recalcitrants he could succeed where others had failed in "de-Peronizing" the labor movement. Though no sudden transformation of loyalties was expected, he did assume that once the shock of stabilization had passed, many of the rank and file would come to accept the new democratic order, concentrate their energies on peaceful wage negotiations with

TABLE 4.4
Labor Protests and Wage Responses, 1959–61

	1959	1960	1961
Strikes			
1. Frequency	.008	.0046	.0078
2. Duration	7.14	12.78	7.42
3. Size (thousands)	31,357.00	5,002.00	5,499.00
4. Volume	1,791.67	293.98	318.26
Wage Response			
1. Change in Monetary Wage of Industrial Worker (percent)	58.8	35.1	26.9
2. Change in Real Income of Industrial Worker (percent)	− 25.8	6.4	11.6

Sources: *Strikes* computed from República Argentina, Secretaria de Estado de Trabajo, *Conflictos del trabajo,* junio de 1970, cuadro 25.

Wages taken from Lorenzo Juan Sigaut, *Acerca de la distribución y niveles de ingreso en la Argentina* (Buenos Aires: Ediciones Macchi, 1972), p. 57, cuadro 16.

employers, and integrate themselves into one of the existing political parties or a moderate, democratic one of their own creation. But the sting of stabilization did not pass quickly. Peronist labor leaders adroitly exploited it, along with the memories of the good years under Perón, to preserve their control over the rank and file and sustain their campaign for the restoration of Peronist political rule.

Although he was disappointed with the obstinancy of his working-class opponents, Frondizi could not help but be pleased by the general performance of the Argentine economy once the initial shock of stabilization had passed. Most impressive was the fact that the recession and record inflation of 1959 were followed by economic growth rates of 8 percent in 1960 and 7.1 percent in 1961, and a decline in the rate of inflation from 27.1 percent in 1960 to only 13.7 percent in 1961.[23] He also attracted record levels of foreign investment to Argentina, most of which was used to build new industries and accelerate petroleum production. In fact, if there was a bright spot in the government's program, it came from the performance of Argentine industry. The country's larger industrialists had initially been suspicious of Frondizi's opportunism, especially after he had campaigned on an industrialization platform and then rewarded organized labor with a huge wage increase, restored the CGE to legal status, and resurrected Perón's old labor laws. Nevertheless, the large industrialists of the UIA praised his stabilization program (despite its obvious recessionary character) because for them it represented a long awaited attempt to restore the kind of free market that offered opportunities for the expansion of their well-financed enterprises.[24]

The smaller firms of the CGE, in contrast, did not welcome the new order. They complained that a stringent monetary and credit policy was inappropriate in a country whose small native capitalists required financial support rather than sudden deprivation. The product of stabilization, they argued, would be the bankruptcy of the smaller and more fragile nationally owned industries and their absorption by foreign capitalists taking advantage of the country's capital shortage.[25] The plight of the small firm was not among Frondizi's immediate concerns, however, for it was the larger investor—and especially the foreign one—whose cooperation he needed in order to finance the nation's recovery. He was not to be disappointed, for as we can see from Table No. 4.5, after a recessionary decline of 10.3 percent in 1959, industrial production increased by 10.1 percent in both 1960 and 1961, with most of the growth coming in the new, and often foreign-financed, automotive, metal, and chemical industries.

TABLE 4.5
Industrial Product Growth Rates, 1959–61
(Percent)

	1959	1960	1961
Food, Drink, and Tobacco	– 10.7	– 0.1	5.3
Textiles, Leather, and Clothing	– 12.5	5.3	2.3
Metals, Metal Products, Machinery, Vehicles, and Electrical Goods	– 9.3	28.1	14.7
Total Industrial Production (not summed)	– 10.3	10.1	10.1
Nonagricultural Wholesale Price Increase	127.1	16.8	9.3

Computed from: Organización Techint, *Boletín Informativo no. 188* (octubre-diciembre 1972), p. 26, cuadro 5.

The apparently successful fight against inflation, the rise in
GNP growth rates, and the addition of new foreign-financed industries were only one side of the government's performance. If
one looked beyond these indices there was another, less reassur-
ing side. The government's heavy borrowing abroad trebeled
the country's foreign debt. The balance of payments, which had
taken a positive turn in 1959, experienced a deficit of $572 mil-
lion in 1961.[26] Most embarrassing, Alsogaray's pledge to reduce
the public-sector deficit by cleaning house in the bureaucracy
and state enterprises fell far short of fulfillment. In fact, the deficit, which had been only 9.9 percent of total expenditures in
1956 and 1.9 percent in 1957, rose to 27 percent in 1958 and
averaged 23.1 percent during Frondizi's four years, as the government was repeatedly forced by union opposition and its own
electoral ambitions to abandon its bureaucratic reforms.[27] Finally, at the time of Frondizi's overthrow in 1962, Argentina was
faced with both payments and liquidity crises. Defenders of
Frondizi would later argue that the economic crisis of 1962 was
not of his making, but had resulted from the failure of his successors to respond to the devaluation-recession-recovery cycle
due to begin in 1962 with measures aimed at making full use of
the country's increased productive capacity.[28] His critics, in contrast, claimed that the seeds of the 1962 crisis had been sown
long before by his underestimation of the foreign exchange costs
of import-substitution industrialization and his failure to make a
dent in the fiscal deficit.[29]

Frondizi might have overcome his foreign-exchange problems
were it not for the disappointing performance of the rural sector.
When he launched his program in 1959, Perón had been gone
for three years, most commodity price controls had been removed, and nearly all exchange dealings were in the process of
being freed. His original development plan had included among
its objectives the mechanization of agriculture to increase production over the long term, but in the face of the payments
problems he inherited, he was forced to turn immediately to the
rural sector with offers of price incentives in exchange for their
rapid expansion of commodity exports. Specifically, he had
hoped to increase rural production by doubling commodity
prices through devaluation and the elimination of price controls,
anticipating that higher prices would encourage cattlemen to

retain animals and rebuild their herds, while at the same time discouraging enough domestic consumption to permit a steady supply of beef exports despite the short-term decline in the cattle available for market. Though his plan did succeed in increasing the cattle population by 5 percent and reducing domestic beef consumption by 25 percent in two years, it did not prevent a decline in exports, as we can see from Table No. 4.6. In fact, what Frondizi did was encourage an expansion of cattle production at the expense of grains as changing relative prices induced farmers to convert cropland into pastures.[30]

TABLE 4.6
Annual Growth Rate of Export Commodity Production, 1959–61

	1959	1960	1961
Beef Production			
(tons slaughtered)	– 23.5	– 3.0	13.3
Wheat and Corn Production			
(tons)	9.8	– 14.6	– 9.0
Total Rural Production			
(tons)	– 1.0	1.7	0.7
Beef Exports			
(tons)	– 20.1	– 25.5	3.0
Wheat and Corn Exports			
(tons)	45.5	– 8.3	– 44.7
Total Export Value	1.5	6.9	– 10.7

Source: Computed from: Centro Internacional de Información Económica, *La economia argentina: treinta años en cifras* (Buenos Aires: CIDIE, 1971), p. 24.
——, *La economía argentina: comercio exterior 1940–1971* (Buenos Aires: CIDIE, 1971), p. 13, cuadro 4.
Organización Techint, *Boletín Informativo no. 188* (octubre-diciembre 1972), p. 20.

In their defense, rural producers, led by the SRA and CAR-BAP, complained that Frondizi had failed to deliver on his promises and had undermined the farmer's confidence in his effort. Not surprisingly, they were displeased when exchange retentions of 20 percent on grains and 10 percent on beef were imposed in conjunction with the December 1958 devaluation, claiming that the government's arguments about preventing inflationary windfalls masked another treasury raid on rural income.[31] They also denounced his demotion of the Ministry of Agriculture to the status of a secretariat within the new Ministry of Economy as another step in the government's campaign to remove rural policy from the farmer's hands. Thus, what to government officials was a measure aimed at greater coordination of economic policy making, came to be seen as the subordination of rural issues to the increasingly nonrural concerns of the powerful minister of economy.

In the end it was rural attitudes toward the new price incentives that was most damaging. When export retentions were added to existing taxes, they argued, one discovered that the government was taking 31.5 percent of the value of their exports. Moreover, that which was not taken by taxes was being absorbed by inflation. While wheat and corn prices had risen by 60 and 85 percent respectively, the cost of a tractor had increased by 122 percent and gasoline by 300 percent during the same period, negating many of the benefits acquired in 1959.[32] To be sure, rural complaints were probably exaggerated, but they did reflect a decline in rural-sector confidence in government policy and with it the loss of the producer's willingness to assume the risks required to expand export commodity production.

It was Frondizi's misfortune that he failed to convince farmers and cattlemen that the restoration of some of the elements of the traditional export strategy was not intended to signal a return to a political economy in which rural demands prevailed. Because the Argentine economy had changed so much in fifteen years, Frondizi had to contend with a greater variety of competing policy demands than any president before him. He could not have met every rural demand without depriving other sectors of the economy. For example, even though he was well aware that farmers would protest his use of exchange retentions, he could not abandon them without cutting back in public expenditures. Like most Argentine presidents in the 1960s, he had found himself forced by his own failure to cut the costs of public enterprises, like the deficit-plagued railways, to grasp at revenues from the most readily available sources. If Frondizi failed with the rural sector, then, it was in not communicating his policy options and assessments to them so that they would at least understand, if not fully accept, his choices. Instead, his and Alsogaray's propensity to make policy without consulting anyone, and then to exhort the public to comply with it, merely reinforced rural suspicion and distrust of policy makers who seemed to be too preoccupied with the demands of their urban, foreign, and industrial constituents to care about the plight of the Argentine farmer.

Concern about Frondizi's program suddenly became academic in early 1962 when the military stepped in once again to remove an elected Argentine president. As had been the case throughout Frondizi's tenure, it was the question of resurgent Peronism and the military's opposition to it that brought him down. Frondizi wanted to carry through with the construction of a legitimate democratic system and in the process restore his damaged civil authority by winning Argentina's first completely free elections since the mid 1940s. As the March 1962 gubernatorial and congressional elections approached, he came face to face with the question that was to haunt all Argentine presidents during the post-1955 period—whether to cling to a precarious democratic process that excluded one of the country's largest political movements from the competition or to restore full electoral participation (and strike a blow for democratic rule by defeating the Peronists, or risk military intervention if the latter won). Despite the failure of his integration strategy, he nevertheless gambled that his party could defeat the Peronists in the congressional and gubernatorial elections of March 1962 and thereby gain a more secure foundation for his government. But the gamble did not pay off. By winning victories in several provinces, the most critical of which was their capture of the governorship of strategic Buenos Aires province, the Peronists brought immediate military intervention and an end to Argentina's democratic experiment.

The Democratic Policy Maker as Survivor

As a politician operating in a relatively normal constitutional democracy Frondizi might have done well, for he was an experienced and skillful political leader. But the political conditions that he faced could hardly be described as normal except within the context of post-1955 Argentina, where normality included unpredictability and sudden governmental change. Consequently, he took office with one economic program only to be forced by economic and political conditions to pursue another and watch the men he had brought with him displaced by others not of his choosing. Nevertheless, Frondizi did occupy the

Argentine presidency for four years and during that time he implemented a host of policies, including the country's most severe economic stabilization program, several impressive infrastructure and industrial projects, and a remarkable increase in petroleum production. It is the policy-making process used to formulate and implement these policies that we must now assess.

If one judges Frondizi's policy learning on the basis of the development strategy that he and Frigerio designed before taking office, the performance is impressive. It reflected a sincere search for new policy alternatives, and involved a critical assessment of the errors of previous strategies that yielded a creative response to the desire for industrialization. To their credit, Frondizi and his associates demonstrated that Argentine economic thinking did not have to be limited to only the two alternatives prescribed by the export strategists and the Peronists, but that it could lead in new directions if one was willing to experiment and take some economic and political risks. Unfortunately, he never had the opportunity to implement fully his creative new scheme, but was forced to modify it according to the requirements of his stabilization program. How then does one assess the creativity of a policy-making process that substitutes a conventional program recommended by foreign advisors for a creative one of national design?

First, the adoption of the measures recommended by the International Monetary Fund in response to an unanticipated economic emergency should not detract from the process that produced the original development program. Even though it may have been inappropriate for the conditions Frondizi faced immediately after his inauguration, and in the end may have contributed to the country's foreign exchange problems, it remains an impressive effort when compared to those of his predecessors. Second, the intervention of the IMF into the policy process raises another question, namely, what were the domestic political costs of importing an economic program, especially from the IMF?

A government that agrees to IMF stabilization measures obviously sacrifices the opportunity to formulate a program of its own choosing. This may be especially costly if it also relinquishes its freedom to incorporate domestic political considerations into its choice of economic policies. Of course, those who advocate stabilization measures argue that disregard for domestic political conditions is one of the strengths of an IMF advised effort, for it provides the means by which expertise can be applied directly to critical economic problems without dilution by political timidity. But this argument, though persuasive in the abstract, ignores an essential point, the sensitivity of policy implementation to political conditions.

The economic problems that lead to the adoption of an IMF stabilization program by the government of an industrializing nation frequently include an intense competition for scarce resources that has forced local authorities to resort to deficit financing or payments deficits to buy temporary social peace. One of the goals of stabilization is to halt this wasteful process; yet, by demanding the redistribution of scarce resources into more "productive" activities, stabilization temporarily accentuates the zero-sum qualities of the competition and intensifies social conflict. To succeed in an open, competitive society, stabilization programs require a Herculean effort that mobilizes public support and cooperation by convincing citizens that they will be eventually rewarded for their short-term sacrifices. Economic authorities must employ not only inspirational rhetoric but also engage in an effective dialogue with those whose cooperation is needed to make stabilization work. But if they begin without the reservoir of public trust needed to inaugurate cooperative problem solving, and lack the institutions, processes, and political strategies that might generate it, authorities who must adopt stabilization measures will find it difficult to resist the temptation to resort to autocratic methods to force public compliance with their objectives. Autocratic methods may, however, only provoke more opposition to stabilization. Thus, far from solving the development problems of industrializing nations, an IMF stabilization program, when unsupported by appropriate policy management strategies, may actually increase them.

Frondizi, as we have seen, was not willing to undertake the kind of effort required to build public confidence and generate cooperation with his stabilization program. He had hoped to create a broad governing coalition through his integrationist electoral strategy and a development program that promised something for almost everyone over the long haul. But he split his party and alienated the military through his pursuit of Peronist votes, lost working-class and small-business support when he adopted economic stabilization measures, and never completely dispelled the suspicion and distrust of farmers and cattlemen. Only the UCRI stalwarts and the larger, foreign-linked industrialists remained loyal to the president throughout his tenure.

His principal policy management problem stemmed from the fact that almost overnight he was forced to shift from using economic policy to further his political ambitions to implementing an emergency economic program without consideration for its political consequences. It was a change from which he never fully recovered. But the tragedy of the Frondizi adminstration was institutional as well as personal, for it was the Argentine policy-making process, as well as the president, that was found wanting between 1959 and 1962. Economic stabilization required bold leadership and the mobilization of diverse clienteles into a well-coordinated attack on fundamental economic problems. What it got were the exhortations of the president and his minister of economy and very little central coordination or conflict resolution, convincing many observers, especially those in the Argentine military, that liberal democratic institutions were ill-equipped for the demanding task of restoring the market economy to Argentina. Indeed, the institutions and processes that had seemed appropriate for the management of a development program appeared unsuited for the task of stabilization. To execute his original program, Frondizi had counted on his political party, his presidential authority, and the support of those who were to benefit from his policies. Like Perón he did not bother to augment conventional legislative and executive processes with more informal modes of consultation and decision making. As a result, when he adopted the IMF program, Frondizi had only his personal authority to draw upon to enforce it and, after the military forced cabinet changes in mid 1959, even that was reduced. So, with neither well-established conciliatory practices nor adaptable institutions to fall back on, he merely retreated into his presidency and marked time until the opportunity to improve his sagging political fortunes arrived with the 1962 elections.

Finally, we must recognize that many of Frondizi's difficulties were not unique to him. They are examples of the more general problem of conflict resolution in scarce-resource, competitive societies where citizens come to distrust public authorities and each other. In Argentina one finds traces of public cynicism and distrust dating as far back as the early postindependence struggles over regional autonomy and economic privilege. But it was in the tough years of the early 1930s and during Perón's controversial reforms in the 1940s that such attitudes came to prevail. The critical question that must be answered is how economic authorities can chart and carry out economic development programs under such conditions. Frondizi's answer, it turned out, was not too different from the one given by Perón. One must adopt the measures recommended by one's economic advisors and then absorb the public wrath that they provoke, hoping that, despite popular discontent, the economic forces you set in motion will prevail and the development problems you have addressed will be solved. According to this view, it is not the job of economic authorities to build a broad agreement on policy objectives in advance of their implementation or to resolve policy conflicts through negotiating with one's opponents; rather, policy managers should ignore conflicts in the hope that the economic conditions that caused them will be overcome. But political and economic realities were not that simple in postwar Argentina, and the more policy managers ignored or bypassed social and economic conflicts, the more they removed themselves from the farmers, laborers, and businessmen they claimed to serve. Moreover, the longer such conflicts survived, the more difficult their solution became.

5

Illia and the Limits of Partisanship

It is tempting to view Arturo Illia's presidency as a replay of Frondizi's and conclude that constitutional democracy failed for similar reasons in the two cases. After all, both men came from the Radical party, were elected under procedures that excluded Peronist parties, were haunted by questions of their own legitimacy, and were overthrown by the military after defeats by Peronists, whom they had challenged in congressional and gubernatorial elections. It would be a mistake, however, to build one's case on these similarities, for the two presidencies differed in important ways.

While it is true that both men came from the Radical party, the nature of their electoral victories differed significantly: Frondizi received 52 percent of the popular vote in 1958, including the votes of many Peronists, while Illia and his UCRP, in contrast, were supported by only 26 percent of the electorate in 1963. Frondizi's congressional opposition consisted primarily of the UCRP, which controlled one-third of the Congress, whereas Illia faced an opposition made up of nine different parties, which controlled almost two-thirds of the seats.

If we turn to economic policy, we find even greater differences. Where Frondizi had dedicated his administration to economic stabilization and foreign-financed industrial development, Illia chose nationalism and economic expansion. In part their respective policy choices were dictated by the conditions

112

they inherited; Frondizi had to induce a recession in order to deal with a severe payments crisis while Illia inherited an economy emerging from a recession and ready for expansion. But they were also influenced by their contrasting assessments of the country's economic problems and strategies for solving them. In the Illia experience, then, we have an opportunity to discover how an elected government executed policies that differed sharply from those implemented by Frondizi.

The Search for Prosperity

Unlike Frondizi, Arturo Illia did not draw on the services of an International Monetary Fund team of experts or other foreign advisors to assist in the design of his economic policies. Nor, at first, did it appear that he had his own plan for curing the country's economic ills. Instead, Illia and the little-known slate of Radical party officials who won the July 1963 election seemed as surprised by the outcome as everyone else.[1]

Few elections in Argentine history have involved more political parties, were surrounded by more last minute intrigue, and were as unpredictable in their results, even to the candidates themselves, than the one held in July 1963 to restore Argentina to civilian rule. With deposed President Arturo Frondizi still imprisoned, and the Peronist party struck from the ballot at the last minute, the victory fell to a country doctor and former provincial governor named Arturo Illia, who led a long list of presidential candidates with only 26 percent of the popular vote. Of course, his People's Radicals were not alien to political rule. They were, like Frondizi's Intransigent Radicals, direct descendents of the Radical party that had governed Argentina between 1916 and 1930 and they had occupied legislative seats ever since. But the well-worn platforms of the past were obviously inadequate for solving the problems of the 1960s and the wisdom accumulated as a perpetual critic of other governments was not easily translated into affirmative programs. It is no surprise then that Arturo Illia, even more than his predecessors, responded to the country's economic ills not with a well-defined strategy but with short-term measures that only gradually took the shape of something that resembled an economic program.

In part, the range of economic policy options open to Illia was limited by the economic conditions he inherited from the interim military-controlled government of former Senate President José María Guido, who had replaced the overthrown Frondizi in March 1962. Plagued by yet another deteriorating payments situation, Guido gave the legendary Federico Pinedo, then in his late sixties, one final try at saving the Argentine economy by appointing him minister of economy and authorizing a shock treatment that included a 29.3-percent exchange devaluation and the tightening of monetary and credit supplies in April 1962. But in his eagerness to solve the external problem, Pinedo only hastened the arrival of an emerging liquidity crisis. When it became clear that few of his countrymen had been persuaded by his call for short-term sacrifice, Pinedo was unceremoniously dropped from the cabinet and his successor, the resurrected Alvaro Alsogaray, was directed by the military to soften the impact of his harsh measures.[2]

By the time Illia was inaugurated eighteen months later, conditions had improved somewhat. The economy appeared to be coming out of its 1962 recession. The termination of a two-year drought and the prospect of an excellent grain harvest bolstered expectations of a short-term improvement in exchange reserves and a likely trade surplus. At the same time, the new administration inherited a serious budget deficit, substantial back-up debts to suppliers, unpaid government salaries, a large foreign debt, and continued social unrest due to unemployment and a steady rise in the cost of living.

There was, of course, no shortage of freely offered advice regarding how Illia should deal with the problems he confronted. Industrial, financial, commercial, and rural spokesmen demanded an immediate attack on the budget deficit and rising costs as well as a sustained effort to stimulate greater domestic investment, arguing that if the new government resisted the temptation to seek popularity by relaxing monetary and fiscal policies, private-sector confidence would be restored and the negative growth rate of 1962 would be reversed in 1963. Many labor leaders and UCRP strategists and economists, in contrast, advised Illia that an expansionary economic policy was required to restore domestic consumption, reduce working-class unrest, and attract some working-class votes to the People's Radicals in future elections.[3] Thus, like so many postwar Argentine presidents, Arturo Illia was confronted by a pair of policy options, each of which was supported by some important economic interests and vigorously opposed by others, making intersectoral cooperation in the implementation of either program problematic from the outset.

When it came time to choose among the various options available to him, Illia, not unexpectedly, accepted the recommendations of his closest advisors. The UCRP economists took their inspiration from two sources. One was the structuralist doctrine developed by the Economic Commission for Latin America and advocated by the ECLA-trained economists assigned to CONADE, the national planning agency; it called for a long-term program of rural and industrial modernization directed at increasing productivity. Unfortunately their five-year development plan was a year away from completion at the time of Illia's inauguration and therefore could be of little help in solving the pressing problems immediately before him. The second source of advice was the economists who manned the ministries of economy and treasury and the Central Bank; they, in contrast to the planners, were preoccupied almost entirely with the problem of generating an economic recovery as quickly as possible. Drawing on conventional Keynesian principles, as well as on their own statist and nationalistic beliefs, they advocated the broad application of governmental resources and authority to the stimulation and regulation of economic expansion. Although they stopped far short of Perón's blind faith in rigorous economic controls, they were quite willing for the government to assume a much more active role than it had under Frondizi in financing economic recovery and promoting full employment. The free-market ideology of Alsogaray and the stabilization measures prescribed by the IMF had led to income inequities and excessive indebtedness to foreign financial institutions, they contended, and only through a more centrally planned allocation of resources could these imbalances be rectified.[4]

To the frustration of his supporters and opponents alike, the new president announced no economic program in his inaugural address or in other public speeches immediately thereafter. Instead, he proceeded in a cautious, incremental manner, reinforcing the popular impression that Argentines had elected a man with no program at all. Nevertheless, as the pieces of his economic puzzle began coming together during the first half of 1964, it became evident that in their own gradualist way, Illia and his Minister of Economy Eugenio Blanco were taking economic policy down the expansionary path once again. By increasing consumption and controlling its adverse effects on prices and the balance of payments through the reintroduction of selective controls, he hoped not only to reignite the Argentine economy by putting its record harvests to good use, but also to attract working-class voters to the first government since Perón to elevate the expansion of their share of national income to a position of high priority. Accordingly, after he fulfilled his party's campaign pledge to annul the petroleum contracts signed by Frondizi with foreign companies, Illia cautiously implemented a series of expansionary measures in early 1964. Rather than reduce the public deficit, as demanded in industrial and financial circles, he drew on Central Bank credit to bring the government's salary and pension obligations up to date, increasing the public deficit by 140 percent in 1964 alone. To stimulate demand, wage increases up to 30 percent were permitted through collective bargaining, and the minimum wage was raised and made adjustable with the cost of living. Then, in response to the rising prices that followed, price controls were imposed on most consumer goods and exchange controls were reinstituted for the first time in over five years after the peso was devalued 58 percent in April 1964.[5] (See Table No. 5.1.)

By adopting some of the expansionary measures that many considered discredited by the Peronist experience over a decade before, Illia, much like Perón in the mid 1940s, initially did succeed in reigniting economic growth. Yet, once these similarities are granted, one also discovers many differences between the economic policies of Perón and Illia. They differed, first of all, in their initial purposes. Illia was guided almost entirely by a desire for short-term economic growth whereas Perón sought a long-term reorientation of the nation's economy. As a result, Perón's attempts to stimulate significant income shifts though extensive state intervention far exceeded Illia's more moderate, incremental approach to income redistribution and state intervention. Second, and perhaps most crucial to their implementation of policy, Perón and Illia enjoyed very dissimilar bases of political

TABLE 5.1
Illia's Economic Policy, 1964

Objectives	1. Full employment
	2. Progressive income redistribution
	3. Expansion of production
	4. Economic independence
Instruments	
Fiscal	1. Increase current expenditures
	2. Increase transfers
	3. Increase taxes on upper income groups and rural sector
Money and Credit	1. Expand money and credit supply, especially for public sector
Exchange	1. Successive minor devaluations
	2. Exchange control
Controls	1. Price controls on consumer essentials
Income Redistribution	1. Minor shifts in favor of workers and consumers
	2. Foreign to domestic investors

support. Perón began not only with labor-union backing but also with impressive electoral and legislative majorities. Illia was a minority president whose party could claim only a plurality in the legislature. To succeed, then, it appeared that Illia would have to strengthen his political base by adopting a coalition-building strategy that tried to consolidate the support of those who benefited from his polices and to overcome the resistance of those who initially opposed him.

The Partisan Policy Process

If Frondizi seemed the consummate reformmonger when he took office, Illia appeared to be his opposite. A subdued, white-haired man who looked more like the country doctor that he was than the political leader he had suddenly become, Illia was out of step with the postwar trend of calculating, activist presidents. But he never apologized for leadership style, preferring instead to contend that after two decades of internal conflict and attacks on public authority the country needed a soft but steady hand.

He sincerely believed that if left to their own devices, Argentines could work out their differences and in the process make democratic institutions work in an orderly and productive manner. He was aware that he had gained the presidency in an election that had excluded the Peronists from the competition, but he was also convinced that through his deeds he could convince the Argentine working class that their support for democratic government was in their own best interest.

If there was one thing that appeared to be essential for UCRP governance in 1963, it was an intense effort to attract other parties in the legislature to the administration's side. Yet, contrary to the apparent dictates of political necessity, Illia refused to consider the creation of a coalition government. Instead, he took his chances on getting his legislative program through Congress with the help of sympathetic minor parties, while making it clear that after thirty-three years in the opposition, the UCRP was not about to share its newly acquired status with anyone, no matter how tenuous its hold on it. To understand why he appointed only close associates and party stalwarts to his cabinet when some attempt at coalition building seemed essential, the character of the Radical party and its struggle to regain power must be understood.

Organizationally the party was similar to most modern middle- and lower-middle-class parties, with a national organization composed of active constituency units. The Radicals had never been a wealthy party and had depended instead on the hard work of loyal activists for their electoral success over the conservatives in the 1920s. The one thing that survived their years in the opposition after 1930, and their occasional internal divisions, was the strong sense of fraternity that bound party activists together. To be sure, a belief in democratic government, party patronage, a moderate nationalism, and a defense of middle-class interests were also principles around which Radicals rallied, but it was their emotional bond to each other that led to the UCRP belief that only party loyalists deserved to make policy in the Illia government.[6]

Congress was to play a more active role for Illia than for any president since 1943, largely because of the president's dedication to party government and democratic institutions. Its function, however, was limited primarily to the ratification of policies designed by executive officials in close consultation with UCRP legislators and did not include the building of a broad policy consensus through which the UCRP could govern. The legislative process actually went through two distinct phases during Illia's presidency. The first lasted from his inauguration until early 1965, when the Peronists won several legislative seats by narrowly defeating the UCRP in mid-term congressional elections. It was during this period that Illia rescinded some of Frondizi's legislation, such as the petroleum exploration law, and gained passage of his own price control, minimum-wage, and tax-reform measures with support from various minor parties. During the second phase the Peronists used their legislative clout to challenge the government by obstructing such measures as its budget proposal in early 1966 and making the enactment of its program impossible. Despite such setbacks, Illia held fast to partisan rule until the military overthrew him in June 1966.

Finally, one of the greatest disappointments of Illia's policy-making process, especially for the economic interest groups who sought direct representation of their views within the government, was the president's failure to use the national planning agency (created in 1961) to develop a process through which private-sector leaders and government economists could debate and chart the country's long-term development. UCRP leaders were enthusiastic about economic planning and had reorganized and expanded the planning agency (CONADE) and staffed it with a dedicated group of ECLA-trained economists, who were directed to design the country's first five-year plan since that of Perón in the early 1950s. But the principal concern of the CONADE economists was not consensus building; it was the solution of the many technical problems associated with creating a plan for the 1965–69 period. Starting virtually from scratch with the collection and analysis of economic and social data, they had little time, and no toleration, for public hearings and policy debates and therefore ignored the pleas of several economic-interest-group leaders for the opening of the planning process.[7] Of course, even had they participated in the design of the five-year plan, the influence of interest groups over the UCRP's policies would have been minimal, for the plan was not completed until 1965 and was only going into effect when Illia was overthrown in mid 1966. Nevertheless, in bypassing this oppor-

ing the return of economic disaster by ignoring the lessons of the Peronist years and abandoning sound economic reasoning.[8] But such criticism, which continued throughout 1964 and 1965, had little effect on official confidence in policies which, after declines in the gross national product of 1.7 percent in 1962 and 2.3 percent in 1963, had raised the growth rate to 10.4 percent in 1964 and 9.1 percent in 1965. Moreover, prosperity had brought increased income to wage earners without penalizing rural producers. (See Table No. 5.3.) To be sure, the government had been forced to resort to price and exchange controls once again, but it appeared to have done so to good effect, keeping the annual rate of inflation just below the 1962 rate of 26 percent. Consequently, there was much to cheer about in the UCRP performance and those who failed to join the chorus, and they were many, were summarily denounced by the president as self-serving foes of the country's economic expansion.[9]

TABLE 5.3
The Income Effects of Expansion, 1963–65

	Salary Income as % of National Income[a]	Real Income of Industrial Workers (Percent Change)[b]	Relative Agricultural Prices* (Base 1960 = 100)[b]	Beef Production Real Income (Percent Change)[c]
1963	38.2	+ 0.8	110.43	+ 17
1964	39.1	+ 12.0	112.45	+ 83
1965	39.8	+ 8.4	94.34	+ 7

Sources: a United Nations, Economic Commission for Latin America, *Economic Development and Income Distribution in Argentina* (New York: United Nations, 1969), p. 170, Table 39.

b Lorenzo Juan Sigaut, *Acerca de la distribución y niveles de ingreso en la Argentina* (Buenos Aires: Ediciones Macchi, 1972), p. 66, cuadro 21.

c Banco Ganadero Argentino, *Temas de economía argentina: mercados y precios del ganado vacuno* (Buenos Aires: Banco Ganadero Argentino, 1966), p. 45.

Nevertheless, producers and laborers, much like the financial press, saw only what they wanted to see in the government's performance, preferring to emphasize the features that hurt them most in the hope of evoking more favorable policy responses to their narrow demands. Take the rural sector, for example. We can see from the data in Table No. 5.3 that their relative price position improved under Illia; and thanks to excellent weather in 1964, the production and export of grains

reached record levels, leading many to believe that his rural policy was one of his greatest achievements. (See Table No. 5.4.)

TABLE 5.4
Annual Growth Rate of Export Commodity Production, 1964–66

	1964	1965	1966
Beef Production			
(tons slaughtered)	− 22.5	− 1.2	16.3
Wheat and Corn Production			
(tons)	42.0	14.8	− 20.0
Total Rural Production			
(tons)	7.0	5.9	− 3.3
Beef Exports			
(tons)	− 20.1	− 14.1	16.7
Wheat and Corn Exports			
(tons)	64.7	34.3	− 14.6
Total Export Value	3.3	5.9	6.7

Source: Computed from: Centro Internacional de Información Económica *La economía
Argentina: treinta años en cifras,* (Buenos Aires: CIDIE, 1971), p. 24, p. 30, p. 44.
————, *La economía argentina: comercio exterior 1940–1971,* (Buenos Aires:
CIDIE, 1971), p. 14, cuaderno 4.
Organización Techint, *Boletín Informativo no. 188* (octubre-diciembre 1972), p. 20.

UCRP economists were aware that farm commodities, especially grains and meat, still accounted for 90 percent of the country's exports and that the expansion of rural production was
essential to short-term economic growth, especially if rising consumer demand for imports was to be met. Accordingly, when
many farmers reacted to droughts in 1961 and 1962 by shifting
from cattle to crops and bringing in bountiful harvests in 1964,
the government tried hard not to undermine the rural sector's
newfound confidence. It did not succeed, however; despite its
efforts on the farmers' behalf, it came to be perceived by conservative rural leaders as a well-intentioned but misguided government whose loyalty to its constituents had led it to place the
interests of urban consumers and small farmers above those of
the traditional rural elite.[10]

The Rural Society and CARBAP were especially upset by
Illia's favoritism toward tenant farmers. As a result of Peronist
legislation and subsequent reforms, many tenant farmers had become landowners by the early 1960s, yet several thousand still
retained their tenant status and, through the Agrarian Federation, continued to demand land-tenure reforms. Though he

stopped short of enacting the coveted reforms, Illia did come to the aid of tenant farmers by freezing land rents from 1963 to 1965 (despite the bitter objections of the Rural Society).[11] The SRA also fought hard before congressional committees and in the press against the restoration of exchange and price controls as well as against a special five-percent tax on agricultural profits, but again it met with little success. Despite the president's reassurances to cattlemen, they could not help concluding that the restoration of the regulatory measures that had been abandoned by Frondizi would turn today's prosperity into tomorrow's losses when, after growth rates declined, the government put the squeeze on rural producers once again.[12]

In fairness to Illia, he was frequently faced with agricultural policy problems that defied simple resolution, such as those raised by the "beef cycle" that had haunted most of the country's presidents. After suffering losses brought on by the liquidation of stock during the drought of 1961 and 1962, those still raising cattle were forced to rebuild their herds by retaining their marketable female stock for breeding, doing so at a time when Argentina's growing population, historically accustomed to beef as its daily fare, continued to consume even greater quantities. The beef crisis that resulted was not the country's first (Perón had also faced the disappearance of his export surplus after droughts in the early 1950s) but it was certainly the most severe. The reduced offers in the market in the face of unrestrained domestic consumption led to record liveweight quotations and soaring retail beef prices, causing the packing houses, especially those serving the British chilled trade, to face financial losses as volume dropped and prices rose. As a result, the trade in chilled beef was reduced by one-half in 1964.

The options available to Illia, though unwelcome, were certainly not unclear. First, he might permit prices to rise to discourage domestic consumption; but the inelasticity of domestic beef demand, as well as the disastrous effects of high prices on the packing houses, seemed to rule out this free-market alternative. What remained was a choice between sacrificing internal consumption in favor of exports through rigorous controls on domestic sales or, vice-versa, satisfying domestic consumers at the expense of exports. Neither alternative was calculated to appeal to cattlemen, who naturally preferred the use of higher prices.

Illia, as was his habit, initially tried to have it both ways, placating consumers by holding down prices, while simultaneously limiting domestic consumption and freeing some beef for export. After unsatisfactory experimentation with partial controls, full controls were instituted in June 1964, and the sale of beef to the public was prohibited on Mondays and Tuesdays of each week. Both measures brought denunciations from the country's cattlemen and, not unexpectedly, stimulated a thriving black market. In the end no one was satisfied—consumers complained of the beef ban, cattlemen saw themselves victimized once again, and, despite an increase in activity, packers continued to operate below capacity, making it impossible for Argentina to fill the orders of its foreign customers.[13] Perhaps the cattlemen's sense of frustration might not have been so great had Illia bothered to involve them in the charting of his hazardous course, but like his predecessors, he chose to remain aloof from the cattlemen, convinced that an equitable policy could be designed only if he ignored their narrow demands.

Industrialists, like farmers, contributed much to Argentina's prosperity in 1964 and 1965. (See Table No. 5.5.) But here, too, assessments of Illia's program were divided. The UCRP had not hidden its preference for the smaller, domestic firms represented by the General Economic Confederation (CGE), many of whom were owned by the party faithful, including Secretary of Commerce Alfredo Concepción. The CGE had welcomed the

TABLE 5.5
Industrial Product Growth Rates, 1964–66

	1964	1965	1966
Food, Drink, and Tobacco	2.2	7.3	6.2
Textiles, Leather, and Clothing	21.3	15.1	– 2.9
Metals, Metal Products, Machinery, Vehicles, Electrical Goods	31.4	15.9	– 2.1
Chemicals, Rubber, and Petroleum Products	18.6	15.8	3.0
Total Industrial Production (not summed)	18.7	13.8	1.0

Source: Computed from: Organización Techint, *Boletín Informativo no. 188* (octubre-noviembre 1972), p. 26, cuadro 5.

UCRP's victory as marking the end of the tight credit and monetary policies tried by Frondizi in 1959 and the interim government in 1962, and as signalling the beginning of easier credit and greater protection against competition from foreign firms. It also hoped to realize its dream of a social-economic council where the small national firms that lacked economic clout could have a voice in the formulation of national development policy. But the CGE did not get its council, nor was it satisfied with Illia's tendency to use credit expansion to finance the public rather than the private sector. Nevertheless, in later years its leaders would still refer to the UCRP government as the most favorable of all postwar administrations.[14]

The larger industrialists of the Industrial Union, on the other hand, shared the concern of their rural colleagues over the expansion of state controls. They had hoped in 1963 for a government strong enough to maintain economic and political order; instead, they found themselves with one whose minority status, toleration of labor militancy, and potentially inflationary monetary and credit policies threatened economic stability. To make matters worse, the UCRP, which was unwilling to leave industry to its own devices, insisted on meddling in the market place and with wage rates through its enactment of a minimum wage law that included a cost-of-living escalator clause.[15] But what contributed most to the disillusionment of conservative industrialists with Illia was his apathy in the face of labor protests in 1964 and 1965. Though the volume of protests was actually less than in the recent past, and wage increases were not abnormally high, it was the government's failure to make an effort to protect industry against its working-class foes that disturbed the larger industrialists and contributed to their eventual encouragement of the military coup that overthrew him in 1966.[16]

This brings us to the working class, whose reintegration into the democratic process Illia had cultivated. The president had wanted to appeal to the self-interests of Argentine workers and win with economic policy what he could not gain through politics. Accordingly, he tolerated monetary wage increases of more than 36 percent, which brought workers impressive real income gains. (See Table No. 5.6.) But higher income was not enough to win over CGT militants, so Illia was forced to look for other ways of attracting working-class support.

TABLE 5.6
Labor and Wage Responses, 1964–65

	1964	1965
Strikes		
1. Frequency	.005	.006
2. Duration	4.41	2.90
3. Size	5,342.00	6,362.00
4. Volume	117.79	105.18
Wage Response		
1. Change in Monetary Income		
of Industrial Worker (Percent)	36.8	39.3
2. Change in Real Income		
of Industrial Worker (Percent)	12.0	8.4

Sources: República Argentina, Secretaria de Estado de Trabajo, *Conflictos del trabajo*, junio de 1970, cuadro 25.

Lorenzo Juan Sigaut, *Acerca de la distribución y niveles de ingreso en la Argentina* (Buenos Aires: Ediciones Macchi, 1972), p. 57, cuadro 16.

The CGT's opposition to Illia actually predated his election and reflected its displeasure with the military's proscription of Peronist parties in the 1963 election as much as it did opposition to Illia himself. At its January 1963 convention, where the CGT was reconstituted as a national confederation for the first time since 1955, a Plan de Lucha, or battle plan, was adopted calling for successive waves of strikes and demonstrations directed at forcing a return to civilian rule and the adoption of more favorable wage and welfare policies.[17] When, at the last minute, the military prohibited the participation of the Peronists' Popular Union party in the July elections, the CGT asked its members to boycott the elections and reject its results as illegitimate. But with the surprise triumph of Illia and the UCRP, and the new government's adoption of consumer-oriented policies, the CGT leaders found themselves suddenly faced with an unexpected choice between cooperation with a government that had secured passage of a good part of the CGT's own economic platform and opposition to the government because of the illegitimate manner of its election. After a brief but bitter struggle within the CGT, the hardliners, arguing for ultimate political control over immediate economic objectives, prevailed, and the the Plan de Lucha was continued.

Rather than give up on the CGT, Illia made one last effort to bring it closer to the government by offering its leaders seats on the newly created, but relatively uninfluential, price and wage council in mid 1964. The CGT leaders were unimpressed by the government's offer and soon thereafter reaffirmed their Plan de Lucha and its use of demonstrations and work stoppages to force officials to admit union leaders to the highest policy-making councils, where they could redirect economic policy.[18] Consequently, labor peace was not attained by the UCRP. Even though they would boast with some justification that the volume of strikes was lower in 1964 and 1965 that it had been under Frondizi, they could not hide the fact that strikes were on the average larger than before and, more important, were directed not just at securing higher wages and better working conditions, but also at undermining the government and its policies. (See Table No. 5.6.) Although UCRP officials would continue to argue that the working-class rank and file was gradually coming to accept their rule, their conservative opponents concluded that the country was being governed by leaders who had failed to gain control over the disruptive working class.

The scene of battle between government and labor shifted in early 1965 from the factories and streets to the ballot box. With their expansionary program in full swing, UCRP leaders decided to gamble that the Peronists could be defeated in the March congressional elections by an incumbent administration that had deliberately raised working-class real income over the previous year. It was a gamble that failed once again; despite dissention within their ranks, the Peronists put together a last-minute campaign that quickly mobilized supporters by promising that an electoral victory would pave the way for the movement's return to power and Perón's eventual reconquest of the presidency. To the government's embarrassment, the Peronists secured 30.3 percent of the vote, to the UCRPs 28.9 percent. Since only one-half of the seats in the Chamber of Deputies were at stake in the elections the UCRP managed to retain a slight plurality. It was not, however, the size of the Peronists' victory that was important, but the mere fact of their resurgence, for it convinced the more conservative elements in the military that once again a civilian government had failed to reduce the electoral strength of Peronism. After a year of deliberation, a year in which the government was persistently harassed by the new Peronist congressional delegation, the military removed Illia and the UCRP in late June 1966.

It was also a bad year for the government's economic program. Like the Peronists in 1949, the UCRP discovered that the gains of publicly financed economic expansion are usually short-lived. Even before they had concluded what appeared to have been a successful attack on unemployment and stagnation, government economists were forced to admit that inflation had again become a problem, despite efforts to contain it with price controls, and that the public-sector deficit had gotten out of control. To make matters worse, investor confidence, shaken by the new problems that loomed on the horizon, declined rapidly, leading to a virtual collapse of capital markets in 1966. The fall in the value and volume of shares traded on the Argentine exchange began under Frondizi in 1961, accelerated after 1963, and reached its lowest point in 1966, just before Illia was overthrown, as the issuing of new shares came to a halt and working capital eroded and made the payments of dividends almost impossible.[19]

Illia's economists recognized their deteriorating situation and acted much sooner than had Perón's advisors. Therefore, when they did take action, they could afford to do so in a more gradualist manner. While still accusing his critics in the SRA and UIA of exaggerating the shortcomings of government policy in the hope of undermining public confidence in it, during the third quarter of 1965, Illia began to tighten the flow of new money and credit, especially to the public sector, in order to stem the rising tide of inflation. Most embarrassing, he was forced by declining exchange reserves to set aside his strident nationalism and ask the Paris Club nations for five years of grace and installment financing on some $190 million in debts maturing in 1965 and 1966.[20] Nevertheless, as 1966 approached, most economic indicators showed little improvement. To make matters worse, the government's much publicized campaign to reduce the public deficit by reorganizing the railways had to be abandoned in the face of union resistance in late 1965. As if to emphasize the government's failure, the railway deficit, already quite large, rose by 34 percent in 1965 alone. Finally, as the year ended, Illia announced that he would try to limit price increases to 12 percent in 1966, while keeping wage increases at 15 percent, by urging restraint in wage negotiations.[21] At the same time, he, like Perón, refused to relinquish exchange and price controls as demanded by his critics or to abandon his hostility toward foreign capital. His stubbornness eventually provoked ACIEL, the free enterprise propaganda arm of the SRA and UIA, to launch a public relations campaign directed at undermining support for the UCRP and paving the way for a military coup.[22]

Nowhere are the differences between the politics of Perón's and Illia's governments more apparent than in the ways in which they went about salvaging their expansionary programs. The critical difference, it turned out, was not their respective abilities to gain the confidence of farmers and industrialists, for neither succeeded in winning the acceptance of either sector; rather it was their ability to command labor support in their efforts to hold the line on wages in the fight against inflation. Without labor compliance the wage-price spiral could not be halted, but with it there was a chance that it could be slowed and the way cleared for a return to the government's original objectives. Having built a large political following that included organized labor, Perón managed to hold down wages without losing significant CGT support, as we saw in Chapter 3. Illia, in contrast, viewed the Peronist unions as major competitors rather than allies and, after his party's defeat at their hands in the March 1965 congressional elections, he abandoned his even-handed labor policy, apparently convinced that he could subdue with force those whom he had failed to win over with his stands on wages and civil liberties. Accordingly, in September 1965, he prohibited union political activity, revised the labor laws in an attempt to break the monopoly of single unions over entire industries, and began auditing union funds and regulating union elections.[23] It is no wonder then that when he asked labor to limit its wage demands to 15 percent in 1966, he was almost completely ignored. Instead unions rushed to sign contracts with average wage increases of 25 percent during the first six months of the year.[24]

Few things disappointed Illia and the People's Radicals more than the discovery that political freedom, unconstrained collective bargaining, and rising wages could not win labor support for their experiment in democratic government. Throughout their rule a majority of the working class remained devoted to the exiled former president, who persistently reminded those who might forget of the illegitimacy of the president whom only 26 percent of the Argentine electorate had supported in 1963. The lesson of the Illia experience, i.e., that economic gains alone would not win labor's cooperation, was not lost on his military successors who seized power in mid 1966. Unwittingly, this latest try at civilian rule had demonstrated the futility of depending on wage policy as the principal means of dividing and conquering the working-class movement. Moreover, these same military observers, along with their many civilian advisors, found no support in Illia's performance for the traditional populist argument that policies that are good for labor are also in the short run good for economic growth and stability. The deductions to be drawn from his performance seemed quite clear to those who overthrew him: either you include labor leaders in the formulation and implementation of economic policy (at the risk of becoming their captive), or you exclude them and compel, through force of arms if necessary, their compliance with whatever economic strategy you choose to follow.

The Democratic Policy Maker as Partisan

Economic policy innovation was not one of the virtues of the UCRP regime. Nor was political inventiveness among its strengths. Three decades in the opposition had taught the People's Radicals more about what they opposed than what to do about the country's economic and political problems. At the outset they rejected Frondizi's resurrection of the free market and his dependence on foreign capital and, although sympathetic with some of Perón's social and nationalistic objectives, they wanted nothing to do with the autocratic means by which he had achieved them. Unable to complete their development plan in time to influence their choice of economic policies, they retreated to the tarnished but not completely discredited doctrine of state promotion and regulation of economic expansion, which they used with some skill in managing an economic recovery ignited by record harvests. These short-term successes could not, however, hide Illia's failure to generate new solutions for the Argentine condition. One might have expected policy learning to reach new levels in the mid 1960s after a decade of post-Peronist policy experiments and the restoration of competitive politics. Instead, the insecure but proud People's Radicals withdrew behind a screen of partisanship that distorted their analysis of previous economic programs and greatly reduced the range of policy alternatives they considered.

The UCRP government was plagued by an image of indecisiveness in economic policy matters as a result of the president's cautious, incremental manner, his frequent currency devaluations, and his lack of a single, coherent program. But indecisiveness was due more to the style than the substance of UCRP policy making, for until late 1965, the government deviated little from the policy course it had charted at the beginning of 1964. Its incrementalism came primarily from Illia's determination to secure congressional passage of his price control, minimum wage, tax reform, and other measures and the lengthy debates and negotiations that were required to secure the support of various minor parties for each bill. Had he controlled Congress, or merely resorted to decree powers, he too could have made the dramatic announcement of an economic program within a few months after his inauguration. That he did not do so says more about the costs of minority government, as well as his devotion to democratic processes, than about official indecisiveness. Delay is the price one pays for constitutional rule and, even though it would tarnish his image, Illia believed it was a price worth paying.

The principal obstacle to UCRP success, as it had been for Illia's predecessors, was the restoration of public confidence in economic authorities and their policies. Illia was handicapped by his minority status and the doubts about the legitimacy of his election, both of which made his task of policy management extremely difficult. Yet, rather than adopt a coalition-building strategy to broaden his base of support, he sought security within the familiar confines of the UCRP. Like Frondizi, he had begun with a political strategy aimed at electoral victory, but when it proved inadequate for the task of policy implementation, he had no other to replace it. In many ways he was the victim of his own campaign to rebuild Argentine democracy. Although admirable in principle and purpose, his scheme was really a simple attempt to turn back the political clock to the heyday of partisan Radical party rule rather than a campaign to adapt democratic processes to the changing social and economic conditions of the mid 1960s in a country that had grown cynical about traditional forms of party government.

UCRP leaders had been taught to believe that there was only one way to govern their country democratically and that was through a competitive electoral process in which Argentine voters chose the party they wanted to govern them. This noble view rested on three assumptions, all of which had become invalid by the time the UCRP had returned to power in 1963.

First, it assumed the existence of strong, representative political parties capable of gaining majority support or forming relatively stable multiparty coalitions; second, it assumed that those responsible for the management of private economic activities accepted their representation through politicial parties and were satisfied with the influence over economic policy such representation provided them; and third, it assumed that opposition parties and groups would play by the democratic rules, waiting patiently for their legal opportunity to capture public office for themselves. Yet, as we have seen, Argentine political parties were not strong. They had been weakened and much discredited by their behavior during the preceding two decades. Most economic interest groups had long before turned away from political parties in favor of direct pleas to the executive, where nearly all economic policy was made. Moreover, the Peronist opposition, despite the government's valiant effort to induce its cooperation, never accepted the UCRP's right to govern.

In the end, the government's activist economic policy could not compensate for its partisan but passive political strategy, which had assumed, erroneously it turned out, that Argentines could solve their conflicts if left to their own devices. In fact, Illia and the UCRP so discredited the idea of laissez-faire democracy that few Argentines, outside of the UCRP, mourned his overthrow by military officers who made clear their intention of strong-arm rule.

The Democratic Experience: Lessons and Legacies

The virtues of democratic policy making are said to rest with its consideration of diverse interests, its toleration of different kinds of policy influence, and the institutionalization of conflict resolution through bargaining and compromise. Unfortunately, these strengths were seldom in evidence during Argentina's brief experiments with democratic rule where some interests were deliberately neglected by those who formulated national policy, certain modes of influence were denied particular competitors, and bargaining was often sacrificed to narrow-minded partisan rule. Frondizi and Illia were not, of course, entirely to blame for the form of their rule. They were elected under rules that excluded the Peronists from the competition and were haunted by the question of their own legitimacy throughout their tenures. Yet neither man was particularly inventive in adapting his policy-making process to such conditions; instead each relied on the conventional practices of partisan-party government.

Undoubtedly the most aggravating problem that haunted both Frondizi and Illia was the opposition of organized labor to their rule. Each required some means for winning the cooperation of a political group whose own candidates had been excluded from the electoral process. Frondizi tried to do it by inviting organized labor into his electoral coalition and restoring its collective-bargaining rights. Illia, in contrast, used economic policy to win the support of the rank and file, hoping that his promotion of bread-and-butter issues and higher worker income would compensate for the exclusion of labor's spokesmen from the electoral process. Unlike the military rulers that came after them, Frondizi and Illia's goal was not the subjugation of the labor movement, only the attraction of the rank and file away from its Peronist leadership and toward their own parties. They had hoped to satisfy not only the demands of their military guardians for the demise of Peronism as a political force, but also their own political ambitions. In the end neither succeeded, since they could not compete with Peronist leaders, who pledged a return to power if the rank and file held fast in its support of their exiled leader. In a country where the occupancy of public office is essential to policy conquests, the promises and policy gestures of Radical party governments were no match for the expectation of the return of Perón to office.

The weakness of Argentina's democratic experiments was more fundamental than an inability to attract labor support. Two shortcomings in particular proved damaging to the execution of development policy. The first was the very narrow and partisan character of the country's dominant political parties, and the second was the lack of institutional linkages between interest groups and policy makers.

Despite the rise and fall of many political parties since 1945, Argentina has remained essentially a two-party system composed of Peronists and Radicals. Only when the Peronists were excluded from elections did minor parties gain more than token representation in the legislature, and even then their influence over policy was negligible. It has also been an extremely partisan two-party system where, once in office, neither the Peronists nor the two wings of the Radical party worked closely with other parties. The Peronists ignored and abused the Radical party opposition when they were in office and, as a result, they never completely regained their trust. Unfortunately, the kind of partisan politics that might have succeeded in polities where the regular exchange of public office was an established practice, took on a narrow, destructive character in Argentina. Since 1930, the triumph of one party has usually meant discrimination against all others. Consequently, instead of fostering cooperative solutions to development problems, party government only reinforced the cleavages that separated political groups and compounded the difficulty of securing compliance with government policy.

In addition, Argentina's democratic presidents failed to generate any lasting solutions to the problem of interest-group participation in the policy-making process. Traditionally, liberal democracies have relied on the participation of economic interest groups either through their membership in political parties or more informally through their contacts with legislators and administrators. But in Argentina, political parties included few economic groups, and administrators often tried to insulate themselves from the influence of such groups. Rather than search for suitable alternatives to these traditional forms of interest-group involvement in the policy process, Argentina's elected presidents refused to give up their faith in their already discredited system of party democracy.

Not unexpectedly, interest-group leaders, with the occasional exception of those in the CGT and CGE, came to view political parties not as a means of channeling their policy demands to public authorities but as obstacles to the communication of their demands. If they had hoped for some alternative channels for influencing policy decisions, they were to be disappointed, for

Argentina's insecure democratic presidents consistently turned a deaf ear to their pleas for institutionalized access to the executive. This in part explains why many interest-group leaders supported the military coups that removed elected officials in 1962 and 1966. If they could not get elected presidents to listen to them, they were willing to give military leaders a try.

PART THREE

The Military Authoritarians

6

Aramburu and the Military as Founding Father

Our knowledge of military intervention in Latin American politics and its causes has increased rapidly in recent years, but we still know little about military rule, especially with regard to the military's management of development policy. Increasingly, Latin American militaries have not been content to intrude into the political arena only long enough to depose public officials, but have seized public authority in order to reorganize political institutions and implement sophisticated development programs. Their ideological purposes and policy objectives have varied from country to country, but their continued presence at the center of the policy-making process clearly differentiates their current from their past interventions.

Unlike constitutional administrations, which inherit governmental organizations and policy processes from their predecessors, military officers who reject the use of political parties and formal legislative processes must devise their own means of formulating and executing public policy. Either through deliberate decisions or by inaction they define new rules for political participation, establish the degree and form of contestation, and determine the amount of coercion used to execute government decisions. But unlike the more rigid rural societies of the nineteenth and early twentieth centuries, where a simple, heavy-handed paternalism was sufficient for the maintenance of orderly rule, far more sophisticated forms of military governance

139

are required in late twentieth-century Latin America to manage increasingly urban, semiindustrial societies where diverse domestic and foreign interests compete vigorously for scarce political and economic resources.

To prevail in complex societies, military leaders, in addition to using their conventional tools of violence must also develop more subtle means for directing sophisticated public agencies and mobilizing the support of those who contribute to the process of industrialization. The true measure of their success as development policy managers is not their ability to bring disruptive political conflicts to a halt, but their performance in solving the economic problems that frustrated their civilian predecessors. There is no reason to believe, however, that the military is any more qualified than civilian politicians to accomplish the latter. Nevertheless, military rule continues to be favored by many industrialists, traders, bankers, farmers, and foreign investors in industrializing nations like Argentina and Brazil. Its appeal, it seems, rests primarily on the military's ability to create, even temporarily, the kind of political order that allows native and foreign entrepreneurs to operate unmolested by demogogic politicians, militant labor unions, and persistent economic uncertainty.

Like most Latin American countries, Argentina has not escaped military intrusions into its domestic politics during the postwar era. In fact, in few countries has the military been as continuously and deeply involved in a nation's public affairs as in Argentina. Excluding Perón, who, though an army general, did gain the presidency through elections in which he defeated several civilian candidates, six army generals have served as president of the country between 1946 and 1978. Between 1955 and 1978 the military has controlled the executive for fourteen years and civilians only nine. Moreover, as we saw in the two preceding chapters, military involvement in Argentine politics has not ceased with the election of a civilian president; on the contrary, seldom did a day pass that elected officials were not subjected to pressures from officers or haunted by the possibility of a military coup.

What makes military rule in Argentina particularly interesting to the student of policy making is the seriousness with which Argentina's soldiers have taken themselves and their role in governing the country. They are not officers who have intervened casually in order to gain only personal advantages but individuals who have come to view the supervision of the nation's political life as one of their principal responsibilities. Some have seen themselves as arbitrators who must use their power periodically to end conflicts among civilian political forces that threaten public order. Others have sought to purify the political process by purging it of particular political groups whose presence threatens the traditional order as well as the military itself. And still others have from time to time decided that the Argentine political system required a complete overhaul and that they were the only ones capable of achieving it. Still, one cannot help but wonder if the military really has anything special to offer a country like Argentina. That is, is it any better equipped to govern than its civilian rivals? Does it possess unique attributes that allow it to deal effectively with the problems of economic growth and political conflict that plague industrializing countries? And what about the costs of military rule; are they so high that they negate any of the contributions that they may make to the governance of a country? It is to the search for answers to these questions that we must now turn.

While all postwar Argentine military regimes shared a commitment to ending disruptive political conflict, they differed, as did military regimes elsewhere in Latin America, in their long-term political objectives. One type of regime, which included those headed by General Pedro Aramburu (1955–58) and General Alejandro Lanusse (1970–73), sought to govern only long enough to purge political processes of particular groups and institutions and then restore constitutional government. The other type, which is exemplified by the regime created by General Juan Carlos Onganía (1966–70), represented a more ambitious approach to the resolution of societal conflict. Rather than reforming the constitutional process according to demands of particular civilian groups, Onganía sought to create a new political and economic order through the use of a military-led and civilian-advised authoritarian regime.

The advantages of military rule in Argentina have proven more apparent than real thus far. Neither Aramburu nor Lanusse generated enduring constitutional governments and Onganía failed to sustain the new order that he launched in 1966.

Consequently, in our examination of Argentina's military regimes we must not only assess the generals as policy managers but also ask why military governance appears to have failed in its political objectives. To this end we will compare the military's ability to deal with short-term economic problems with its apparent inability to solve long-term political ones by focusing on its ill-fated attempts to institutionalize durable processes for resolving societal conflicts. In this chapter I will concern myself with General Pedro Aramburu's reconstruction of post-Peronist Argentina and in the next will examine Onganía's campaign to replace liberal democracy and Lanusse's efforts to restore it.

Purging the Peronist Economy

We must step back in time for a moment from the year 1966, where we left Arturo Illia and his overthrown UCRP government at the end of Chapter 5, to 1955 in order to examine the presidency of General Pedro Aramburu. The latter's tenure began two months after the overthrow of Juan Perón and ended with the election and inauguration of Arturo Frondizi in 1958. Many of the issues that troubled the presidencies of both Frondizi and Illia arose during Aramburu's tenure when Argentines were trying to create a new political order to replace the Peronist one that had just been ended. Moreover, many of the political constraints that circumscribed Argentine democracy after 1955 were imposed by Aramburu and his military col-. leagues in 1956 and 1957. An examination of Aramburu's presidency will not only tell us something about policy making in the transitional military regime, but will also help complete our understanding of the peculiar conditions under which the Argentine military forced elected presidents to operate after 1958.

We can begin by asking the question that Aramburu must have asked himself in 1955: how does a military president purge his country of its largest political movement, restore constitutional government, and reignite a sluggish economy? And how does he do all this in a country where democratic institutions were abused by a conservative elite during the 1930s and then further discredited by Perón between 1946 and 1955? He tries to do so, Aramburu decided in November 1955, through the use of a civilian-advised, autocratic regime capable of repressing the followers of Juan Perón, imposing unpopular economic policies on a defiant working class, and setting down the rules for the partial restoration of constitutional government.

After taking the presidency from General Eduardo Lonardi, the leader of the September coup that removed Perón, General Aramburu faced two immediate problems. First there was a need to decide the fate of the Peronist movement. Although it was too large to be eliminated entirely from the body politic, something had to be done with it if the government was to prevent a Peronist victory in an election called to restore constitutional government. For Aramburu the most appealing solution was to find some way of destroying Peronism as an organized political movement while at the same time reintegrating the Peronist rank and file into other political parties. Needless to say, this "Peronist problem" transformed an already difficult exercise in political reconstruction into the hazardous task of restoring insecure and much abused democratic institutions to a country whose citizens disagreed over who had the right to participate in them.

An economic crisis demanding immediate attention was the second problem left behind by Perón. Although Perón had managed a short-term recovery after 1953, it had been accompanied by an increasingly demoralized private sector, a bloated and decapitalized public one, and, in mid 1955, a renewed foreign exchange crisis which, according to a United Nations survey at the time, would end in national bankruptcy if not dealt with immediately. Aramburu could not march his countrymen down the path to constitutional government without also dealing with the destabilizing effects of his deteriorating economy. More important, he could not isolate his response to the economic crisis from his task of political reconstruction since his economic policies and their distribution of rewards and deprivations would affect public acceptance of his regime and support for his reorganized constitutional order. Already faced with a working class that was hostile to him because of his involvement in the overthrow of Perón, he needed the support of anti-Peronist politicians and interest group leaders to help with the restoration of constitutional government and, therefore, could not afford to alienate them with his economic policies. Thus, no matter how compelling, technical economic considerations alone could not be allowed to determine his choice of economic policy measures. What he required instead was a skillful blend of economic policy and political strategy that could simultaneously relieve the economic crisis while mobilizing support for the restoration of civilian rule by 1958. It was to the design of such a program that he turned immediately after assuming the presidency.

If there was one thing on which the military and their political party and economic interest group supporters agreed in 1955, it was the immediate overhaul of the Peronist economy, with its heavy-handed and arbitrary interventionism and encouragement of progressive income redistribution. There was less agreement on what form the reconstructed economy should take. As expected, each private-sector spokesman concentrated his demands on immediate compensation for his particular sector or industry rather than on the global requirements of economic recovery. Yet Aramburu was not without an economic model to guide him; he only had to look back to the pre-Peronist economy of the 1930s and listen to the demands of conservative rural, financial, and foreign interests for its restoration to find an easy solution to the policy-design problems that he faced.

Chastened by the depression and Peronist experience, rural elite spokesmen, exporters, and free-trade ideologues admitted in 1955 that Argentina had indeed been treated rudely by the international market and her trading partners after 1930. The persistent foreign-exchange and price-stability problems of the past decade, however, were not due to the country's export vulnerability, they were quick to argue, but were caused by the Peronists' inept campaign to subvert the country's natural trading relationships. Instead of a strong industrial economy, their ill-conceived nationalistic policies had created a bloated and inefficient bureaucracy, overprotected industries, disillusioned and apathetic farmers, and an undisciplined working class whose inflated appetites had undermined productivity and financial stability.[1]

The advocates of the old export strategy demanded an immediate campaign to combat price instability and a growing balance-of-payments deficit. If one began with the assumption that the international trading system was the constant in the Argentine political economy, and internal fiscal, monetary, wage, and price policies were the variables, as did the proponents of

this view in 1955, then clearly any solution to price and payments problems had to come from a change in internal rather
than external conditions. In the short term this meant a reduction in domestic consumption, in accord with the financial constraints imposed by the country's level of exports. To be sure, if
adequate export-stimulating policies had been pursued in the
first place, periodic foreign-exchange crises and their accompanying cutbacks in domestic consumption would have been avoided
altogether, except in times of natural calamities. But it was use-
less to dwell on what might have been; instead, it was argued,
the government must give highest priority within its hierarchy of
economic policy objectives to price stability and the improvement of the balance of payments. The measures required to
achieve these objectives would be harsh ones, including substantial exchange devaluations to reduce imports and encourage
raw-product exports, severe monetary and credit restraint, a
temporary decline in wages, the acceptance of large doses of
foreign assistance, and cutbacks in public services. If the government did not induce a reduction of consumption, Argentines
were warned, the economy would continue to be plagued in the
years ahead by payments deficits and high rates of inflation.[2]

Obscured by the rhetoric, yet of paramount political importance, were the income effects of a sudden return to the political
economy of the 1930s. The restoration of resource allocations to
prewar patterns would obviously require a significant regressive
redistribution of income. Devaluation, for example, if not modified by exchange taxes, would transfer vast amounts of income
to the traditional commodity-export sector. Similarly, a reduction
in real wages would shift income from labor to capital; and
tighter monetary policies offered new opportunities to foreign
financiers and investors while depriving small business and wage
earners. Regardless of how temporary these income shifts might
be, they would deprive many who had gained under Peronism,
and therefore could expect their vigorous opposition. The ways
in which economic authorities responded to this opposition,
whether through the modification of their policy designs, or
through the use of administrative and political strategies during
their implementation, would become critical to the success or
failure of the reconstruction effort.

Thus, in 1955, the economic strategy that had begun as the

child of nineteenth-century doctrines of free trade and comparative advantage, and had guided Argentina's impressive economic
development until 1929, once again was made available to
Argentine leaders. This time its advocates were not naive op-
timists, promising instant prosperity, but prophets of doom, who
warned that Argentina must now pay a price for the sins of
Peronism. Like old Puritans confronting unrepentant sinners,
they scolded their countrymen for their excesses and promised
redemption in return for discipline and sacrifice.

Despite the temptation to resurrect the old export strategy in
its most primitive form, Argentina's new leaders did not do so.
They recognized that a sudden return to the pre-Peronist political economy was plagued by hazards, not the least of which were
the immediate political costs of a drastic reduction in consumption on top of the government's purge and reorganization of the
working-class movement. Moreover, the Argentine economy in
1955 differed far more from that of the 1930s than the export
strategy's proponents cared to admit. Not only had the working
class grown in size, power, and militancy under Perón. Argentina now had an enlarged industrial sector with a growing demand for energy and raw-product imports, and had become part
of a world economy that had witnessed the postwar decline of
Great Britain (the country's traditional trading partner), the rise
of the United States, an embryonic European Common Market,
and a new international financial order.

What the new government needed most, but did not have,
was time to deliberate calmly over the relative risks and benefits
of various courses of action. The country's financial crisis could
not be postponed, nor could the demands of aggrieved farmers,
bankers, and foreign creditors be ignored while officials carefully
designed a long-range development program. Nevertheless, economic authorities did formulate an integrated emergency plan,
which they adopted only three months after Perón had departed.
They did so by drawing on the services of the United Nations
Economic Commission for Latin America (ECLA), which dis-
patched a team under the supervision of Secretary General Raúl
Prebisch, to assess the Argentine condition and recommend appropriate emergency measures. The decision was fortuitous, for
by turning to outside experts the military not only gained some
time but also secured an economic program more in line with

their political objectives. Moreover, by clothing their rescue operation in the garb of United Nations expertise, they added an authoritative ally with whom to share the burden of unpopular economic measures.

Raúl Prebisch was an Argentine economist who had left his Central Bank post when Perón took over in 1946 and had become secretary general of ECLA after its creation in 1949. In a very short time he developed a reputation as a defender of Latin America's economic interests within the world economy and as a proponent of economic development through programmed structural change. But despite his preoccupation with the larger issues of hemispheric development, Prebisch was delighted to set them aside long enough to return home in 1955 and lead the rescue operation.[3]

In seeking to fill Argentina's economic policy vacuum, the Prebisch report became the object of a heated debate that has raged to this day. Its prescriptions, which came after a month of study, were predicated on Prebisch's conclusion that the Peronist development program had failed, since the 1954 per capita gross national product was only 3.5 percent higher than it had been in 1946, a dismal outcome due primarily to the fact that most of the gains made during the early boom years had been lost during the later recessionary years.[4] Of more immediate concern was a decline in rural productivity, a deteriorating balance of payments, and enormous short-term debt obligations totaling $757 million at a time when gold and monetary reserves had declined to only $450 million.[5] To deal with these ills, Prebisch recommended a two-pronged plan of attack: first would come the termination of the economic controls, which, contrary to the Peronists' intentions, had discouraged innovation, investment, and higher productivity; and second, an assault on the balance-of-payments crisis through the stimulation of a rapid expansion of agricultural exports. In view of his reputation as an advocate of state planning, his call for an end to most of Perón's regulatory schemes surprised many of Prebisch's followers.[6] But for him the shift was more apparent than real, for, as he later argued, while state planning was necessary to allocate resources to crucial sectors and correct distortions and inefficiencies, it should not take the form of the kind of bureaucratic suffocation that had arisen under Perón.[7]

Prebisch's advice, it turned out, was exactly what the new leadership wanted to hear because it supported their taking a middle position between a return to the export doctrine of the 1930s (with its high political costs) and the continuation of the abhorent statist system of the 1940s (with its obvious deficiencies), while at the same time giving the appearance of favoring the former without totally abandoning all elements of the latter.

IAPI, the state trading monopoly, was the first of many institutions abandoned in an attempt to restore agricultural commodities to freer trade. But to the displeasure of Argentine farmers, not only did the government delay the restoration of the meat and grain boards until mid 1956, but, in order to continue government control over commodity marketing, it reorganized them so that half rather than only one-third of their directors (as was the case before 1945) came from the public sector.[8] Also in 1956, the Central Bank was returned to its semiautonomous status, but this time with a governing board appointed entirely by the president rather than partially by the private sector as had occurred before Perón.[9] At the same time, the nationalized railways and public utilities, along with military industries, remained in government hands even though the railways had become an immense drain on the treasury. Aramburu did not want to take on the Radicals over the issue of nationalism since their cooperation was essential to the restoration of constitutional rule.

One only has to read the vigorous denunciations of the Prebisch program by the advocates of prewar economic strategies to appreciate the fact that, although he had turned Argentina away from Peronism, Aramburu stopped far short of a restoration of the prewar rules of the game.[10] The government's caution was due not so much to its rejection of the export strategy per se as to its recognition of the social and political costs of the sudden redistribution of income that would result from a hasty retreat to the past. Whatever the excesses and mistakes of the Peronists, they had concluded, the habits and expectations built up during their tenure prohibited an immediate restoration of free-market pricing and open competition in an unsubsidized market place. Moreover, if the government were to maintain public order in preparation for a peaceful return to elected civilian rule, it could not risk provoking the social tensions that might undermine its campaign.

The short-term objective of expanding commodity exports dictated the government's initial choice of economic policies. (See Table No. 6.1.) Because the Argentine peso was far out of line with internal costs and prices, it was devalued by 260 percent (from 5 to 18 to the dollar) and a Special Reconstruction Fund was created to transfer the proceeds from exchange taxes to those most disadvantaged by devaluation.[11] Commodity support prices were also increased significantly, a move which, though too late to effect greater plantings in 1955, was intended to bolster rural confidence and encourage expanded sowings in 1956. Devaluation was also used to discourage imports and, in combination with higher taxes and a tighter monetary policy, was expected to reduce domestic consumption generally.

TABLE 6.1
Aramburu's Economic Policy, 1956

Objectives	1. Improve balance of payments
	2. Expand export production
	3. Price stability
Instruments	
Fiscal	1. Reduce deficit
	2. Increase taxes
	3. Increase prices of government services
Money and Credit	1. Tighter money and credit
Exchange	1. Devaluation
	2. Export earning exchange retentions
Controls	1. Wage controls
	2. Gradual ending of price controls
Income Redistributions	1. Transfers from consumers to rural producers and investors

The elimination of price controls on domestic foodstuffs proved more difficult than Prebisch had anticipated. He had recommended the gradual elimination of price controls, but when Aramburu's announcement of a decision to decontrol some consumer items in early December 1955 produced an outburst of protest from political party leaders and their supporters in the press, the government rescinded its measures, preferring to continue its subsidization of a few critical foodstuffs rather than risk alienating large segments of the population.[12] Throughout the remainder of his tenure, Aramburu continued to employ some price controls in an effort to sustain enough domestic tranquility to permit elections in 1958, an objective that increasingly assumed a higher priority than that of freeing the domestic market.

The costs of exchange devaluation were borne not only by Argentine consumers but by raw-material-importing industrialists as well, though the latter could take some consolation in the added protection devaluation afforded them against competition from imported products. Industry was not sacrificed to the rural wolves by Prebisch as some feared. The ECLA report clearly acknowledged industry's new prominence in the post-Perón economy even though it conceded that some time would elapse before the balance-of-payments situation would permit any considerable increase in capital-good imports. Short-term increases in industrial production were still possible due to the existence of idle or underutilized capacity accumulated during Perón's last years in office. If there were any obstacles in industry's path to recovery, then, they would not include a lack of short-term factory supplies but rather the possible failure of agriculture to relieve the long-term balance-of-payments problem and finance the restocking of raw materials and capital goods.[13]

Finally, Aramburu also adopted an incomes policy of sorts. Prebisch had argued that without greater wage restraint, inflation, already on the rise as a result of devaluation, would get out of control, destroying producer confidence and undermining any long-term solution to the balance-of-payments problem. At the same time, officials recognized that they could not ask the country's workers to bear the entire burden of income redistribution. Prebisch had warned against punishing the rank and file for the sins of their leaders and called instead for some minimal justice in the implementation of his harsh prescriptions. Accordingly, Aramburu permitted some upward adjustment in wages before imposing an eighteen-month wage freeze in early 1956.

The Policy Process in Transition

The adoption of the Prebisch program solved Aramburu's policy-design problem but he still needed a political strategy to help with its implementation. How does a government that has seized power through violent means implement a program of institutional reform and regressive income redistribution when it is opposed by nearly half of the electorate and besieged with demands for preferential treatment by the rest? If the 1930 coup against the Radicals had served as a guide, brutal repression of workers and political party opponents, followed by the restoration of rule by a military-backed financial and exporter elite would have been likely. Despite the similarities between the Aramburu government and that of General José Uriburu in 1930, however, no simple transfer of political strategy was possible in a country changed by ten years of Peronist rule. Organized labor, though on the defensive, could not be pushed aside as it had been during the 1930s, nor could a government determined to encourage non-Peronist political parties manipulate and repress them as the military had done two decades before.

TABLE 6.2
Aramburu's Policy-Making Process

Phases	Political Institutions and Techniques
Initiation	Foreign Advisors: Raul Prebisch and the ECLA economic team
Formulation	ECLA team and inner ministerial circle
Consultation	Inner circle and informal contacts with entrepreneurs
Ratification	Political parties in National Consultative Council and non-Peronist economic interest groups in National Economic Council after brief discussion and little dissent
Execution	Repression and reorganization of labor movement Gradual reduction of bureaucratic regulation Increase in economic incentives
Feedback	Largely informal through personal contacts and interest group protests

Aramburu's solution was both innovative and subtle: instead of resorting entirely to autocratic rule and risk offending his non-Peronist supporters, he initially sought to blend firm governmental leadership with a support-building campaign that involved political parties and economic associations in the informal ratification of the policies that most directly affected their interests. He had actually inherited the solution to his political party problem from his predecessor General Eduardo Lonardi, who had created a National Consultative Council in late October

1955, a month before Aramburu deposed him. Its twenty members included leaders of the Radical, Progressive Democrat, Socialist, and minor parties who functioned as a rump legislature on constitutional and electoral reform matters, meeting regularly in the national congress building under the chairmanship of Vice-President Admiral Isaac Rojas.[14] The Council did not concern itself with economic policy matters, but devoted nearly all of its energies to preparing the way for the 1958 elections.

As might have been expected, the country's industrial, commercial, and rural interests, most of whom enjoyed no formal ties to political parties, demanded separate representation within the new government. Accordingly, Aramburu created the National Economic Council in early January 1956 and appointed to it four representatives each from industry, trade, farming, finance, and professional economists, and added two from journalism, three from the cooperative movement, and seven from the recently purged labor movement.[15] Led by its chairman Eustaquio Mendez Delfino, later to become a Central Bank president in the Frondizi administration, and Executive Secretary Adalbert Krieger Vasena, who would serve as the controversial economic czar of the Onganía regime in the late 1960s, the Council was ostensibly created to assist Prebisch in the final design of his prescriptions for the ailing economy. In fact, its principal task was not policy formulation but ratification; Aramburu adroitly used the Council during his first year to legitimize the measures that Prebisch recommended rather than to initiate or consider other policy alternatives. To the president's delight, the gambit worked. Private-sector representatives, pleased with the official attention they were suddenly receiving after a decade of neglect by the Peronists, gladly gave the Prebisch report their blessing. Not long thereafter the Council quietly fell into disuse and Aramburu turned his attention from the formal matter of policy ratification to the more complex and difficult one of policy implementation.[16]

Thus, Aramburu blended selective repression, cooptation, and limited consultation in an attempt to purge the economy and polity of Peronism while regaining the confidence of the country's rural, industrial, and financial interests along with that of Argentina's traditional trading partners. Excluded from the government deliberations were representatives of the Peronist party, the General Confederation of Labor, and the General Economic Confederation, all of which were closed in the hope that their constituents would be driven into non-Peronist parties, unions, and economic associations. At the same time, Aramburu restored the legal rights of the Industrial Union and CARBAP, re-creating the pre-Peronist system of rural, commercial, and industrial interest groups. While this strategy of selective consultation and repression served well in weakening the Peronists and in generating entrepreneurial ratification of economic policy, as well as political party cooperation with constitutional reform, it did little to reduce the government's vulnerability to the attacks of a growing number of critics during the process of policy implementation.

Managing Reconstruction

No matter how much he talked of softening the impact of income redistribution, Prebisch could not hide the fact that painful income shifts would result from devaluation, higher commodity prices, and the freezing of wages. As we can see from Table No. 6.3, the claim of salaries on national income, already down from 46.9 percent in 1952, declined to 41.4 percent by the end of 1957. Moreover, as intended, relative agricul-

TABLE 6.3
The Income Effects of Economic Reconstruction, 1955–57

	Salary Income as a Percent of National Income[a]	Real Income of Industrial Workers (Percent Change)[b]	Relative Agricultural Prices (Base 1960 = 100)[b]	Beef Production Real Income (Percent Change)[c]
1955	43.0	− 1.6	74.37	− 5
1956	42.6	4.6	90.17	6
1957	41.4	− 0.2	90.75	− 24

Sources: [a] United Nations, Economic Commission for Latin America, *Economic Development and Income Distribution in Argentina* (New York: United Nations, 1969), p. 170, Table 39.

[b] Lorenzo Juan Sigaut, *Acerca de la distribucion y niveles de ingreso en la Argentina* (Buenos Aires: Ediciones Macchi, 1972), p. 57, cuadro 16 and p. 66, cuadro 21.

[c] Banco Ganadero Argentino, *Temas de economía argentina: mercados y precios del ganado vacuno* (Buenos Aires: Banco Ganadero Argentino. 1966), p. 45.

tural prices rose by 22 percent in two years. Critical to the smooth implementation of the government's program was the Argentine worker's acquiescence to income shifts from consumers to producers, because if the government did not escape relatively unscathed from labor protests, its campaign to restore entrepreneurial confidence and create a new political order would be seriously impaired.

The military government's preoccupation with the labor movement was apparent when General Aramburu, largely because he and his hardline colleagues disagreed with Provisional President General Lonardi's more conciliatory attitude toward the CGT, deposed Lonardi in early November 1955. Lonardi had devised a simple but risky strategy to reintegrate labor into the political process. He assumed that the labor organizations fostered by Perón would remain a significant and permanent fixture on the national scene and reasoned therefore that it would be self-defeating to deny them the opportunity to affect economic policy. There was more to be gained, he believed, by quickly reintegrating labor into the new regime. Success, of course, would come only if Lonardi could persuade the CGT rank and file to replace its Peronist leaders with less politicized officials, who could maintain labor discipline while delivering working-class support to the new government. In essence, Lonardi hoped that, despite an atmosphere filled with demands for revenge against Perón's followers, cooperation between labor and those who had deposed its political leaders could be established. It was Lonardi's misfortune, however, that few shared his assumptions. Labor came to view his scheme as little more than a disguised means of subjugating workers to the new government, while anti-Peronists made it clear that they would settle for nothing less than the breaking of the spirit of the entire labor movement. With little support for his plan, Lonardi quietly gave way to Aramburu after less than two months as the chief executive.

Aramburu relied on repression and intimidation to accomplish what Lonardi had failed to do through negotiation. The government's attack on the CGT unions, which began with their intervention in November 1955, was sustained during the first half of 1956 by a series of decrees that froze wages and postponed the renewal of wage contracts for eighteen months, prohibited anyone who had held union office after 1952 from doing so again in the future, and cancelled the Peronist statutes regulating union organization, which had fostered the growth of a strong central confederation like the CGT.[17] In contrast to Perón, who had used carefully crafted labor laws to force the merger of disparate unions so that he could control them more easily, Aramburu sought to use a new set of labor laws to divide the labor movement and undermine Peronist control over it. The final triumph of his campaign to purge the CGT was to have come during an August 1957, government-supervised union convention "normalizing" the CGT under non-Peronist leadership. But the convention had hardly begun before participating unions, Peronist and non-Peronist alike, fell to bickering over the structure of the new organization and adjourned without electing a new executive committee to govern the reconstituted confederation.[18]

Instead of eliminating Peronist control over the CGT, Aramburu only managed to reopen old conflicts between anti-Peronist commerce and transport unions and the Peronist industrial ones. His jailing of the men who led the CGT before 1955 generated a new corps of union leaders who quickly rose from the lower ranks to hold together what was left of the Peronist movement. Since these new leaders retained a large following that remained loyal to its exiled leader, the normalization of the CGT eluded Argentine authorities.

As we can see in Table 6.4, the principal result of Aramburu's divide-and-conquer strategy was not labor peace but continued working-class protest, with most of it directed at securing compensation for the hardships imposed by the government's incomes policy. Despite the administration's attempts to cushion the impact of its wage policies with controlled food prices, most Argentine workers found little reason to comply with the policies of a government that had jailed their leaders and set wage rates without consulting CGT leaders. With the conventional channels of communication closed to them, and their national confederation dismembered by government intervention, the individual unions took up the challenge of protecting the rank and file by leading strikes that secured a succession of wage increases in 1956 and 1957, despite the official ban on new collective agreements.[19] In 1956 labor gained an 18.3-percent boost in monetary income and a 4.6-percent increase in real wages. The price had to be paid the following year when less liberal wage agreements and rapidly rising prices resulted in a slight loss in real income. Clearly, neither labor nor the government emerged the victor from this bitter two-year struggle. Labor managed to cushion some of the blow of the government's measures, while the government's repressive tactics and tough wage policy, which secured a slight income shift from consumers to producers, increased rank-and-file alienation from non-Peronist political authority.

TABLE 6.4
Labor Protests and Wage Responses, 1956–57

	1956	1957
Strikes		
1. Frequency	.0098	.0100
2. Duration	6.05	11.15
3. Size (thousands)	16.4	5.4
4. Volume	973.84	605.41
Wage Response		
1. Change in Monetary Income of Industrial Worker (percent)	18.3	24.7
2. Change in Real Income of Industrial Worker (percent)	4.6	– 0.2

Sources: *Strikes* computed from: República Argentine, Secretaría de Estado de Trabajo, *Conflictos del trabajo,* junio de 1970, cuadro 25.

Wages taken from: Lorenzo Juan Sigaut, *Acerca de la distribución y niveles de ingreso en la Argentina* (Buenos Aires: Ediciones Macchi, 1972), p. 57, cuadro 16.

The second critical element in the government's program was the response of the rural sector to income shifts in its favor. If labor posed the greatest threat to recovery, the producers of commodity exports were expected to be its most enthusiastic and cooperative boosters. Of course, one might argue in Aramburu's defense that no dramatic increases in rural production could have been expected during his brief tenure since several years of renewed effort was needed to restore full-scale rural production after a decade of decapitalization under Peronism. Yet Aramburu had counted on a sudden turnaround in rural production, at least by 1957, to improve the country's trade balance. He was therefore disappointed by the performance of export commodities that is revealed in Table No. 6.5. On the positive side, beef production rose in 1956 and declined only slightly in 1957, but corn

and wheat dropped sharply in 1956 and then recovered somewhat in 1957. What resulted was an increase in total exports of
only 1.6 percent in 1956 and 3.3 percent in 1957.

TABLE 6.5
Annual Growth Rate of Export Commodity Production, 1956–57

	1956	1957
Beef Production		
(volume slaughtered)	15.3	– 1.0
Wheat & Corn Production		
(volume)	– 10.9	7.4
Total Rural Production		
(volume)	– 4.6	– 0.5
Beef Exports		
(volume)	45.1	– 3.0
Wheat & Corn Exports		
(volume)	– 9.8	– 4.0
Total Export Value	1.6	3.3

Source: Computed from: Centro International de Información Económica, *La economía
argentina: treinta años en cifras* (Buenos Aires: CIDIE, 1971), p. 24.
————. *La economía argentina: comercio exterior 1940–1971* (Buenos Aires:
CIDIE, 1971), p. 13, cuadro 4.
Organización Techint, *Boletín Informativo no. 188* (octubre-diciembre 1972), p. 20.

The sluggishness of the rural recovery can be explained in part
by economic conditions, e.g. insufficient credit, decapitalization,
inadequate storage, and inefficient transportation. It was no
doubt also affected by rural attitudes toward public officials.
Where once they had seen policy makers as close allies, rural
spokesmen now viewed them with suspicion and hostility after
what they perceived to have been a decade of abuse and neglect.
While the Aramburu government was a vast improvement over
the Peronists as far as farmers and cattlemen were concerned,
they refused to embrace it enthusiastically. They welcomed the
closure of IAPI and the lifting of commodity price supports, but
they were quick to oppose the new government on most other
matters. Take export taxes, for instance. Farmers were delighted
with the elimination of price controls on all grains except wheat
and the devaluation of the peso, but they complained of betrayal
when a 25-percent tax on foreign exchange was added by Aramburu after it had been recommended by Prebisch in order to
soften the inflationary impact of the rural sector's exchange
windfall. Rather than grant the government its case, the leaders

of the Rural Society and CARBAP denounced the measure as another attempt by greedy public officials to confiscate legitimate rural profits in order to finance the operations of overextended public enterprises.[20]

The wealthier and more conservative cattlemen and farmers were also displeased by Aramburu's failure to dispose of Perón's onerous system of land rent controls. But here again Aramburu tried to establish himself on the middle ground and in so doing pleased neither the large landowners, who desired greater freedom to set the conditions of tenancy, nor the tenants, who had hoped to retain the gains of the past two decades. First, to the surprise and displeasure of the SRA and CARBAP, Aramburu decreed the extension of rent contracts on all land except that immediately sold to tenants.[21] Soon thereafter he retreated somewhat by permitting the eviction of tenants who refused to buy their plots when owners offered to sell at market prices. It had been Aramburu's hope that he could stabilize the land-tenure situation by creating many new title holders, while at the same time restoring tenancy contracting to the rules of the market place. Though he did manage significant progress toward the first objective—the Agrarian Federation estimated that 30,000 tenant farmers became landowners under Aramburu—his suspension of the practice of freezing land rents lasted only until President Arturo Illia renewed it eight years later.[22]

What appeared to upset rural interest groups most after Perón's overthrow was their failure to regain the degree of influence over economic policy that they had enjoyed prior to 1943. Their access to authorities, which had been drastically reduced by Perón, was not completely restored by Aramburu, Frondizi, or Illia. All three recognized that rural concerns had to be balanced with urban ones. Moreover, each in his own way sought to insulate himself from interest-group pressures in order protect his policies from partisan demands. Aramburu even refused to restore the meat and grain regulatory boards to complete farmer control in order to leave himself and successive governments more room to maneuver.[23] To be sure, most of Aramburu's farm policies were aimed at helping the rural producer by raising his income. Nevertheless, by limiting the access of rural interests to the process by which economic policy was made, Aramburu and his civilian successors reinforced farmer distrust of those who occupied the inner circles of the policy-making process.[24]

In contrast to the sluggish rural recovery, industrial production rose impressively during Aramburu's presidency. Total industrial output, which had increased by 12.2 percent in 1955, rose by 6.9 percent and 7.9 percent in 1956 and 1957, respectively. (See Table No. 6.6.) Increased production was not Aramburu's only goal, however. De-Peronization also required the reorganization of industrial interest groups. It will be recalled that Perón had closed the Industrial Union in 1946 and thereafter substituted the General Economic Confederation as the official spokesman for industrial and commercial interests. Like the CGT, the CGE came to be regarded by Perón's opponents as a crude instrument used by the regime to control and exploit the private sector; the small businessmen who had launched the CGE, in contrast, credited it with influencing the government's decision to adopt high tariffs and easy credit to promote national enterprises. Both views were somewhat exaggerated, for the CGE was neither a major instrument of government control nor a critical influence on policy. Nonetheless, its association with the Peronists dictated its closure by the new government, and its replacement as industrial-sector spokesman by the resurrected Industrial Union. With the return of the free-market-

TABLE 6.6
Industrial Product Growth Rates
1956–57

	1956	1957
Food, Drink, and Tobacco	9.2	0.4
Textiles, Leather, and Clothing	6.1	0.0
Metals, Metal Products, Machinery, Vehicles, and Electrical Goods	9.0	19.2
Chemicals, Rubber, and Petroleum Products	5.6	11.6
Total Industrial Production (not summed)	6.9	7.9
Nonagricultural Wholesale Price Increase (percent)	21.4	23.6

Computed from: Organización Techint *Boletín Informativo no. 188* (octubre-diciembre 1972), p. 26, cuadro 5.

oriented UIA came demands for an immediate end to economic controls. Like their colleagues in the rural sector, the conservative industrialists of the UIA were too resentful of the Peronist experience to accept anything less than a complete break with it. Consequently, rather than praising Aramburu for his efforts, they too frequently criticized his timidity on economic matters and concluded their assessment of his performance in early 1958 by observing, with obvious hyperbole, that by failing to halt the economic and social decline begun under Perón, Aramburu had paved the way for the country's economic bankruptcy and spiritual decadence.[25]

Despite pressures from all sides to depart from the program outlined by Prebisch, Aramburu held his middle ground firmly throughout his brief tenure. More than once he appeared to veer away from his original course only to return to it when it became apparent that his change of course might threaten his march toward new elections. The most notable of his swift retreats from the temptation to change policy occurred in early 1957 when, under constant attack from a host of free-market economists and conservative interest-group leaders for not going far enough with the liberalization of the economy, Aramburu dismissed Finance Minister Eugenio Blanco, a widely respected economist from the Radical party who had executed most of Prebisch's recommendations. To solve the continuing foreign-exchange and fiscal problems facing the government, the president called upon Roberto Verrier, an economic consultant known primarily for his advocacy of a freer market and tougher austerity measures.[26] The victory of Prebisch's conservative opponents was short-lived, for once Verrier's intentions became clear and their political costs fully assessed, Aramburu fired his new minister and retreated hastily back to his original program. Verrier's downfall came after the unauthorized publication of his confidential review of Blanco's performance, in which he charged that his predecessor had gone farther than Prebisch had recommended in softening the blow of austerity and de-Peronization. What was now required, he insisted, was even tighter fiscal and monetary restraint, tougher wage controls, and freer prices. Embarrassed by the premature publication of the report and the immediate opposition of the election-minded political parties, who warned that Verrier's scheme would prevent the mobilization of Peronist voters into non-Peronist parties, Aramburu dropped Verrier only two months after his appointment. He replaced him with Adalbert Krieger Vasena, the economist who had served as the executive secretary of the Economic Council.[27]

In the year that followed, few policy changes were made despite the fact that the country's payments and price problems remained acute. Aramburu continued to be convinced that his course was the correct way to achieve long-term political stability and economic growth, even if its immediate outcomes were unsatisfactory. The proof of his success was to have come when he turned over the presidency to elected civilians on May 1, 1958. But the election of a new government, it turned out, did not assure the kind of stability and growth that Aramburu had promised. Instead, as we saw in Chapter 4, his elected successor, Arturo Frondizi, was handicapped from the outset by the rules Aramburu had imposed on the 1958 elections. By excluding the Peronists from the competition and leaving fundamental economic problems unsolved, he made the task of democratic governance incredibly difficult, if not impossible, for the civilians who succeeded him.

The Military Autocrat as Founding Father

In assessing the performance of the transitional military regime, we are not as concerned with its ability to solve long-range development problems as its responses to immediate economic crises and its skill in orchestrating a return to constitutional government. The transitional regime does not seek to eliminate major societal problems. Instead it tries to create the political and economic conditions it believes will facilitiate the efforts of its successors to deal with them. In the case of General Pedro Aramburu, these conditions included the restoration of minimal domestic and foreign confidence in the Argentine economy through the gradual termination of Peronism's stifling economic controls, and the holding of peaceful, democratic elections in which Argentine voters would participate through one of several non-Peronist parties. We must now assess how well Aramburu used the economic and political instruments available to him in pursuit of these objectives.

The reconstruction of a liberal democratic, market-oriented Argentina in the wake of ten years of regulated, welfare capitalism under the Peronists required a government that could quickly design emergency measures to stabilize prices and improve the balance of payments, successfully purge Peronist institutions, and reintegrate the working-class rank and file into the reformed political system, while retaining the support of those who had been united by their opposition to Perón. What Aramburu and his military colleagues created was a civilian-assisted autocratic regime which brutally repressed its working-class opponents and gradually insulated itself from its industrial, rural, financial, and political-party supporters after drawing on their initial support and collaboration to launch a program of economic and political reconstruction. It never did, however, resolve the issue of how to create a democratic regime while excluding the candidates of nearly half of the voting population from elections; it tried to finesse instead, guided by the belief that once the new constitutional order had been launched, the Peronist rank and file would be gradually, if reluctantly, drawn into it.

Although he closed or reorganized many of the state agencies created by the Peronists, Aramburu did not resurrect the entire pre-Peronist political economy. He stopped short primarily because the Argentine state and its regulatory authority had come too far too fast to retreat to the narrow confines of the promotional state of the 1930s. He was also influenced by the advice of economic moderates, who warned that politically intolerable social and economic dislocations would result from the sudden liberalization of the Argentine economy.

Equally significant in the short run was the special role played by Prebisch and his ECLA team in filling policy void left by the sudden eviction of the Peronists. Foreign consultants had advised Argentine authorities in the past but seldom had they dominated the scene the way they did in 1955. The optimism and self-confidence that had characterized Argentina's economic authorities before 1930 was gone in 1955, victims of depression, war, and the onslaught of Peronism and its associated problems. Argentine officials faced unusual problems that could not be solved with the kind of fine tuning that had rescued the economy in decades past. Moreover they possessed no special knowledge or experience to guide them in the unusual task of dismantling a host government agencies and creating others in their place. Unprecedented problems required unprecedented solutions, and by turning over the task of policy design to the ECLA team, Aramburu and his colleagues temporarily filled the policy vacuum that had arisen after Perón's departure.

As they have elsewhere, foreign economic advisors offered certain advantages to a government in need of instant solutions to its economic problems. Not only did the ECLA team come up with a program very quickly, but it also provided one that could be sold to the Argentine people as an authoritative solution to their immediate problems. In comparison with Argentine economists, who had become embroiled in the heated controversies that surrounded Peronist economic policy, the ECLA team, despite the fact that it was headed by an Argentine known to oppose Perón's methods, appeared to bring a less politicized expertise to bear on the country's difficulties. Unlike the conservative economists, who demanded the restoration of the free market regardless of the social and political costs, the ECLA economists, though not reluctant to point out the many errors of past policy, were careful to eschew simple-minded policy prescriptions merely for the sake of ridding the country of Peronism. They therefore appeared to offer Argentines less drastic remedies at a time when moderation was dictated by the military's political objectives.

But what about the costs of turning to foreign advisors? Here, too, the Aramburu experience is illustrative. In addition to the obvious embarrassment that results from asking others to solve one's internal problems, those who import their policies from abroad also invite accusations of being controlled or manipulated by interests alien to the country. Prebisch may have been an Argentine, but that fact did not save Aramburu from appearing to have sold out the country's national interests. For the ardent nationalist it was easy to believe that Argentina had gone the way of the Roca-Runciman pact once again. It was not important whether or not Aramburu actually capitulated to foreign interests; it was appearance that counted, and by appearing to sacrifice a decade of efforts to increase national autonomy for the expediency of short-term economic assistance from abroad, Aramburu helped deepen the division between nationalist and internationalist that had arisen in the 1930s.

In the end the autocratic, manipulative regime created by

military officers in 1955 proved to be an ineffective means for dealing with economic reconstruction and laying the foundation for a new consensus on the political rules of the game. There were primarily two reasons for the latter. First, in 1955 one could not generate a meaningful political consensus in Argentina by excluding Peronist organizations from the councils that made and ratified economic and electoral policies. To hope that some-how the country's workers could be liberated from Peronist leadership and would lend their support to the recovery effort was to ignore the essential fact that the deep political loyalities that had been formed during Perón's ten years in office could not be eradicated overnight. By using brutal repression against loyal Peronists, while appearing to make concessions to anti-Peronists, Aramburu made a mockery of his campaign for na-tional unity. Second, once the Prebisch program had been ratified, Aramburu expended little effort trying to retain the support of non-Peronist economic groups. All that sustained the regime was political-party devotion to its campaign to restore elected government. By mid 1956 those who disagreed with the pace or direction of reconstruction began to find themselves cut off from a president who, in his zeal to avert the slightest devia-tion from the drive toward a new constitutional order, preferred to ignore his critics rather than consult with them. But as he became more isolated, Aramburu found it increasingly difficult to assess the intentions of his opponents and judge the serious-ness of their threats. This became especially evident with the Verrier case in 1957. Early that year he had discovered that his economic policies were not succeeding and in desperation turned to his conservative critics for assistance. Yet, because he had no reliable means of assessing probable responses to the harsh measures they prescribed, he was surprised by the fierce opposition of political parties and economic interest groups and was forced by them to beat a hasty retreat back to his original economic course in order to avoid upsetting his march toward peaceful elections. Had he not abandoned reliance on the con-sultative mechanisms he had used in early 1956, he might have avoided the entire embarrassing episode.

Finally, one of the most important things to result from Aramburu's brief tenure was the lessons that others derived from his travails. On the economic front they learned how a moderate version of the familiar export strategy could be adapted to the conditions of the late 1950s and how a simple but flexible set of rather orthodox instruments could be applied to payments and price problems by reducing consumer demand and improving the relative prices of commodity exports. Even though the strategy's weak performance under Aramburu did little to bolster confidence in it, several Argentine economists and political leaders, who would later govern the country, came away from the experience convinced that with more skilled economic management and more time for implementation this rather orthodox approach to economic management could restore order and set the stage for sustained growth. There were political lessons as well that were learned from Aramburu's ordeal, especially by those who were determined to eradicate Peronism and the influence of the labor movement over public affairs. Unnoticed at the time, the Aramburu regime served as the classroom for a generation of military officers and economists, who observed that the spirit and cohesion of the Peronist movement could survive the dismantling of the CGT and that commitments to the restoration of constitutional government could compromise and undermine the implementation of stabilization policy. By adding these insights to those gained during the Frondizi and Illia years, General Juan Carlos Onganía and his supporters would decide a decade later that a much harsher treatment was required to restore economic and political order to their divided country.

7

Onganía and the Revolution that Failed

We can now return to 1966 and the military coup that overthrew the constitutional regime of Arturo Illia. History appeared
to repeat itself in June of that year when the Argentine military,
as it had done to Perón in 1955 and Frondizi in 1962, abruptly
ended the life of another elected government. In the events
leading up to the coup we find several familiar conditions, including the threat of Peronist resurgence, the failure of the governing party to solve the nation's economic problems, and the
deterioration of civil-military relations. It seemed once again that
the military had entered the political arena to purge it of discredited politicians in order to replace them with others more to
their liking.

But the military regime that was created in June 1966 was
unlike any Argentines had known before. The officers who led
the coup made it clear at the outset that, unlike Aramburu and
his colleagues a decade before, they had not rid their nation
of one set of civilian leaders so that they could pave the way for
the election of others. Quite the contrary: General Juan Carlos
Onganía and his fellow officers announced that they had no intention of relinquishing their control over the government until
after they had restored the country to economic prosperity
and reconstructed its political processes. Since 1958 they had
watched in frustration as two democratic regimes had failed to
resolve the country's social conflicts, cure its economic ills, and

rid it of Peronism. With democratic rule discredited, and the restoration of Peronism ruled out, only sustained rule by the military, they reasoned, could save the country.

The military's approach to political rule was influenced not only by the generals' loss of faith in liberal democracy and their opposition to Peronism, but also by their intense desire to promote rapid economic growth. Perón had given the country a consumer-goods industry in the 1940s, but his efforts at import substitution had also yielded persistent inflation, foreign-exchange shortages, and social conflict. Frondizi had added iron, steel, automotive, and petro-chemical industries, but the country's industrialization still remained incomplete and its external problems acute. What the country needed, Onganía and his advisors concluded, was not more of the inflation-inducing, nationalistic, expansionary policies of the UCRP government, but a centrally directed campaign to complete its industrialization, with the assistance of large multinational enterprises that could supply the capital and technology that Argentina lacked. They also were convinced that Argentina could not attract foreign investors as long as its politics were chaotic and its economic policies inhospitable. What was required, it seemed, was a strong government that could guarantee political order and a friendly investment climate. And that kind of government would come, the coup leaders were convinced, only through the efforts of the military to create a regime that dedicated itself to imposing the will of the state on the unruly Argentine people.[1]

With the consent of the Argentine military, General Onganía created an authoritarian regime that he personally supervised, in the manner of an eighteenth-century monarch. He was assisted by a corps of internationally respected Argentine economists, who welcomed the opportunity to deal sternly with the country's economic problems when backed by a government that could keep the popular classes in check. For the next three years Onganía governed the country with a firmness and determination seldom before seen in Argentina, convincing many that military authoritarianism was indeed capable of ending an era of economic instability and political conflict. But in the end, he too failed to achieve his objectives, a victim of his own inability to construct durable political institutions that could be used to manage the nation's economy and resolve its social conflicts.

The Restoration of Investor Confidence

The emerging recession and recurring inflation that the military inherited in mid 1966 were no strangers to Argentine policy makers. But to the conventional arsenal of measures that were normally used to deal with such conditions, Onganía added another—the heavy hand of a strong state. In contrast to free-market liberals such as Alvaro Alsogaray, who had placed their faith entirely in the market's ability to drive out inefficiency and waste, Onganía and his advisors concluded that the market mechanism could not change the habits or resolve the conflicts that had been nurtured by the postwar experiences with inflation, subsidization, and regulation. What Argentina needed, they reasoned, was a central authority strong enough to make the market rules of the game operate smoothly, for only by forcing competitors to follow the rules and accept less than total satisfaction of their demands could a government hope to create the conditions necessary to build stable economic growth. Therefore, once the rules of the economic game were set by the president and his ministers, all debate over them would cease so that private producers could get on with the task of economic development.

Given the conventional view that Onganía took office with a comprehensive plan of action in hand, one is surprised to discover that it took him almost a year to formulate his new program. During his first six months he proceeded cautiously, concentrating on the suppression of recalcitrant labor unions and minor changes in monetary and fiscal policy. But he offered no global attack on the economic problems that he had inherited. It was during this initial stage, however, that he commenced discussions with a select group of distinguished Argentine economists noted for their articulate criticism of the nationalistic schemes of Perón and Illia. After reviewing the programs of the past decade, they concluded that errors had been made not only in the expansionary programs of the past but also in the stabilization efforts of 1959 and 1962, which had placed too much faith in monetary restraint and currency devaluation and too little in fiscal management and wage and price controls. This view, expressed most persuasively by Dr. Carlos Moyano Llerna in his prestigious quarterly *Panorama de la Economia Argentina*, and echoed by Drs. Adalbert Krieger Vasena, Roberto Alemann, and José Martínez de Hoz (h), ministers of economy in the Aramburu, Frondizi, and Guido adminstrations respectively, recommended that the government carry out a nonrecessionary attack on inflation by carefully applying selective economic controls through a global scheme of economic management.

Onganía proved to be an attentive student. In January 1967 he replaced Minister of Economy Jorge Salimei with Krieger Vasena and assigned him responsibility for designing and implementing a comprehensive economic program. Krieger Vasena and his aides recognized in early 1967 that they were faced with an economy characterized structurally by slow and irregular growth in real production, significant annual increases in the level of prices, low international reserves, and an appreciable and recurring fiscal deficit.[2] But rather than slavishly adhering to past policies or the dictates of the International Monetary Fund, they sought to fashion an innovative global program that coordinated measures dealing with price, exchange, wage, agricultural, and industrial objectives. Central to this approach was Krieger Vasena's conviction that Argentina's fundamental problem was its gross inefficiency in both the public and private sectors and that its elimination would require the reallocation of resources among activities within each economic sector rather than among the sectors themselves. In selecting his polices, the new minister also drew on the experiences of other nations, believing, as he later asserted, that in addition to what one could learn from Argentina's past failures, the recuperation of Western Europe after the war, and the experiences of Mexico in 1954, of France in the mid 1950s, and of Brazil in the mid 1960s offered valuable lessons that should be applied to Argentina in 1967.[3]

Before a national television audience on March 13, 1967, Krieger Vasena announced his "Grand Transformation" of the Argentine economy, which included a wide-ranging program that was to affect nearly every economic activity as supplemental decrees were implemented in the year that followed.[4] It began with a 40-percent devaluation of the peso: this was intended to create an undervalued currency that would stimulate an influx of foreign capital and, once and for all, end speculation based on expectations of future devaluations. To prevent exchange windfalls and abrupt income redistribution, an export tax, ranging from 16 to 20 percent, was imposed on traditional exports; and to promote greater industrial efficiency, import duties were relaxed in the hope of increasing foreign competition. Simultaneously, a host of tax incentives was provided to encourage investment in the industrial sector and foster a rapid expansion of nontraditional exports; within the public sector the prices of public services were increased, sales and property taxes were raised, and redundant public employees were transferred to more productive activities. (See Table No. 7.1.)

TABLE 7.1
Onganía's Economic Policy, 1967

Objectives	1. Price stability
	2. Improve balance of payments
	3. Industrial growth
	4. Improve economic efficiency
Instruments	
Fiscal	1. Reduce deficit
	2. Reduct current expenditure growth rate
	3. Reduce import tariffs
	4. Increase income taxes and improve collections
	5. Increase prices of government services
	6. Increase public investments
Money and Credit	1. Expand money and credit for private producers moderately
Exchange	1. Devaluation
	2. Export earning retentions
Controls	1. Wage controls
	2. Voluntary price controls
Income Redistribution	1. Maintain existing internal distribution but shift from domestic to foreign investors

What distinguished Krieger Vasena's plan from those of his predecessors were not its fiscal or exchange measures, but its use of monetary policy and wage controls. To the surprise of hardline monetarists, the government, in its determination to avert a recession, actually expanded the country's financial liquidity in 1967, though at the same time it reduced the public sector's share of Central Bank credit. And, on March 31, when he froze wages for the first time since 1957, Krieger Vasena added what his admirers came to consider the most critical component of his strategy. The decree that permitted wage increases ranging downward from 24 to 8 percent until November 1967, prohibited further increases until December 31, 1968.[5] Clearly, this measure, more than any other, set the tone of the new program. It was not just a declaration of the government's intention to combat one of the principal causes of inflation, but also notification that this time a wage freeze would be backed by a president capable of enforcing it. The government's tough stand on wages also increased the probability that its voluntary price controls would succeed, for it made it easier for industrialists to control their factor costs.

There is no doubt that the measures announced in March 1967 represented Argentina's most sophisticated and comprehensive attempt to combat inflation. It was also a program that defied traditional labels. With conventional stabilization programs it shared a tough incomes policy and a desire to encourage foreign investment, yet it also reflected expansionary policy's disdain for recession-inducing monetary stringency. Of equal interest was its apparent reluctance to give special favors to any of the domestic economic sectors. Rural producers, for example, were asked to relinquish much of their windfall profits from devaluation through export taxes; domestic industry was told to compete with less expensive foreign-made goods; and organized labor saw its wage issues declared nonnegotiable. To all appearances, Krieger Vasena had designed the most balanced antiinflationary program of the postwar era, one in which he had combined the expansion of production, price stability, and the improvement of the balance-of-payments objectives with an effort to increase the level of aggregate consumption, albeit, very gradually. It was truly an effort born from displeasure with the excesses of Peronist rule, nurtured on the shortcomings of strict stabilization in 1959 and 1962, and made possible by a bold assertion of government authority.

One should not be surprised by the early optimism of Onganía's advisors, who were convinced that they had at last unlocked the door to Argentina's political stability and economic growth. Clearly theirs was the country's most sophisticated economic program and, more than any of their predecessors, they appeared to have freed themselves from debilitating political constraints. One must ask, however, if their optimism was well founded; that is, was it possible suddenly to terminate deep social conflicts by using the threat of force against those who transgressed the new rules of the game? Was the policy itself so well balanced and finely tuned that it could avoid conflicts among its own objectives as well as protests from its opponents? If not, could it survive such conflicts and protests? Certainly Onganía could take hope from the success of his military colleagues in Brazil, who in 1967 were solidly entrenched, despite the initial hardships imposed by their recession-inducing stabilization policy. Yet, only by means of the utmost self-delusion could Onganía believe that Argentina, with its postwar experience of domestic conflict and distrust of public authority, could be tamed as easily as had less deeply divided Brazil three years before.

The New Autocrats as Policy Managers

Onganía initially justified his coup by pointing to the failure of the Argentine political system to cope with critical economic and social issues and to maintain public order. His task of self-justification was more difficult than that of previous military regimes. Whereas Aramburu could point to Perón's authoritarian excesses and middle-class opposition to him to justify military intervention in 1955, Onganía had to argue that it was liberal democracy that had failed Argentina and that only through long-term military rule could the country's deficiencies be corrected. Fortunately for the military, the Illia government greatly facilitated their effort. Even more than its predecessors it had given constitutional government a partisan yet indecisive color, leading most political parties and private-sector groups, including the CGT, to cheer the coup for having rid the country of a naive and misguided government.[6]

To demonstrate that the country's malaise could be cured through military rule, nothing less than a major feat of political and economic engineering was required. There was, of course, no lack of examples to which Onganía could turn in seeking guidance for political reconstruction through military rule. The Spanish military, much admired by Onganía and his colleagues, had long ago imposed a new order on strife-ridden Spain and, more recently and closer to home, the Brazilian military that had deposed João Goulart in April 1964 was in 1966 well along in its campaign to reorganize the country's politics and stabilize its economy. Yet despite the availability of these and other models, Onganía had no comprehensive plan of political reconstruction in mind when he deposed Illia, but instead could offer his countrymen only indefinite rule using the simplist autocratic means.

From the beginning, the new president said little about what he was going to create to replace the constitutional processes he abandoned or the political parties he banned in July 1966. The Revolutionary Acts, issued by the junta immediately after the coup, were little more than vague pronouncements justifying the coup as a response to civilian political errors, a decline in "spiritical unity," and the danger of Marxist penetration into the political system. The so-called revolution's political, economic, and social objectives were equally vague. Politically, the new government promised that it would promote "tolerance and solidarity," restore respect for authority and individual liberties, and perpetuate the country's Christian tradition. On the economic front, it proposed to eliminate the causes of stagnation and provide as much liberty, prosperity, and security as were compatible with order and social discipline. In the critical area of labor relations, it offered only a "just balance" among the interests of labor, capital, and the public good.[7]

The first to be disappointed with the new government were those who had hoped it would create some new form of public participation in the political process to replace the political parties and legislatures it had closed—a consultative body or corporatist council admitting representatives along functional lines, for example. But Onganía initially confined his political reorganization within the executive branch where he reassigned policy-making responsibilities to two coordinating bodies, each composed of five ministers, with one responsible for economic and social planning and the other for national security.[8] Not until mid 1967, ten months and two ministers of economy after the original coup, did he finally give some indication of the government's long-range political strategy. To the disappointment of those who had anxiously awaited the announcement of some kind of new constitution, Onganía offered only vague proposals

for the gradual transformation of the country's economic and
political life. He informed his countrymen that the first stage of
a three-stage program of national reconstruction had begun with
the announcement of the new economic policy two months before. After the completion of this economic stage, a social stage
aimed at restoring harmony and cooperation to Argentine life
would be initiated, and after that would come a final, though
undefined, political transformation.[9] This vague three-stage
strategy was the closest Onganía came to announcing a plan to
guide his campaign to lead the country out of the wilderness.
Unfortunately, it revealed little about the form that Argentine
politics would take under his leadership.

Onganía's basic idea seems to have been drawn from a very
simple linear view of social change popularized by admirers of
the early work of historian Walt Whitman Rostow and other
"stage" theorists.[10] What he failed to appreciate, however, was
that the utility of such theories in interpreting history has not
been equalled in their application to the transformation of political systems. First of all, large gaps remain between the analyst's
ability to demonstrate how particular economic and social conditions have shaped the growth of political institutions and his ability to prescribe programs aimed at effecting such changes.
Moreover, it offers no guidance about how a country like Argentina should organize its government in order to implement the
required social and economic changes, without hindering the
consequent growth of desired political institutions. That is, it
says nothing about whether the use of authoritarian techniques
during the first two stages will help or hinder the growth of
other institutions during the third.

To complicate matters, Onganía did not govern a society unfamiliar with most forms of political participation and contestation, but one accustomed to widespread, if often raucous and
distorted, political competition. Thus, even though he had suspended political parties, he could not thereby eliminate the conflicts that had plagued the country, nor could he ignore the
country's very active interest groups, each of which continued to
advance its well-articulated claims on public policy. Organized
labor, although still torn by internal divisions that the government might exploit to its advantage, threatened to obstruct the
implementation of wage and price policies; in industry, the In-

dustrial Union and the General Economic Confederation each hoped to secure advantages from the new government; and in the rural sector, disillusionment with the ever-changing, counterproductive policies of the previous decade gave rise to a renewed urgency for the renovation of agricultural policy. Unfortunately, his elementary stage theory offered him no scheme for securing the cooperation of such groups in the implementation of his program of reconstruction.

The institutional simplicity of Onganía's autocracy is clearly revealed in his initial solutions to the problems of political participation and contestation. Rather than create new organizations and processes to resolve social and economic conflicts and mobilize the support of critical interests, Onganía and his inner circle preferred to insulate themselves from the influence attempts of private groups and use force instead of negotiation to deal with domestic conflict. They acted not so much from a lack of concern with the causes of such conflicts but from a strong desire to impose order as quickly as possible so that government technocrats and foreign investors could get on with the job of completing the country's industrialization.

Political party conflict was abruptly terminated through the closing of all parties and a prohibition against political activity. To deal with economic interest groups a less drastic approach was taken. Onganía was convinced that he could not allow interest groups to meddle freely in the policy-making process since he believed that government concessions to their narrow demands had undermined the economic programs of his predecessors. At the same time, he needed the cooperation of their members in order to attain his economic objectives. Something had to be done to protect decision makers from the give-and-take of interest-group bargaining without provoking the hostility of most entrepreneurs and laborers. His solution, it turned out, was quite elementary, like most aspects of his rule. Instead of reorganizing interest groups or bringing them under direct government control, he chose to isolate the executive branch as much as possible from them and treat them as subjects who were expected to expend their energies executing government policy rather than debating or influencing its content. In this arrangement, communication flowed in only one direction because there was no need to receive and process the demands of subjects who existed primarily to carry out the will of the state. What made it so simple was that it did not attempt to control interest groups or rule through them. Cabinet officials confined themselves primarily to charting the country's economic course and dictating the rules and conditions under which individual firms and citizens would participate. Neither the rules nor the economic policies adopted by the government were subject to debate or review by the private sector, but once the latter had accepted them, it was free to follow its economic self-interests wherever they might lead.[11]

Some students of the Onganía period have concluded that his authoritarian regime represented a clear break with past policy-making practices. Actually, it is more accurate to describe what he did as an extension of a familiar pattern of presidential behavior to a new extreme. In previous chapters we observed how Argentina's postwar presidents had from time to time tried to isolate themselves from the demands of certain economic groups in the hope of protecting their economic policies from critics. Perón ignored conservative rural groups, Aramburu the labor movement, and Frondizi and Illia nearly all groups at one time or another. The idea of the insulated president did not begin with Onganía; what he did was formalize a process that had been present since the 1930s. By freeing the president from any obligation to bargain with private citizens over the policies he selected, Onganía and his associates believed that they had at last made it possible for the nation's chief executive and the technocrats who assisted him to make policies for the society as a whole rather then according to the demands of a few selfish groups. It was the triumph of rationality over politics, and long-term economic policy making over crisis management, that they thought they had achieved in 1967.

Finally, much was made by Argentine and foreign writers of the composition of Onganía's cabinet as an indicator of his preference for either a liberal or a corporatist approach to policy matters. Most of this speculation centered around the roles of Adelbert Krieger Vasena, his "liberal" economics minister, and Dr. Guillermo Borda, his "nationalist" or corporatist minister of interior.[12] While we will never know what might have occurred had Onganía remained in office after 1970, it is quite clear that neither of these views came to dominate his political strategy. He was liberal only insofar as he sought to manipulate the mar-

ket place to reallocate economic resources to more efficient activities. In politics he neither restored the semilibertarian participatory process preferred by most political liberals nor did he
adopt the corporatist alternative demanded by others. Throughout his tenure he never altered the rather simple autocracy he
created at the outset, in which policy was made by a small group
of ministers who were known more for their technical expertise
than their ties to political or economic groups. Krieger Vasena,
for instance, had been a minister in the Aramburu government
and a frequent advisor to the United Nations thereafter. His
successor, Dr. José María Dagnino Pastore, was a researcher
with the Di Tella Institute before his elevation to the planning
agency and later to the Ministry of Economy and Labor. Similarly, the Secretariat of Agriculture was headed first by Dr.
Lorenzo Raggio, a well-known leader of Argentina's more progressive and technically minded cattlemen, and thereafter by
Dr. Rafael García Mata, an agricultural engineer and long-time
ministerial functionary.

TABLE 7.2
Onganía's Policy-Making Process

Phases	Political Institutions and Techniques
Initiation	Krieger Vasena and his economic team
Formulation	Same
Consultation	Limited to small circle of "liberal" economists
Ratification	By the president alone
Execution	Mix of bureaucratic controls and market incentives Selective repression of labor unions
Feedback	Informal contacts with individual entrepreneurs and labor leaders

Onganía's choice of a political strategy was in part the product
of his assessment of the one employed a decade before by
Aramburu. Where Aramburu had tried to rebuild the country's
political process by purging it of a host of undesirable participants, Onganía, having witnessed the shortcomings of Aramburu's
approach to political reconstruction, concluded that the restoration of economic and political order required the elimination of
the Peronists and all political parties and the subordination of
partisan economic interests to the will of the state. Policy bar-

gaining, party coalitions, and the cooptation of potential opponents had no place in such a scheme. Only those who were willing to play by the rules of his new autocratic game would be allowed to participate, and even their activities would be confined primarily to the economic market place rather than government chambers. Ultimately, it was hoped, this new system, which was initially sustained by force and fear of repression, would prove so rewarding to most participants that their fear would give way to acceptance and even support.

The Bubble that Burst

It is understandable why many Argentines expected a harsh, regressive redistribution of income from their new autocratic government. After all, had not that been the result of Aramburu's and Frondizi's stabilization efforts and was not this a government even more determined than its predecessors to enforce the rules of the market place? But contrary to such expectations, income was redistributed less severely under the Onganía program than under those of his predecessors. It will be recalled that Krieger Vasena was determined to avoid the economic dislocations and recessions that had been caused by previous stabilization programs. To the surprise of his critics, he kept his word, as we can see from Table No. 7.3. At the same time, while he held

TABLE 7.3
The Income Effects of the New Stabilization, 1966–69

	Salary Income as a % of National Income[a]	Real Income of Industrial Workers (Percent Change)[b]	Relative Agricultural Prices (1960 = 100)[b]	Beef Production Real Income (Percent Change)[c]
1966	43.7	1.4	95.78	– 6.2
1967	45.4	0.0	96.68	0.0
1968	44.4	– 0.5	96.93	6.8
1969	43.3	3.8	99.80	– 5.0

Sources: [a] United Nations, Economic Commission for Latin America, *Economic Development and Income Distribution in Argentina* (New York: United Nations, 1969), p. 170, Table 39.

[b] Lorenzo Juan Sigaut, *Acerca de la distribución y niveles de ingreso en la Argentina* (Buenos Aires: Ediciones Macchi, 1972), p. 66, cuadro 21, and p. 57, cuadro 16.

[c] Banco Ganadero Argentino, *Temas de economia argentina: mercados y precios del ganado vacuno* (Buenos Aires: Banco Ganadero Argentino, 1966), p. 45.

back on the redistribution of income within Argentina, he did not hesitate to encourage significant redistributions from domestic to foreign investors by lowering tariff barriers and increasing incentives that attracted substantial foreign capital to Argentina in 1968, more than in any year since 1961.[13]

Onganía was not surprised that his economic program was greeted warily and unenthusiastically by the country's farmers, urban entrepreneurs, and labor leaders. Krieger Vasena had deliberately avoided singling out any group or sector for special favor. Of course, he did offer domestic producers some short-term benefits. But what he gave with one hand, he often appeared to take back with the other. Perhaps the best example is what occurred in the industrial sector.

The steady but slow industrial growth reported in Table No. 7.4 testifies to the increasing responsiveness of industrialists, especially the larger, foreign-financed ones, to the opportunities opened up by the new program. Many of those who had been frustrated by the uncertainty of public policy under democratic governments had welcomed the creation of the no-nonsense authoritarian regime which left economic policy matters to the experts who understood the needs of modern industry. At last it seemed that Argentina had a government able not only to suppress unwanted strikes but also to freeze wages during the initial phase of its economic program. Moreover, Onganía had also promised to end featherbedding and waste in the national railways and invited private participation in the petroleum industry

TABLE 7.4
Industrial Product Growth Rates, 1967–69

	1967	1968	1969
Food, Drink, and Tobacco	4.3	3.0	3.9
Textiles, Leather, and Clothing	0.1	5.4	4.2
Metals, Metal Products, Machinery, Vehicles, Electrical Goods	0.1	8.5	17.1
Chemicals, Rubber, and Petroleum Products	1.5	8.4	15.2
Total Industrial Production (not summed)	1.3	6.9	11.1

Source: Computed from: Organización Techint, *Boletín Informativo no. 188* (octubre-diciembre 1972), p. 26, cuadro 5.

once again, all of which earned him the enthusiastic endorsement of the Industrial Union.[14] But even Onganía was not perfect. On closer inspection, industrialists discovered that the obvious benefits thrown their way had to be weighed against some significant costs. Krieger Vasena, it will be recalled, had been disturbed by gross inefficiencies within the Argentine economy and set out to improve the performance of the industrial sector by lowering tariffs and subjecting industrialists to greater foreign competition. Naturally, the UIA cried foul as soon as the policy took effect, claiming in its defense that the high cost of industrial goods was due primarily to the country's inflated social security system, high taxes and interest rates, extravagant wage contracts, and an appalling economic infrastructure, all conditions that competition with cheaper imported goods would not alleviate.[15]

It was not the large industrialists of the UIA who would suffer under foreign competition, however, but the smaller firms associated with the CGE. They were not as well equipped financially or technologically to withstand the challenge. For many small firms easy credit and tariff protection had meant the difference between economic survival and disaster. Consequently the CGE, which had been one of the loudest critics of the laissez-faire approach taken by Frondizi, came to view Onganía with even greater alarm. Not only had he abruptly terminated the more preferable policies of Illia and the UCRP, but, after setting off on his new course, he was more immune to private-sector influence than any of his predecessors. It is therefore not surprising that the CGE soon abandoned any hope of altering the design of Krieger Vasena's program and devoted itself instead to a campaign directed at embarrassing the government by drawing public attention to what it claimed was the "denationalization" of Argentine industry and finance through increasing foreign takeovers of weakened national firms. Thus, having lost the battle over the formulation of policy, the CGE turned to attacking its effects in the hope of building sympathy for the vulnerable small producer who, it claimed, was being forced by government policy to relinquish his enterprise to foreigners.[16] Though Onganía was initially immune to such criticism, the CGE campaign, joined later by the CGT, gathered momentum in 1969 and 1970 and finally culminated in some restrictive, antiforeign-investment legislation in 1974.[17]

A similar ambivalence characterized rural assessments of Krieger Vasena's program. On the one hand, conservative rural interests were pleased to have a government dedicated to holding popular forces in check, economizing in the public sector, and increasing Argentina's integration into the international economy. Yet, this had to be weighed against the decision to impose yet another distasteful 20-percent exchange tax after a currency devaluation. Moreover, without notice, Krieger Vasena also promulgated an emergency land tax in December 1968. The national, in contrast to the traditional provincial, land tax was one of the measures least expected from the military government, for such taxes had been associated in the past only with the demogogic populist governments. The new law, whose stated purpose was to end widespread tax evasion by landowners, was designed not as an appeal for popularity but simply as a technical solution to a fiscal problem that had long plagued the government. It fixed a rate of 1.6 percent of the assessed land value, free of improvements, which, if not already paid in income taxes, would have to be paid as a land tax.[18] Nevertheless, rural spokesmen were outraged that an authoritarian government, whose creation they had cheered because of its apparent dedication to the promotion of economic growth, had ignored the wishes of the rural producers whom it had been expected to serve.[19]

The government's unilateral decision to apply the land tax served to emphasize how much influence cattlemen and farmers had lost during the previous two decades. Under Onganía, more than ever before farm policy was placed under the control of a powerful minister of economy, who regarded the secretary of agriculture as only one of many subordinates. It was this centralization of control over agricultural policy that led to the resignation of Dr. Lorenzo Raggio, Onganía's first secretary of agriculture, in July 1967, after he had tried unsuccessfully to persuade Krieger Vasena to reduce export retentions. In much the same way, the Rural Society and CARBAP in December 1968 withdrew their representatives from the Agricultural Advisory Council (created by Onganía three months before), protesting that their participation had been used only as window dressing for the government's small inner circle, the same circle that had imposed measures like the emergency land tax on rural producers without consulting them.[20]

The one policy decision from which conservative landowners could take some encouragement also divided them again from the tenant farmers with whom they had long disputed the land-tenure issue. After Illia's overthrow, the SRA and CARBAP resurrected their demand for an end to the practice of rent freezes and contract extensions. This time they were supported by government economists, who argued that Perón's and Illia's intervention into the land market had discouraged capital improvements and long-range production planning by creating a climate of uncertainty for tenants and landowners alike. Not surprisingly, Onganía's efficiency-minded advisors drew on such arguments when they drafted a new tenancy law in April 1967, which, in the words of the very pleased Rural Society, "paved the way for increasing productivity by removing the unjustified legal advantages long enjoyed by tenants."[21] The new law, which restored the landowners' right of eviction and control over contracts and was one of the few causes for celebration by the SRA and CARBAP during Onganía's tenure, brought immediate protests from the Agrarian Federation. Though only about 36 percent of the FAA membership of 100,000 was still tenant farmers in 1966, the issue of land tenure continued to absorb the attention of its leadership, and they campaigned throughout the remainder of Onganía's rule against his "expulsion law."[22]

Since he had not relied as much on the rural sector to rescue the Argentine economy as had his predecessors, Onganía's program was not seriously impared by the sluggish rural recovery in 1967 and 1968. (See Table No. 7.5.) In fact, the gross national product increased by 4.7 percent in 1968 and 8 percent in 1969. Equally impressive, the public-sector deficit, which had risen astronomically under Illia, was reduced by 31 percent in nominal terms due to a remarkable 58-percent increase in public revenues through new taxes and more effective collections.[23] By restoring investor confidence in the Argentine economy, Krieger Vasena also succeeded in financing the remaining deficit almost entirely from domestic savings and external borrowings.[24]

It was the containment of the economic appetite and political ambition of Argentina's working class, however, that was the most critical variable in Krieger Vasena's equation and it was here that the government claimed its greatest success by 1968. Not only were wages held constant for almost two years, and the

TABLE 7.5
Annual Growth Rate of Export Commodity Production, 1967–69

	1967	1968	1969
Beef Production			
(tons slaughtered)	8.6	2.0	12.6
Wheat and Corn Production			
(tons)	12.5	− 5.9	− 9.2
Total Rural Production			
(tons)	4.3	− 3.9	4.2
Beef Exports			
(tons)	18.9	− 12.8	26.4
Wheat and Corn Exports			
(tons)	− 27.6	− 16.6	19.7
Total Export Value	− 8.0	− 6.7	17.8

Source: Computed from: Centro Internacional de Información Económica, *La economía Argentina: treinta años en cifras* (Buenos Aires: CIDIE, 1971), p. 24, p. 30, p. 44.
———, *La economía Argentina: comercio exterior 1940–1971* (Buenos Aires: CIDIE, 1971), p. 13, cuaderno 4.
Organización Techint, *Boletín Informativo no. 188* (octubre-diciembre 1972), p. 20.

rate of inflation reduced to only 7.6 percent in 1969, but strikes and demonstrations appeared to have become a thing of the past. (See Table No. 7.6.) In short, Onganía appeared to have confirmed the notion that the only way to end domestic social conflict and achieve stable growth was to divide and conquer the

TABLE 7.6
Labor Protests and Wage Responses, 1967–69

	1967	1968	1969
Labor Protests			
1. Frequency	.0010	.0012	.0013
2. Duration	4.49	9.63	22.44
3. Size	91.00	230.00	837.00
4. Volume	0.44	2.66	24.41
Wage Response			
1. Change in Monetary Income			
of Industrial Worker (Percent)	29.6	15.0	11.7
2. Change in Real Income of			
Industrial Worker (Percent)	0.0	− 0.5	3.8

Sources: República Argentina, Secretaria de Estado de Trabajo, *Conflictos del trabajo,* junio de 1970, cuadro 25.
Lorenzo Juan Sigaut, *Acerca de la distribución y niveles de ingreso en la Argentina* (Buenos Aires: Ediciones Macchi, 1972), p. 57, cuadro 16.

working-class movement through the use of physical force and intimidation.

Yet what appeared to have been Onganía's greatest success turned out to be his most costly failure, for it was the working class that rose up to challenge him during several days of riots in the interior industrial city of Córdoba in May 1969 and undermined his quest for political order and economic stability. To understand how an apparently successful labor policy was suddenly transformed into an embarrassing failure, a review of Onganía's labor strategy is necessary.

Initially, Onganía had faced a CGT that had greeted his coup with cautious optimism, hoping that somehow its representatives could find their way into the inner circles of the rather ill-defined new regime. The CGT was in fact among the first to justify the coup publicly, claiming that it was the logical consequence of a UCRP government that had become the victim of its own lack of direction and purpose. As for the future, CGT leaders expressed the hope that the new government could be persuaded to join with labor in the implementation of the social and economic reforms it had long advocated.[25] The CGT's cautious optimism proved ill-founded, it turned out. After some initial hesitation, the government systematically set out to subjugate the labor movement so that it could no longer obstruct the execution of economic policy. Its antilabor policy, which in the end proved unsuccessful, went through three distinct phases: (1) June 1966 to March 1967, during which time the government expanded its formal authority over labor organization and collective bargaining and sought to gain the support of some unions while repressing others who tried to obstruct its economic policies; (2) March 1967 to May 1969, during which a weakened and divided labor movement was forced to accept a wage freeze and the suspension of collective bargaining; and (3) May 1969 to July 1970, when a wave of labor violence led to a retreat from hardline policies, culminating in Onganía's own overthrow by military colleagues disillusioned with his autocratic rule.

Despite the swiftness of the June 27, 1966, coup, Onganía was slow to define the role of labor in the new order. He appeared to reach out for labor support when, not long after the coup, he suspended for 120 days some of the repressive labor regulations adopted by Illia during his last year. Then in late August he reversed himself with the announcement of a compulsory arbitration law, authorizing the government to arbitrate labor disputes whenever it wished. There followed in October the government's intervention of the port workers union in order to put an end to its refusal to accept the government's reorganization of the port operations. In early 1967, there was the intervention of the railway unions, which, as they had done back in 1961 under Frondizi, tried, unsuccessfully this time, to block the government's reorganization of the state railways. Clearly on the defensive, the CGT decided to make its stand with an antigovernment Action Plan, to begin with a general strike on March 1, 1967. But unlike his vacillating predecessors, Onganía met labor's attack head on, first by declaring the strike illegal and then by intervening several unions, thus forcing the CGT into an embarrassing retreat.[26]

With the government's authority firmly established and the CGT's morale at its lowest point in over a decade, Krieger Vasena froze wages and suspended collective bargaining. As the program took effect in the two years that followed, Onganía's supporters came to believe, prematurely it turned out, that at long last the principal obstacle to the government's fight against inflation had been removed. They were especially pleased with the Balkanization of the CGT under the pressure of government repression. Labor leaders quarrelled among themselves throughout 1967 and 1968, dividing among those ready to collaborate with the government, others, including some Peronists, who were prepared to talk with authorities only when it served their purposes, and a third group, composed of unions intervened by the government and many hardline Peronists, who wanted to continue the attack, however futile.[27] The last two fought for control over the CGT at its March 1968 convention. The hardliners won and their opponents withdrew from the CGT in anger.[28] By skillfully exploiting these divisions through on-again, off-again promises of concessions to opposing factions, Onganía exacerbated conflicts within the labor movement and made organized obstruction of his program virtually impossible; or so it appeared.

There is little doubt that Onganía's moderately regressive wage policies sowed some seeds of discontent among the Argentine working class. This fact alone though does not explain why a violent confrontation emerged and why it came in Córdoba rather than in Buenos Aires, where the power of the CGT was concentrated. The explanation, it would appear, rests, at least in part, with the unusual character of the labor movement in Córdoba, a condition which Onganía's labor policy, predicated as it was on assumptions drawn from observations of the bureaucratized CGT unions of Buenos Aires, failed to take into account. He had sought to neutralize CGT unions by sowing divisions among them and by encouraging the pursuit of government favors by union leaders, whose traditionally strong control over their rank and file permitted such opportunism. But these tactics served the government's cause well only so long as they were confined to the traditional union leadership of the Balkanized CGT. Replication of their success was more difficult when the same tactics were applied to the Córdoba unions, as Onganía unexpectedly discovered.

Industrialization had come later to Córdoba than Buenos Aires, reaching a significant level only after the arrival of large automotive firms in the mid 1950s. As a result, unlike the industrial unions formed during the war years, Córdoba's labor movement was not indebted heavily to Perón for its bargaining advantages, and therefore felt little loyalty toward the CGT leadership. Unlike the larger and more bureaucratized unions of Buenos Aires, those of Córdoba remained smaller and more close-knit. Union leaders maintained strong ties with the rank and file, which constrained their ability to wander from their unions' militant stance in order to gain favor with public authorities.[29] So while the CGT unions continued to bicker among themselves, playing the government's game of political opportunism, those in Córdoba held fast to their militancy; and when the opportunity for a violent expression of frustration with the isolated, authoritarian government arose during student protests in May 1969, the workers of Córdoba seized it to provoke the kind of military response that could not help but undermine a government that justified itself by its ability to maintain public order.

The Cordobazo did not bring Onganía's regime or his policies to an immediate halt. It did, however, compel the president to dismiss Krieger Vasena and his economic team in the hope of restoring confidence in the government and its economic course. But in casting his minister to the wolves, Onganía only further undermined investor confidence in his determination to carry through with his orginal program. Most Argentine and foreign businessmen were bewildered by the Cordobazo as well as by the president's response to it and looked with envy upon the Brazilian government, which appeared to have harnessed labor in the process of successfully implementing its own economic revolution. To some, the cause of Argentina's new plight had been Onganía's failure to replicate all of the stern repressive measares employed by the Brazilians when he was challenged by the Cordobazo. Such criticism was misplaced, however, for it ignored some essential differences between Argentina and Brazil, as Roberto Campos, the designer of the Brazilian program, reminded Argentines in an interview in 1971. Not only were the economic problems faced by the two countries in the mid 1960s and the resources available for dealing with them dissimilar, but they also had quite different political structures. This was especially true in the area of working-class politics. As Campos noted, Argentine authorities had faced a well-organized and well-financed labor movement since 1946, while their Brazilian colleagues confronted a less well-mobilized working class that had traditionally been subject to greater public control by the paternalistic Brazilian state. This made it much easier for the Brazilian military to subdue and dominate its country's workers after 1964 than it had been for the Argentine military to gain control over theirs throughout the 1950s and 1960s.[30]

Argentina's brief experiment with autocratic military rule ended on June 8, 1970, nearly four years after it had begun, when military colleagues deposed Onganía and began a hazardous three-year journey that would return the country to constitutional rule. The Cordobazo had weakened Onganía's authority by undermining his claim to have stabilized the country using autocratic methods but it was a lingering dispute with fellow officers over matters of political strategy that finally brought him down. Led by Army Chief of Staff Alejandro Lanusse, service chiefs demanded that Onganía share presidential power with them and embark on a course leading gradually to the restoration of democratic government. But when Onganía refused and dismissed Lanusse on June 8, 1970, the military commanders, after a brief show of strength, forced the president to resign.[31] In deposing Onganía, the military leaders were also rejecting military authoritarianism in favor of a more traditional political solution to popular discontent. Moreover, where Onganía had subordinated his political strategy to the dictates of his economic policy, his immediate successors would do the opposite, using economic policy to mobilize support for a peaceful return to civilian rule through elections.

The Transition to Constitutional Rule

The transition from the military authoritarianism of Onganía to constitutional rule by the Peronists three years later was neither smooth nor well-mapped in advance. When the military commanders replaced Onganía with a little-known intelligence officer who had been stationed in Washington, D. C., since 1968, they again had no plan to guide immediate political reconstruction. The best that General Roberto Levingston could do was promise elections within four or five years, after the government had prepared the way economically for the kind of electoral outcome desired by the military. Foremost among the military's goals was the compensation of Argentine workers for past economic losses in order to still their protests and avert their turning once again to the Peronist party for rescue. Only if the condition of the Argentine consumer were rapidly improved, it was believed, was there any hope of a victory by a moderate coalition of Radicals and minor parties in future elections.

Levingston began cautiously by appointing Carlos Moyano Llerena, a widely respected economist who had been close to Kreiger Vasena, as minister of economy and directing him to loosen economic policy gradually, beginning with an across-the-board wage increase of 7 percent on August 15, 1969. The CGT was not satisfied with this meager effort and proposed instead its own program calling for the nationalization of banks, much higher wages, restrictions on foreign investment, and immediate elections, and took to the streets with general strikes on October 9 and 22 to make its point. Conflict within the administration over the rate of economic expansion soon followed with Moyano arguing that the new president should not sacrifice the stability gained under Onganía in order to pursue illusive political objectives, and others, like Minister of Public Works Aldo Ferrer, advocating a more nationalistic and expansionary course that, he claimed, was not only expedient politically, but also wise economically. The battle was cut short when Levingston sided with the latter, forcing Moyano to relinquish his ministry to Ferrer on October 14.

On October 27, Ferrer announced his own recovery program. He promised first to accelerate the rate of economic growth to a steady 8 percent. He, like Illia and the UCRP before him, considered economic expansion critical to the reduction of social unrest and the creation of full employment. Second, in order to combat the growing presence and power of foreign capital, he proposed to stimulate domestic industry and its exports through the use of the government's Development and Foreign Trade Banks. And third, he announced his intention to let up temporarily in the fight against inflation so as not to deter accelerated economic growth. That is, he was prepared to tolerate some wage and price compensation for past losses but hoped to protect against the sudden return of galloping inflation through the use of scheduled "minidevaluations" and adjustments in interest rates, capital valuations, and wages, much as the Brazilians had done since 1964.[32] In sum, Levingston and Ferrer decided to gamble that by igniting the economy through the compensation of Onganía's victims, they could restore national confidence and foster the kind of public optimism that would permit the maintenance of a high rate of growth while holding inflation to 10 or 15 percent.

It was, unfortunately, a strategy that was doomed at the outset, not only by the inherent difficulty of keeping inflation below 15 percent while stimulating 8-percent growth rates, but also because neither Ferrer nor Levingston possessed the political authority needed to enforce the program in the face of concerted opposition. Repeatedly, the president, unsure of his course or the degree of his support within the military, backed away from the tough enforcement of measures taken by his minister of economy. Ferrer, for example, had asked unions to comply voluntarily with a 19-percent limit on wage increases, but the president stood by idly as agreements of 30 and 40 percent were secured.

Inflation reared its head again in 1970 and 1971. The annual rate, which had averaged only 6.6 percent during Krieger Vasena's ministry, rose to 29.6 during Ferrer's. In fairness to Ferrer, it should be noted that the new surge in prices was not entirely of his making. Much of it was due to a single cause: the beef cycle and Onganía's failure to compensate for its effects. The domestic price of beef increased rapidly after 1969, rising by 80 percent in 1970 alone. By depressing the relative price of beef to compensate the beef-eating Argentine consumer for his stagnant wages, Onganía had encouraged cattlemen to sell off stock, as low prices have repeatedly tended to do, and thereby reduced cattle stocks by approximately 1 million head in 1969. The supply reduction that followed, coupled with a sharp rise in foreign demand, contributed to a rapid increase in beef prices in 1970. Because beef is so central to the Argentine diet—one estimate puts it at 15 percent of family expenditures—consumers were immediately hurt by the price increase and after Onganía's departure demanded substantial wage compensation. When Ferrer tried to prevent a new wage-price spiral by limiting beef prices and wage increases, he was opposed by both cattlemen and organized labor and was forced to back down.[33]

By early 1971, a sizeable faction of the military, encouraged by the country's leading industrial, commercial, and financial interests, decided that Levingston's efforts were too quickly leading to the kind of economic chaos that had provoked Onganía's intervention in 1966. Using Levingston's failure to forestall renewed rioting in Córdoba in early March as their excuse, the chiefs of staff deposed him and placed General Alejandro Lanusse, the architect of Onganía's removal eight months before, in the presidency.[34] Lanusse's assignment was not easy, for on the one side he faced those who wanted Ferrer's compensatory measures extended, while on the other there were investors, bankers, and large industrialists who had prospered under Onganía and now threatened to block any extension of Ferrer's program.[35] To complicate matters, each of these views, as well as a synthesis of the two that was favored by Lanusse, enjoyed support among competing factions within the military.

Throughout the remainder of 1971 and all of 1972, Lanusse

steered economic policy along a moderate nationalistic course, which did little to halt the deterioration that had begun in 1970. Mixing toleration of rising wages with selective price controls and very liberal use of Central Bank credits to finance a growing budget deficit, Lanusse saw the annual rate of inflation rise to 59 percent during his first fifteen months.[36] Finally, in December 1972, he announced a 25-point plan to combat rising prices. The plan included a 25-percent limit on wage increases and a 20-percent one on prices, a 30-percent increase in employee family allowances, and a 2-billion-new-peso limit on Central Bank issues.[37] Nevertheless, wage increases in 1972 averaged 35 percent, prices rose by 60 percent, and, by the end of the year, the government still faced $100 million in unpaid bills and $50 million in unpaid salaries (as well as a foreign debt that had passed the $3.5 billion mark).[38]

Lanusse inaugurated one of Argentina's most difficult experiments in political engineering when he announced the new Organic Law of Political Parties on June 30, 1971. For the first time since June 1966, the organization of political parties was permitted. His primary objective was to find a way out of the political stalemate created by the division of the country into the supporters of Onganía's internationalist strategy of development and their populist and nationalist opponents. His dilemma resembled that of Aramburu fifteen years before when he sought to secure the election of a moderate non-Peronist government. But Lanusse rejected Aramburu's anti-Peronist solution in favor of a conciliatory approach similar to that tried briefly by General Eduardo Lonardi after he overthrew Perón in September 1955. Of course, Lanusse knew that Lonardi had failed because of the intense animosities that had resulted from Perón's ouster, and that some of this hostility had persisted into the 1970s, making a repetition of the earlier failure likely. But on the other hand, he believed that if he followed Aramburu's exclusionary route, the victory gained through closed elections would be later lost because of the opposition of the Peronists to the new government, as happened after the 1958 and 1963 elections. If he thought his chances of success with open elections and conciliation were greater in 1973, it was primarily because he was advised that he could design a new electoral system, which, if properly exploited, would increase the probability of the victory of moderate parties over the Peronists.

The government's preelectoral campaign was waged on several fronts during 1971 and 1972. The first order of business was the maintenance of social peace and the mobilization of support for the 1973 elections. To this end, Lanusse held fast to his moderately expansionist economic policy, despite persistent labor charges that he was doing too little and conservative complaints that he was sacrificing economic stability to the political wolves. Labor cooperation was essential to the electoral scheme. Lanusse hoped that by working closely with CGT leaders in setting favorable wage policies, while repressing militant unions like those in Córdoba, the Peronists could be led to the ballot box. At the same time, he continued to reassure the more conservative industrial, rural, and financial interests that their privileges would be guaranteed through the victory of moderates in 1973. In addition, Lanusse tried to follow precedent established by Aramburu in 1956, of increasing private-sector cooperation with his government by resurrecting the device of a social-economic council through which 20 labor representatives, 20 from commerce, industry, and agriculture, and 20 from the public sector could advise the government on economic policy matters. Unfortunately, disputes among competing interest groups over representation delayed the council's inauguration until it was too late to be of much use.[39] Finally, the president sought to seal his campaign by appealing directly to the public through a massive publicity campaign that called for all Argentines to join together in a *gran acuerdo nacional* ("grand national agreement") in support of an electoral solution.

Of course, the entire campaign would come to naught if moderate political parties failed to coalesce and attract some working-class voters in the 1973 elections. It was the job of the designers of the new electoral law to make sure that it would not fail. The result of a brief but intensive effort by a group of distinguished Argentine lawyers, the new electoral law announced in May 1971 was shaped by its authors' fear of the multiplication of parties and the election of a minority government through the use of a system of proportional representation, as had happened in the 1963 election. Their goal, they announced, was to guarantee efficient and stable government by assuring rule by a majority party. Accordingly, they proposed the direct election of the president and vice-president through the two ballot—"ballot-age"—method, the election of senators by province (with two seats going to the party receiving a plurality and one to the second-place party), and the election of deputies through a modified proportional representation system, in which the winner would receive 60 percent of the seats apportioned by population within a district, the second party 30 percent, and the third 10 percent.[40] This unusual system was justified by Lanusse as the best possible compromise between two competing values: majority rule, which would be secured through presidential and, he hoped, senatorial elections, and minority representation, which would be encouraged in both the Senate and the Chamber of Deputies. More concretely, if it worked according to plan, it would lead to the election of a non-Peronist majority and a loyal Peronist minority.

This optimistic election scenario rested on two hopes, neither of which, it turned out, was well founded. First, the moderate parties, led by the Radicals, dissident Peronists, or Lanusse himself, were expected to coalesce into a single bloc prior to the election and, if they did not win the presidency on the first ballot, would do so on the second, after picking up minority-party support. No massive moderate bloc emerged, however. An attempt had been made in late 1971 when a group of Peronists and Radicals formed an alliance called La Hora del Pueblo, but after unsatisfactory discussions with Perón during his brief visit to Argentina in late 1972, the People's Radicals (now calling themselves by the party's original name, Unión Cívica Radical) decided to nominate Ricardo Balbin, the party's elder statesman who had run against Perón 20 years before. Soon thereafter Arturo Fondizi was nominated by his own party, as were the leaders of all minority parties, except those who joined with the CGT to form the Frente Justicialista (FREJULI), a coalition of Peronists. Second, Lanusse assumed that the Peronists, even with Perón urging them to vote for his stand-in, Hector Cámpora, would poll only 30 to 40 percent of the popular vote, as they had done in elections since 1955. What he apparently failed to take into account were the hazards of predicting the results of the 1973 election on the basis of a vote taken at least eight years before. Approximately one-third of those who voted in 1973 had entered the electorate since 1965 and, as several informal surveys had shown, a majority of these new voters favored the

Peronists. Moreover, this was the first presidential election since 1951 that the Peronist party had contested. Because a party victory would pave the way for Perón's eventual return to the presidency, a high Peronist turnout was likely.[41]

But even if Lanusse had admitted the tenuousness of these hopes, there was little that he could have done to avoid carrying through with the course he had selected in 1971. The cancellation of the elections would only have perpetuated a form of military rule which he believed destructive to military institutions. And an annulment after a Peronist victory would merely return politics to the status quo ante of 1962 or 1966. As a result, he was compelled by his own logic to stand by idly while Hector Cámpora, filling in for Perón, received 49 percent of the popular vote and a concession from the second-place Radicals on March 11, 1973. Having exhausted all other options for the moment, Lanusse stepped aside in the hope, shared by many of his countrymen, that an older and possibly wiser Juan Perón could accomplish for Argentina what the military and Radicals had repeatedly failed to do.

Military Autocracy: Lessons and Legacies

Now that we have examined the performance of two different kinds of military authoritarian regime in some detail, we can compare them to establish their strengths and weaknesses as systems for managing development policy in an industrializing, conflict-ridden society. Since they claimed a capacity to solve problems that liberal democracies were believed incapable of solving, we are especially concerned with their ability to live up to such claims. As we noted in Chapter 1, the advantages of the authoritarian mode of policy making are said to rest in its ability to maintain public order, sustain a rational attack on development problems, and swiftly implement bold institutional reform. All of these attributes no doubt appealed to the organizers of Argentina's military regimes and accounts in large part for their enthusiastic support for democracy's replacement by authoritarian forms of rule. In particular, they were impressed by how far autocratic methods might take them toward the demobilization of the Peronist-led popular classes and the execution of harsh economic measures aimed at increasing capital accumulation. There was really nothing mysterious about these preferences; military rule simply appeared to be the most familar, accessible, and effective means for achieving a host of political and economic objectives.

We can begin with the military president's approach to policy formulation. First of all, the military regime does not appear to have enjoyed any particular advantages over other forms of government when formulating policy. As with civilian regimes, the adequacy of its economic policies depends largely on the quality of the advice received from civilian technocrats. Military officers, as one would expect, possess no more wisdom about economic policy than do elected officials. What matters is not their own policy choices but those of the economists they rely upon. Even more than civilian politicians, they must turn to men who are known primarily for their technical expertise when selecting their economic policies. Aramburu, as we saw, drew heavily on the advice of a group from the Economic Commission for Latin America, while Onganía was assisted by a distinguished group of Argentine economists. In both cases they sought the help of experts whom they believed were capable of giving them economic advice undiluted by conventional political considerations.

One of the claims of military authoritarianism is that it can make hard economic judgments unhindered by political constraints. Military presidents claim to be free of the kind of constituency pressures and electorally motivated bargaining that frequently appear to undermine the decisions of democratically elected policy makers. There is undoubtedly some truth to this claim; authoritarian leaders can and often do ignore the claims of political parties and economic interest groups when they design their programs. But they are, nevertheless, not entirely free of constituency considerations. Even though they may not have to negotiate with all interest groups over their choice of policy instruments, they still have to contend with the ideological and policy preferences of the military officers who put them in office and sustain their rule. The latter have their own views of politics and economic development. They may not interfere with day-to-day policy decisions, but they will set boundaries within which policy makers must operate. Both Aramburu and Onganía, for example, rejected socialism and Peronist social welfarism at the outset. It was due neither to accident nor their economic objectivity that they chose policies drawn from the mainstream of contemporary capitalist theories of finance and trade. Their advisors were selected in part because of their well-known belief in such theories and their promise to keep their prescriptions within the boundaries set by their military employers.

There is also the question of how free the military president is of pressures exerted by nonmilitary constituencies when he formulates policy. Of particular interest are the capital-supplying international agencies, multinational firms, and local entrepreneurial elites who play a critical role in the execution of policy. Aramburu and Onganía—much like the officials who led coups in Brazil in 1964 and Chile in 1973—were anxious to improve their country's credit rating in order to attract foreign loans and investments that would help complete the transition to industrial maturity. To succeed they had to shape their policies according to needs and expectations of their foreign benefactors. The same was true of government relations with some domestic constituencies. Although he may not have openly consorted with his country's entrepreneurs and bankers, the military president knew their policy preferences and what it would take to stimulate their activities. Here again, anticipated constituency responses, if not actual policy bargaining, shaped the formulation of economic policy. In sum, it is apparent that military presidents, though well-insulated from popular pressures, can seldom ignore the policy demands of constituents who play a major part in the achievement of official policy objectives.

The miltary regime is, of course, not noted primarily for its strengths as a policy formulator, but for its reputation as a tough executor of unpopular economic policies, and it is on its performance in this area that it should also be judged. Its appeal rests primarily on its ability to impose the will of the state on society over the protests of most social groups. It is not only the military that appreciates this attribute but also the many civilians who desire to see an opponent eliminated or a policy executed over the objections of powerful adversaries. In fact, at one time or another, nearly every Argentine political party and interest group has supported a coup against its opponents. Two types of military regime resulted from such coups; one tried to purge the political process of undesirable political groups, and the other sought to reconstruct economic, social, and political institutions. Initially, each claimed impressive successes, but in the end neither achieved its goals. The reasons for their failures are many, but none is more important than the inherent weakness of military authoritarianism as a means of managing complex political processes.

The strength of military rule is found in its ability to destroy institutions and deter particular kinds of behavior. But the same resources and instruments that strengthen it as a destroyer of political institutions tend to weaken its ability to create new ones. The transitional military regime, for example, seeks to restore the democratic process after purging it of groups it considers undesirable. But in punishing or depriving certain groups, it will often alienate large numbers of citizens whose support it needs to make democracy work. When Aramburu attacked the Peronist movement and imposed regressive incomes policies on the working class, he succeeded in reinforcing its antipathy toward all non-Peronist political parties and interest groups. Even his efforts to reorganize the labor movement under non-Peronist leadership failed because of the opposition of the rank and file to his purges. What he demonstrated was the military regime's greater capacity for destruction than for reconstruction, especially when it is dealing with a well-entrenched popular movement that has little to gain and much to lose from cooperating with the military regime. The legacy that Aramburu left to the democratic presidents who succeeded him was not a revitalized democratic process but one greatly weakened by the constraints he had imposed upon it.

The military's incapacity for political reconstruction in Argentina is even more apparent in the performance of the Onganía regime. The government created in June 1966 was supposed to represent the triumph of the technocrat over the politician, of coercion over compromise, and of global solutions to economic problems over piece-meal ones. It also marked the rejection of liberal democracy and its concept of the political leader's obligation to meet the demands of citizens in favor of a view of politics that directs leaders to concern themselves with the needs rather than the wants of their subjects. The military officers who deposed Illia were convinced that politics, as it had been practiced in Argentina before 1966, had retarded the country's economic development. It was therefore imperative that a new political system be created in which qualified officials could promote the country's economic development, unhindered by legislatures and other democratic institutions.

Onganía demonstrated how easy it was to bring order to a divided society and execute harsh economic measures over the objections of the popular classes. Yet his achievements were superficial and transitory. Economic policy success, in the form of accelerated growth and reduced inflation, contributed much less than had been hoped to the creation of a durable new political system. In fact, the methods used to secure these economic triumphs undoubtedly increased popular resistance to the military government. It was Onganía's misfortune that he mistook temporary acquiescence to his policies for public acceptance of military rule as the only viable alternative to discredited liberal democracy.

The survival of any political regime depends in part on the ability of its creators to institutionalize some form of public involvement in the political process, be it psychological, expressive, or electoral. The principal weakness of military authoritarian government throughout Latin America has been its inability to achieve this objective. Electoral gimmicks and corporatist rhetoric are no substitute for the creation of essential processes to manage political participation, channel policy demands to the appropriate authorities, and coordinate the implementation of public policies. But military autocracies have little experience to guide them in this endeavor; to make matters worse, their strengths as destroyers of political institutions may only hinder their efforts to build new ones. By deliberately cutting themselves off from the popular classes, they reduce the possibility of reorganizing their participation in the political process. And by isolating themselves from interest groups in order to make policy unhindered by private demands, they only increase distrust of the policy-making process and encourage resistance to their decisions.

Where there already exist entrenched political structures and practices to fall back on, as in Brazil, the military may be able to survive for a period by drawing upon old ways to organize its authority and coordinate the activities of diverse social groups. And, as in Brazil, its efforts will be facilitated if improving economic conditions allow it to satisfy the demands of entrepreneurial elites. But sooner or later the military will have to cope with demands for other forms of direct or indirect popular participation, and it is here that it appears to be least equipped to respond. The Argentine, Brazilian, Peruvian, Chilean, Bolivian, and Uruguayan military regimes have not devised a long-term solution to the problem of political participation. Their failure is due in large part to the fact that they have no coherent philosophy of politics to guide them. They have few ideas about how to reorganize channels of political communication or how to manage citizen involvement in public affairs. Instead, they rule defensively, assisted by bureaucrats who can deliver only temporary solutions to a few obvious economic development problems.

PART FOUR

The Reconciliation Regime

8

The Peronists Restored

Only Perón's most ardent supporters would have predicted a few years before that he would return to the presidency in 1973. Of course, it would not have happened at all had civilian and military governments achieved their objectives during the previous two decades. But given their many shortcomings, the country's military leaders reluctantly accepted the inauguration of a Peronist government after stand-in candidate Hector Cámpora won an election carried out under electoral rules that the military had hastily written in 1972.

Three conditions contributed to the unexpected return of the Peronists in 1973. One was the apparent failure of the military to reconstruct the nation's political system. Neither the military's attempts to force the Peronist rank and file to join non-Peronist political parties, nor its later campaign to replace liberal democratic institutions with autocratic ones, significantly altered the nation's politics or reduced the social conflicts that traditionally had plagued the country. Although there were some Argentine officers in the early 1970s who believed that authoritarian rule could yet succeed if given a more thorough application, there were many others whose experience with repeated failures to eradicate Peronism had led them to accept one more try by the Peronists.

Second, the country's largest non-Peronist political party—the Radical party—appeared to have little to offer the country in

1973 that it had not tried several times before. Despite the fact that the Radicals' fall from office in 1962 and 1966 was not entirely of their own making, there was little reason to believe that they would not fall victim to the same conflicts if they tried to rule again. Radical party platforms had changed little from those offered the Argentine electorate in the past and the party's capacity to govern in the face of Peronist opposition seemed no greater than what it had been before. Consequently, the possibility of a Radical victory in 1973 elections brought little hope for marked improvement in the country's strife-torn political life.

Finally, there was the stubborn survival of the Peronist movement. Through a combination of skillful leadership by the exiled Perón, who kept alive hopes for the movement's return to power, as well as the ability of local Peronist leaders to attract to their cause a very diverse assortment of moderates and revolutionaries, who had grown weary of military and Radical party governments, Peronism survived as a political force with the capacity to win national elections. To be sure, it was not entirely the same movement that had governed the country before 1955, for new union bosses had risen in the interim, two decades of factional struggles within Peronism had made unity more tenuous than ever before, and the Peronist ideology was even less coherent than in the past. Nevertheless, it remained a formidable force, which, as long as Perón was available to lead it, could defeat its opponents at the polls.

As election day approached and opinion surveys were tabulated, a Peronist victory appeared to be a certainty to all but a few recalcitrant military officers who still held faint hopes of a Radical party triumph. What was less certain was the Peronists' ability to govern the country after the election. They had been out of office for almost two decades and their capacity for dealing with the complex economic and social problems of the 1970s was unknown. Their campaign had been hastily contrived and their platform was designed more to appeal to a diverse aggregation of aggrieved citizens than to guide a new government. Moreover, it was not Juan Perón, the brash young general, who would lead them, but Juan Perón, the elder statesman, in his seventies and in ill health.

Before the new government could begin, the Peronists had to resolve several critical issues. On the political front they had to

decide whether they were willing to live by the liberal democratic rules of the game set down by the military or were still
determined to reorganize the nation's politics along corporatist or
other lines. Whatever they decided, they would have to take
into account the increased complexity of Argentine society and
the high level of activism of its economic interest groups (as well
as the latter's well-known ability to resist subjugation by the
state). On the economic front they had to offer something new if
they hoped to solve the problems that had plagued the country
throughout the postwar period. The expansionary measures they
had tried in the mid 1940s would no longer do. The simple
transfer of income from farmers and cattlemen to industrialists
and urban laborers would accomplish little in a country where
the rural economy still produced far below its capacity, foreign
exchange shortages were common, and inflation ever present. To
appreciate the difficulty of the economic problems they faced
and the irrelevancy of old solutions, a brief review of the state of
the Argentine economy in 1973 is helpful.

Unsolved Policy Puzzles

We can begin with the rural economy. The apathetic and erra-
tic behavior of Argentine agriculture had been a bitter pill for
the country's presidents to swallow. Simply put, farmers and cattlemen failed Argentine presidents by not increasing their production at the rate required to satisfy both the demand of
domestic consumers and the foreign exchange needs of burgeoning national industries. Between 1945 and 1972, for example, the
value of the country's rural production increased by only 48 percent at constant prices, that of industry grew by 250 percent,
and combined nonagricultural activities by 223 percent.[1] This
disappointing performance would not have been so disturbing
were it not for the fact that, even into the early 1970s, the
Argentine economy still depended on rural products for approximately 85 percent of its export earnings.[2]

No special insight was required for Argentine leaders to recognize that since most of the country's arable land had been settled by the early 1940s, the expansion of rural production would
have to be achieved primarily through the more efficient use of

existing acreage rather than the opening of new lands. Yet, no matter where they looked in 1973, it seemed that Argentine farmers and cattlemen had done little during the preceding three decades to make better use of their existing resources. While North Americans were increasing their grain yields by 140 percent and Australians by 89 percent, for example, Argentines had increased theirs by only 25 percent.[3] Moreover, mechanization, thought by many to be the key to higher production, had only a marginal impact. Despite the fact that Argentine farmers must pay 90 percent more wheat or 300 percent more beef than their North American counterparts for a tractor, they have increased their use impressively. In 1947, there was one tractor per 873 hectares; in 1965, there was one per 187. But tractors have not had significant effects on productivity.[4] According to one survey Argentine tenant farmers have actually overinvested in equipment as a result of their desire to expand contract work as a hedge against the loss of leased land.[5]

In his use of fertilizers, the Argentine farmer's record is even less impressive. By the late 1960s only 2 percent of the country's wheat, corn, or pasture land was being fertilized; large farmers, it seems, prefer to rest land planted to grains for three to five years rather than fertilize it, while the tenant prefers to move on to a new plot after exhausting his land. In this way both avoided paying the high price demanded for imported phosphorus and potassium, a price that amounted to the equivalent of nearly 50 percent more grain per unit of fertilizer than in North America or Australia. But if high costs deterred more liberal use of fertilizers, it was the abundance of land that led to another problem, the cattleman's refusal to expand his land's holding capacity by seeding his pastures. Because he has available pasture land all year, the Argentine cattleman has tended to prefer natural over seeded pastures or the use of grain supplements. It has been estimated that if natural pastures were seeded, their carrying capacity could be doubled and cattle production increased proportionately. Nevertheless, many cattlemen have refused to depart from the easy ways of the past.[6]

One of the most persistent problems faced by economic authorities was the beef cycle, with its wildly fluctuating prices and production levels.[7] Between 1950 and 1970, cyclical fluctuations were particularly well pronounced, lasting from five to seven years, with successive price troughs in 1950, 1957, 1962, and 1969; all but the 1957 low were intensified by droughts, which forced high levels of stock liquidation.[8] Quite obviously, the persistence of the cycle cannot be blamed on any one president or economic strategy since none of the postwar governments succeeded in smoothing out the beef price and production curves, even marginally. Although they did occasionally try to cushion the cycle's blow on exports by restricting domestic consumption or on consumers by imposing maximum prices, Argentine presidents generally resigned themselves to living with the problem and did not undertake any coordinated measures to solve it. Apparently they hoped that they could somehow succeed with their economic programs by compensating for adverse effects.[9] But because of their inaction the Peronists would find themselves in the mid 1970s still plagued by insufficient and gyrating production, protesting consumers and packers, and distrustful and uncooperative producers.[10]

Much has been written by farmers associations as well as agricultural economists about the importance of price as a stimulant to greater investment and production. One is therefore surprised to discover that although the expected relationship between price and beef production is clearly established in Argentina, that between price and grain production still remains clouded. Support prices tell us little for, with few exceptions, they have remained below market prices. World price fluctuations undoubtedly had some influence on the selection of particular grains for planting as well as shifts from livestock to grains or vice-versa, but the expected relationship of higher prices leading to greater grain production does not hold, even when other factors like weather, taxes, exchange rates, and general economic uncertainty are taken into account.[11] It is no wonder then that Argentine presidents have been frustrated in their efforts to use price incentives.

There is also the question of land tenure and its impact on production. Although Argentine farmland was more equitably distributed during the 1960s than it had been at the turn of the century because of the acquisition of land by many of those who were once tenant farmers, there remained a wide disparity between the larger and the smaller units. In 1965 approximately 75 percent of the country's productive land was controlled by only

5.6 percent of its farms.[12] Such findings have led some observers, like the Inter-American Committee for Agricultural Development (CIDA), to conclude that "Argentina's land tenure
structure, according to the evidence so far considered, is responsible to a large extent for the stagnation in farm production."[13]
CIDA's argument was drawn from its discovery that net farm
income per hectare declines as farm size increases, and its belief
that if average yields of the larger units could be increased to
the levels realized by the smaller family farm, total rural output
in Argentina could be increased by as much as 50 percent.[14]

Although the CIDA argument was not unfamiliar to Argentine
leaders, none has acted upon it by implementing a scheme of
wholesale land redistribution. To some observers, this failing is
additional evidence of the subservience of reformer and conservative alike to the dictates of a rural oligarchy. Such assertions,
however, both oversimplify the role of the so-called oligarchy
and underanalyze the means of rural influence over tenure policy. Were the Argentine rural sector composed only of a host of
subsistance farmers and a small but wealthy elite, whose principal concern was social status rather than economic production,
the country's more urban-oriented presidents might have attacked the land-tenure problem long ago. That they did not may
be explained by the fact that the 26,000 farms that control almost three-fourths of the country's productive land, although
grossly inefficient, do nevertheless contribute over half of the
country's beef and mutton exports as well as a substantial proportion of its grains. It is primarily because expropriation, or the
threat of it, might lead to a short-term decline in the production
of such units that economic authorities who have relied on commodity exports to finance their development programs have refused to tamper with existing land-tenure patterns. Instead, they
have sought unsuccessfully to raise productivity with conventional tax, credit, and price incentives.

Finally, whatever the failures of Argentine presidents in matters of land-tenure reform, one thing stands out above all others
in their dealings with the rural sector: repeatedly they failed to
overcome the reluctance of the Argentine farmer to respond to
short-term economic incentives without some assurance that his
gains would not be nullified by rising costs, falling prices, or a
sudden shift in agricultural policy. Having perceived himself as

the frequent victim of antirural policies after 1943, he persistently refused to toss caution to the winds each time a new government promised a return of good times. Instead, he became one of the first to question the government's resolve to carry out its promises. Moreover, as the farmers' disappointments increased throughout the 1960s, so did their propensity to set aside traditional intrasectoral rivalries in favor of unified protests against government policy.[15]

In addition to its disappointments with exchange retentions, the high costs of government, and domestic inflation, the rural elite's frustration was also a result of its failure to regain control over agricultural policy making. Yet, it is doubtful that it could have been otherwise, for although the economy depended heavily on its exports, the rural sector produced only 13 percent of the gross national product in 1969, and could not expect any government, no matter how conservative, to place rural interests above the needs of those who produced the other 87 percent. By the early 1970s, the vast majority of Argentines were urban dwellers more concerned with the domestic price of beef and bread than the level of farm profits. For them the Argentine farmer and cattleman were not the solid yeomen of the pampa who had worked hard and long to supply their countrymen with food and foreign currencies, but the much mythologized estanciero, who had been fortunate enough to secure a piece of land and enrich himself on its bounty. If anyone were to sacrifice for the country's development, the urban argument ran, it was not the factory worker or the industrial entrepreneur but that estanciero, who, among all of his countrymen, could best afford it.

Against the background of a dismal rural performance, the expansion of the industrial product by 250 percent between 1945 and 1972 was indeed a bright spot. Despite the fact that they did not significantly reduce the country's dependence on commodity exports, Perón, Frondizi, Illia, and Onganía did contribute to an impressive increase in manufacturing. But industrialization also had its costs, as the nationalistic critics of Frondizi and Onganía hastened to point out in the early 1970s. In particular they warned of the adverse consequences of growing dependence on foreign capital and an increased concentration of industry during the 1960s.[16] Multinational automotive, chemical, and petroleum firms, rather than private domestic investors, had been primarily responsible for the country's impressive industrial performance. North American industrial investments alone grew from 230 million dollars in 1955 to 789 million in 1969. By 1970 the estimated stocks of private direct foreign investment in Argentina totaled approximately $2 billion, nearly half of which came from North American firms.[17] More significant than the absolute amount of foreign holdings was their impact on the concentration of economic power within Argentine society.

In order to establish the degree of concentration, one first has to take state enterprises into account, since ten of the top twenty firms ranked by sales volume in 1972 were state-owned operations in such areas as oil, steel, gas, communications, electricity, railroads, and airlines.[18] The economic role of the Argentine state has increased significantly since World War II; by 1972 state investment represented 40 percent of the national total (and 9 percent of the GNP) and state firms accounted for 50 percent of the country's imports and the same proportion of its foreign debt. But, if we examine only private firms, we discover that the one hundred largest firms increased their share of the industrial product from 20.8 percent at the time of Perón's fall in 1955, to 28.7 percent at the end of Onganía's first year in office eleven years later. Moreover, just as the vulnerable small businessmen of the CGE had been arguing throughout the decade, industrial concentration rose during the recession years that followed in the wake of stabilization measures and declined when the economy was on the upswing again. Of equal interest is the appearance of an increasing number of foreign firms within the ranks of the top one hundred: in 1957, for example, there were only fourteen foreign firms in this select group, but by 1966 their number had grown to fifty, with 33 percent of them involved in automotive and machinery production, 18 percent in petroleum products, 14 percent in food and beverages, and 12 percent in tobacco products.[19]

If we bring public enterprises back into the picture we discover another interesting fact: by 1972 state enterprises accounted for 49 percent of the sales of the country's thirty largest firms, foreign enterprises 41 percent, and private nationally owned firms only 10 percent.[20] Until 1973, in fact, the trend was toward the increasing acquisition of Argentine firms by foreign ones, especially in manufacturing, and the expansion of state economic activities, resulting in a bifurcation of large industry between state enterprises on the one hand and foreign ones on the other. The Industrial Union, consistent with its traditional receptivity toward foreign capital, a posture reinforced by the inclusion of six of the country's nine largest foreign firms within its membership, accepted the denationalization trend as a blessing rather than a threat, while at the same time vigorously attacking the expansion of state ownership. In contrast, the General Economic Confederation, whose membership was almost entirely composed of domestic firms, continued to champion the cause of restrictive legislation aimed at impairing the easy entrance of foreign capital into Argentine industry, especially through the take-over of existing firms.

The issue of foreign penetration and industrial concentration became a primary concern of the Peronists and their allies, especially after the Onganía experience. And just as with other issues of major importance, this one deeply divided Argentine economic strategists. To those who had fought since 1946 to increase national economic independence by creating a host of state enterprises to replace the foreign-owned transport and utility companies they had expropriated, this increased foreign penetration of the industrial sector represented a more subtle, though equally repugnant, form of foreign economic domination. For those who believed their economy desperately needed foreign capital and technology, foreign penetration was merely another reality that had to be accepted; barring a revolutionary restructuring of the Argentine economy, the country would not prosper without it.

Finally, the issue of income distribution and social equity remained unresolved and the subject of great controversy. From the golden days of Peronism in the late 1940s onward, the working-class movement had struggled in vain to increase and maintain its share of national income. According to one recent estimate, from a high point of 53.6 percent of the national income in 1954, salaried income declined to a low of 39.2 percent in 1959, then rose again to 50 percent in 1967, only to fall to 40 percent in 1972.[21] And the real income of industrial workers, which also rose and fell repeatedly throughout the period, was only 12 percent higher in 1972 than it had been in 1950.

One of the principal shortcomings of Argentine policy makers after 1945 had been their failure to institutionalize a process of continuous income redistribution, especially through the tax system. In fact, less than 1 percent of the national income had been redistributed annually through income taxes, according to a 1969 ECLA study. Nor had the much publicized transfer of income through other means done much better. Income subsidies, for example, transferred only 0.4 percent of total family purchasing power from the upper 80 percent of the income scale to the lower 20 percent, while social security shifted only 3 percent of family income in favor of the lower 90 percent. This sad fact was due primarily to large-scale evasion and underdeclaration of income as well as government timidity in the area of progressive tax reform; it is estimated, for example, that throughout the period, only about 25 percent of the taxable income of entrepreneurs and rentiers was declared for tax purposes.[22]

In the absence of any systematic process of progressive income redistribution, the debate over relative income shares centered almost entirely on effects of short-term wage, price, monetary, exchange, and fiscal policies. This, in part, accounts for the intense interest of labor leaders in almost every policy decision taken by economic authorities. More often than not, they found themselves not fighting for a larger share of the national income, but trying to block the loss of what they already had, as successive governments adopted incomes policies aimed at containing wages in an effort to combat inflation. Incomes policies held a special appeal to policy makers struggling with price instability. Through the use of wage and price measures, they could at least give the appearance of fighting inflation by taking on those who had selfishly caused it. The fact that such measures seldom did anything more than buy a few years of rake's progress for beleaguered officials without solving the larger inflationary problem seldom prevented their use. As long as incomes policy offered an illusory way out of the policy conflicts provoked by inflation, its appeal to officials overtaken by a short-term view of their policy problems remained strong.[23]

The difficulty of applying an incomes policy in Argentina was compounded by the fact that the country lacked many of the conditions believed essential to even short-term success. First, most advocates of incomes policies assume that labor unions are strong enough to hold down the growth of money incomes and, that, in deference to the public interest, they will actually do so when asked. The latter assumes that labor is not especially un-

happy with the existing distribution of income and, more important, that the introduction of an incomes policy would not
change either that income distribution or the state of emotions it
has been generating.[24]

Unfortunately, none of these conditions prevailed in Argentina. Though the CGT appeared to be a strong, centralized organization, not since the early 1950s had it been free of serious
internal divisions, some of which, in fact, were the product of
disputes over the wisdom of cooperating with an incomes policy
of some kind. Moreover, after 1955, labor leaders were clearly
dissatisfied with the existing distribution of income and found no
solace in the reassurances of government officials who promised
that their income share would be preserved or restored under
stabilization programs. To make matters worse, many labor leaders opposed the post-1955 governments not only because of their
wage policies but also because of their exclusion of the Peronist
party from government institutions. Under such conditions, governments could hardly be expected to implement their incomes
policies in the conventional manner.

Second, those who advocate incomes policies believe that social problems that do not yield to competitive pressures arising
from individual activity can be tackled through "quasi government" involving the close collaboration of government officials
and interest groups whose constituents are affected by incomes
policies.[25] But as we have seen repeatedly, Argentine presidents, at least until 1973, refused to rule through such quasi-
governmental arrangements involving multisector collaboration
in the implementation of any kind of temporary social contract.
Instead, they dealt with interest groups separately, securing the
cooperation of a few, ignoring most, and repressing others. But
here more than anywhere else, the Peronists considered themselves uniquely qualified to create the institutions needed to
succeed with incomes policies where others had failed. In fact, it
was their solution to this problem that became the leg on which
their economic program would stand or fall after 1973.

Economic Policy and the Social Contract

It was the economists of the General Economic Confederation,
and not the leaders of the Peronists' FREJULI party or those of

the CGT, who seized the initiative on economic policy matters and supplied President-elect Hector Cámpora with the outline of a program in 1973. The main lines of policy were set by the CGE's Institute of Economic Research in early 1971 and, after securing the approval of CGT leaders, the CGE proposal was made public in September 1972 and incorporated into the FREJULI platform before the March 1973 elections. That the CGE had moved so quickly and convincingly prior to the election is not surprising. Since its creation in 1952, it had enjoyed access to the Peronist leadership, and during the 1960s had developed the kind of technical expertise which the Peronists themselves were not prepared to mobilize immediately before the 1973 elections. In the short run, then, the Peronists needed the expertise of the CGE, and the CGE the political power of the Peronists if the CGE was finally to have an impact on economic policy. Yet, in accepting the CGE proposal, the CGT and Perón were also conceding a great deal, for it tied them to moderate short-term measures to combat inflation and postponed the adoption of the more radical, redistributive measures they had long promised their constituents.

In principle, the CGE program committed the government to a redistribution of income in favor of salaried workers, with a four-year objective of raising the share of national income claimed by wages and salaries from the 40 percent to which it had fallen in 1973 to the 50-percent level attained during the first Peronist administration. At the same time, this long-range objective was accompanied by a short-term commitment to price stabilization. Thus, where previous governments had sought price stabilization through income redistribution in favor of rural producers and investors, the Peronists hoped to stabilize prices while redistributing income in favor of working- and middle-class consumers. They recognized, of course, that in practice the two objectives could not be pursued simultaneously but would have to be approached sequentially, with a very brief stabilization program to be followed by a more progressive redistributive one. What they needed to succeed was not only some finely tuned fiscal, monetary, wage, and price measures but also the means for persuading their constituents to postpone their welfare demands until the attack on prices had achieved its objectives. The solution was found, they believed, in the innovative Social

Contract (Pacto Social), which the CGE designed and the Cámpora administration adopted on June 8, 1973.

Rejecting the strong-arm tactics of Aramburu and Onganía for obvious political reasons, as well as the unpredictability of collective bargaining, Cámpora chose instead a formal agreement among labor, industry, and government, which pledged each party to compliance with a price freeze and, after an initial 200-peso-per-month, across-the-board salary increase, with a two-year suspension of negotiated wage contracts. (See Table No. 8.1.) In essence he had chosen the opposite set of instruments to accomplish price objectives very similar to those pursued by Onganía six years before. Where Onganía used voluntary compliance to limit prices, froze wages by decree, devalued the currency, and expanded money and credit, the Social Contract drew on labor's voluntary compliance with a wage freeze, con-

TABLE 8.1
Peronist Economic Policy, 1973

Objectives	1. Price stability
	2. Progressive income redistribution
	3. National economic independence
Instruments	
Fiscal	1. Public sector austerity
	2. Redistribution of public expenditures in favor of social services
	3. Progressive income and land tax reform
	4. Consolidation of public enterprises
Money and Credit	1. Slow growth rate of monetary supply
	2. Channel credit to domestic enterprises
Exchange	1. Avoid devaluation
Controls	1. Reduce and control consumer good prices
	2. "Voluntary" two year wage freeze
	3. Selective import controls
Income Redistribution	1. Gradual improvement in real working class income
	2. Shift from foreign to domestic investors

trolled prices by decree, refused to devalue the peso but imposed controls on foreign exchange, and limited the supply of money and credit.[26]

To implement the Contract, Cámpora counted on the support of labor through the CGT and industry through the CGE. This left the critical rural sector for separate consideration. In light of their past treatment by the Peronists, the more conservative rural interests naturally anticipated the worst under the new government, an expectation that was reinforced when Cámpora decreed reductions in domestic food prices soon after taking office. But the conditions of 1973 were not those of 1946, and the Peronists, perhaps enlightened by their past rural policy debacles, this time acknowledged the necessity of increasing rural productivity and commodity exports in order to finance economic expansion. Accordingly, in late August 1973 they invited all rural groups to join with them in signing an *Acto de Compromiso del Campo*. The agreement, which was signed by all but anti-Peronist cattle breeders of CARBAP, promised rural producers an increase in minimum commodity prices, more credit, and new tax incentives in exchange for a commitment to double rural production by 1980.[27]

Even the Peronists recognized that their new Social Contract, no matter how bold or innovative, was not self-enforcing. From its inception, it was obvious that at least three conditions would have to be met if it were to succeed. First, not only would the CGT leadership have to remain firm in its support of the wage freeze, but it would also have to keep the rank and file in line by preventing wildcat strikes and blocking attempts by local unions to renegotiate contracts. Second, it was essential that the hardline Peronists tolerate the continued presence of the CGE economic team within the new administration, for it was Minister of Economy José Gelbard and his colleagues from the CGE who sustained the confidence of commerce and industry in the Contract. Should the Peronists evict the CGE, they would invite the renewed suspicion and distrust of those whom they needed to make the scheme work. And finally, something more than a conciliatory attitude toward rural producers was needed to overcome their hostility to price and commodity controls. Only with a sustained effort to maintain favorable prices could economic authorities hope to convince farmers and cattlemen that they were not again being exploited by an antirural government.

Skilled policy management, not wishful thinking or false promises, was needed to hold the Social Contract together, and it was through the use of some old and new political instruments that the Peronists believed they would succeed.

The Politics of the Social Contract

In the efforts of Alsogaray and Krieger Vasena we saw policy makers who acted as enforcers, determined to use public authority to compel compliance with their economic objectives when it was not forthcoming voluntarily. Through the Social Contract, in contrast, the Peronists sought to reach an agreement on policy objectives that would assure compliance in advance of the policy's execution. In short, bargaining and formal agreement were to replace command as the means of controlling economic behaviors in order to reduce the suspicion, hostility, and opposition that came when policy was imposed on citizens without their consent. Yet, to succeed where others had failed, the government had to deliver on its promise to involve private-sector representatives in the ratification and implementation of its program.

Ratification was achieved with little difficulty through the signing of the Contract by the CGT on labor's behalf and the CGE for most industrial and commercial groups and the signing of the *Acto* by the principal rural groups. The Peronists' control over the Chamber of Deputies and the Senate also facilitated formal ratification of the program. In addition to the wage and price agreement, the Contract included nineteen bills directed at the regulation of foreign investment, progressive tax reform, the nationalization of foreign banks, and related matters which required legislative passage. With their overwhelming majorities in both houses, and the probable support of the Radical minority for most of its nationalistic measures, the government anticipated the quick passage of its entire program.[28]

What is most surprising about the signing of the Social Contract and the *Acto* was the government's ability to secure its acceptance by conservative groups like the UIA and SRA as well as nationalistic ones such as the CGE and CGT. Its success in doing so, it appears, was due to its ability to take advantage of several subtle but important changes during the late 1960s in the attitudes of the country's interest-group leaders.

In the past, divisions within the rural and industrial sectors had persistently plagued economic authorities, because policies that satisfied one group often antagonized its rivals. Throughout the 1960s the economic policies that were supported by the Industrial Union were almost automatically condemned by the General Economic Confederation and vice-versa. Rural groups were not as intense in their rivalries, nor as far apart on critical development issues, yet they too contested each other as well as the industrialists and labor unions. But the conditions which had given rise to intrasectoral conflicts gradually changed in the late 1960s, as did the attitudes of the group leaders responsible for them. Many of these changes were minor and almost undetectable at the time, but they were sufficient to encourage a mellowing of rivalries that opened the way for the creation of new coalitions. We have seen, for example, how CGE leaders like José Gelbard had supported the negative interest rates caused by inflation, high tariffs, and restrictions on foreign investors in order to stimulate the growth of domestic industry. Even though he seldom succeeded in securing the adoption of all of his policy prescriptions, Gelbard could take some pride in the fact that many of the businessmen he represented prospered in the 1960s as their firms grew to be as large as some of those in the Industrial Union. With the enlargement of the firms directed by the CGE's leaders came a greater appreciation of the price and wage issues that had traditionally concerned the UIA. As their interests gradually converged, these two old rivals cautiously began to discuss their mutual policy concerns in 1970. When it became apparent to UIA leaders that a common front would be required if they were to have any hope of influencing policy under the Peronists, they initiated a series of negotiations that finally led to the UIA's incorporation into the CGE in early 1973.[29]

Similar changes occurred in the rural sector with equally impressive results. Despite the Agrarian Federation's slavish adherence to the cause of agrarian reform, its membership had been transformed over the past twenty years from tenant farmers to a majority of small- and medium-size landowners. And while conservative cattlemen could still be found within the Rural Society, some of its members had abandoned the traditional life of the estancia in favor of the modern ranch or farm. The transformation was gradual and incomplete, but it was accompanied by

greater recognition of the common interests of farmers and cattlemen in the improvement of policy incentives for more productive operations. Consequently, when all rural groups gathered at
Palermo in late 1970 to present the government with a common
set of demands, there was no debate over land tenure or rural
income distribution, but rather a single rural voice denouncing
the antirural bias of government ministers, exploitation by meat
packers and grain exporters, and the selfishness of urban consumers and public employees. Though few of those present at
Palermo were enthusiastic about the Peronist victory in March
1973, they were, with the exception of CARBAP, prepared to
lend their support to the *Acto*, in the hope that the new government would accede to the demands of a united rural sector.[30]

Perón was indeed fortunate that producer-group rivalries had
been temporarily submerged by the time he assumed the presidency from Cámpora after a special election in September 1973.
His predecessors had turned a deaf ear to such groups or had
picked and chosen among them; Perón had them delivered to
him by his allies in the CGE. If there were any weak spots in
his grand coalition, they did not come initially from the CGE-led
groups but rather from the CGT unions, which he assumed to
be the most loyal of his constituents. It should be recalled that
the CGT leadership had never managed to sustain its control
over all of its member unions but had been plagued by divisions
and rivalries throughout the 1960s. Moreover, dissident unions
had risen up against the Confederation's leaders during the Cordobazo and had taken the political initiative away from them.
CGT leaders never fully regained their control over the locals
and the rebellions that began in Córdoba continued after 1969.
Consequently, even though the heavily bureaucratized and often
isolated leadership of the CGT could deliver the support of a
majority of the unions to Perón on demand, they could not assure the president that all unions would remain loyal to the
terms of the Social Contract. This meant that the government
would be plagued at the outset by the threat of wildcat strikes,
which, if successful, might open the gates to a flood of new wage
agreements that could undermine its fight against inflation. How
the Peronists responded to such dissention in the ranks would
greatly influence the success of their entire program.

Through the mechanism of the Social Contract and the Na-

The Abrupt Collapse of Contrived Consensus

The implementation of the Social Contract can be divided into two distinct phases. The first began with the signing of the Contract and lasted for almost a year, ending just before Perón's death in July 1974. It was marked by steady economic growth, increasing price stability, and a vastly improved external position. The second phase, in contrast, witnessed accelerating political conflict and cabinet instability, the collapse of union discipline, the disillusionment of producers, and spiraling inflation, and ended on March 24, 1976, with a military coup that terminated the Peronist regime. Tragically, in only a few months the chaos of the second phase undermined the achievements of the first.

It was the Peronists' good fortune that they initiated their program in the middle of an economic boomlet that had begun in early 1973. It was an especially good year for commodity exports as high world meat prices and a bumper grain crop brought an 86-percent increase in export value and a rise in foreign-exchange holdings from $465 million in 1972 to $1.3 billion in 1973.[31] The new government also made some headway in its fight against inflation; prices, which had risen by 61 percent in 1972, were held to an increase of only 17 percent during the first twelve months under the Social Contract.[32] And to the delight of Argentine workers, real wages, which had fallen by 3.5 percent during the first half of 1973, actually rose by 13.3 percent during the second half as a result of the pay raises and family allowances granted by the government in June 1973.[33]

But if Argentina benefited from the rise in commodity prices in world markets, it also suffered from them, especially after the OPEC nations raised petroleum prices in 1973. Argentina's postwar governments had alternated between all-out foreign-financed efforts to become self-sufficient in the production of petroleum and nationalistic schemes to go it alone. By 1973 the country was still importing enough petroleum to be hurt by the rise in prices; thus, its petroleum import bill rose from $58 million in 1972 to $588 million in 1974, going from 3.1 percent of the country's total imports to 15.1 percent in only two years.[34] Economic authorities tried to stem the tide of imported inflation by applying import controls in late 1973, but in so doing they contributed to raw-product shortages, the slowing of economic

growth, and the disaffection of raw-product-consuming industrialists.

The rise in the prices of raw materials was not the only problem that threatened the Peronists' stabilization plan. Obstacles to
the implementation of the Social Contract emerged within the
country as well. As policy makers had feared, some of the non-
CGT unions quietly secured new wage agreements, in violation
of the Contract, in early 1974.[35] They were followed by a few
CGT unions, and then, when the minister of labor refused to
intervene, others joined the growing parade of violators. To
make matters worse, just before his death, Perón agreed to double year-end bonuses for all CGT unions, a decision that appeared to make a mockery of the government's fight against rising inflation. Nevertheless, after Perón's death in July, his wife
Isabel and Minister of Economy José Gelbard boasted that the
Contract was still in effect and that new wage agreements would
not be officially recognized until after the Contract expired in
June 1975. And so the first phase of Peronist economic policy
ended, having attacked such problems as rising prices and payments deficits only to discover that the former was now threatened by a breakdown in union discipline and the latter by the
country's continued dependence on the importation of fuels and
other raw materials.

It is not my purpose to review the details of the complicated
and bizarre internal power struggles that followed Perón's death
in July 1974. One irreverent Argentine observer has described
the last days of Perón as something resembling a kingdom from
the Middle Ages, where a wise old king—who had been a famous swordsman in his youth—was surrounded by a kind
queen, a court soccerer, wicked visiers, fauning courtiers, and a
multitude of buffoons. Like the monarchs of old, he was uncriti-
cally loved by his subjects, who cared little for many in his en-
tourage. But once he died, it was the sorcerers, viziers, and
courtiers who fought over his throne by manipulating and deceiving the kind queen.[36] There is more truth to this fanciful
commentary than one cares to admit, for it was in the midst of
Perón's ambitious and quarrelling associates that his wife struggled to carry on his program. Undoubtedly, one of Perón's
greatest failures had been his unwillingness to institutionalize a
line of succession within the Peronist movement. He refused, it

seems, because the choice of successors might have limited his ability to hold the movement together by continually shifting his favor among competing factions. When he selected his wife Isabel as his running mate in the September 1973 elections, he gave up his last chance to settle the issue, but by his actions he only postponed the inevitable power struggle until after his death.

Economy policy became the victim of the government's inattention to the basic requirements of maintaining the Social Contract in 1974 and 1975. To be sure, changes in vital economic conditions, some of which have already been noted, as well as increased opposition from the business and farm communities, exacerbated the difficulties of reaching a new agreement through the renewal of the Social Contract in 1975. But in the end it was the struggle for power within the Peronist movement that undermined the Contract. The year that began with the victory within the cabinet of a conservative Peronist faction, led by Minister of Social Welfare José López Rega, ended in political and economic chaos. López Rega was forced into hiding in exile and Isabel Perón struggled, unsuccessfully it turned out, to prevent the disintegration of the FREJULI coalition and her overthrow by military officers who had grown weary of her chaotic administration.[37]

After her husband's death, Isabel Perón was faced with a choice between two possible courses of action: she could continue the balancing act he had begun by maintaining the uneasy alliance between the CGT and CGE, or she could shift to a position favoring López Rega's conservative faction by breaking with the CGE and repressing CGT dissidents and antigovernment guerrillas. Of course, there was also a third option, namely moving swiftly to the left of the Peronist movement. But little consideration was given to such a move since it threatened the power of the moderate and conservative union officials and the bureaucrats who surrounded the new president.

In October 1974, the choice was made: the president dismissed Minister of Economy José Gelbard, the former CGE president, and thereby broke the alliance of government, industry, and labor that her husband had carefully held together. Although there was no sudden change in policy by Gelbard's replacement, Alfredo Gómez Morales (the economist who had

managed Perón's stabilization program in 1952), the ministerial
change set in motion López Rega's eventually successful campaign to fill the cabinet with his conservative Peronist allies.
Soon thereafter, he persuaded the president to deal harshly with
her working-class critics during the negotiation of a new and
tougher Social Contract in 1975. Thus, under López Rega the
purpose of the Contract was changed completely. It was not
consensus-through-bargaining that he sought, but economic and
political order through the use of force against Peronists and
non-Peronists alike.[38]

The expected confrontation between the government and
labor came during the renegotiation of wage contracts in May
and June 1975. Despite many violations of the two-year freeze,
most unions had refrained from the discussion of wages, working
conditions, or other matters since June 1973. In early 1975,
Isabel Perón gave a tentative go-ahead to all unions to initiate
new wage discussions in anticipation of the signing of new contracts in June. A similar procedure had been followed by the
Peronists between 1952 and 1954, when wages had been frozen
and then new contracts negotiated, without any adverse effects
on the fight against inflation. But in 1975 there were no
memories of a golden past to restrain appetites, nor a Juan
Perón to lend his personal authority to the bargaining process
and reinforce labor confidence in its outcome. Instead, union
leaders saw a deteriorating economy being managed by a man
whose palace intrigues and autocratic ways inspired little confidence in his or Isabel Perón's ability to deliver on their promise
of real wage gains in 1975 and 1976. As a result, when the moment of decision arrived, Argentines witnessed a battle between
economic authorities and union officials such as had never been
seen before under a Peronist administration.

During May and early June, unions bargained hard with management and many came away with a 100-percent increase in
wages. At first economic authorities did nothing. Then on June
2, López Rega replaced Gómez Morales with conservative
Peronist economist and personal ally Celestino Rodrigo, who immediately ordered tough austerity measures—beginning with a
160-percent currency devaluation, a move that pleased neoclassical ideologues more than it did moderate and leftist Peronists.
Then on June 29, Isabel Perón suddenly annulled all labor con-

tracts negotiated during the previous three months and decreed a 50-percent wage increase in place of the 100 percent or more already secured by most unions. Urged on by López Rega, she laid down the challenge to the labor movement and, as one might expect, they immediately responded.

Ignoring the president's pleas for discipline and loyalty to the movement's leadership, the metal, textile, and bank workers, later joined by others, closed or slowed down factories and businesses to protest the presidential decree. Negotiations between CGT leaders and economic authorities ensued, but when López Rega and his associates refused to back down, the CGT leaders abandoned the talks and placed themselves at the head of the protest by calling a 48-hour strike on July 7 and 8. By midday on the eighth, the battle was over, and the CGT victorious. The president revoked her decree and ratified the original wage contracts.[39] Four days later, López Rega was forced to resign by the military high command, and within less than a month, the once-feared conspirator had fled into exile, leaving a shattered Social Contract and a new political crisis in his wake. The power struggle had cost the president dearly. She lost not only López Rega but also her congressional majority when the FREJULI delegation divided in response to her actions; by the end of the year she could count only 115 loyalists among the 243 Chamber deputies.[40]

The economic deterioration that accompanied the collapse of the Social Contract was soon apparent. As we can see from Table No. 8.3, consumer prices rose by a record 183 percent in 1975 and wages nearly as much.[41] The wage increases gained at midyear undoubtedly contributed to the record inflation, though higher prices for public services and raw product imports also were responsible. Before the end of the year, Antonio Cafiero,

TABLE 8.3
Prices and Wages in 1974 and 1975
(Percent increase)

	1974	1975
Consumer Price Index	24.2	183.0
Industrial Wage Level	26.9	180.5

Source: Argentina, Instituto Nacional de Estadística y Censos. *Boletín estadístico trimestral* (julio-setiembre 1975; octubre 1975–marzo 1976; abril-junio 1976).

the fourth minister of economy in as many months, tried to stem the inflationary surge using a system of price and wage indexing, but administrative obstacles, including the lack of precise wage and price data, prevented its implementation. Cafiero too resigned in early 1976.[42]

Industrialists had been less directly involved in the confrontations that destroyed the Social Contract but they were hardly unaffected by them. After Gelbard's dismissal in October 1974, they had turned pessimistic once again, blaming López Rega and his politics of confrontation for the emerging crisis. In 1973 they had hoped for a truce between labor and management aimed at ending the wage-price spiral, but the tactics employed by Isabel Perón and López Rega had made that impossible, leaving industrialists little choice but to raise prices to compensate for the astronomical rise in labor costs, touching off the spiral anew. Moreover, the shock treatment of June, and the confrontations that followed, brought yet another recession as new investment, both domestic and foreign, came to a halt.

Cattlemen and farmers, though skeptical of the Social Contract, had taken some hope from the Peronists newfound sensitivity to the need for realistic commodity prices. They had been especially encouraged when Isabel Perón backed away from a controversial Peronist land-tax proposal in October 1974. The bill, which had been circulating among CGE and CGT leaders since the late 1960s and was favored by some of the more progressive farmers, proposed to tax rural land according to its production potential, thereby encouraging either its efficient use or its abandonment. For reformist economists it had become the panacea to the problem of lagging rural production. But by 1974, even the Peronist leadership believed it too risky to attempt in the face of the warnings of rural conservatives that it would undermine production. Nevertheless, despite its legislative victory, the rural sector continued to be plagued by problems in 1975. The year began with a disappointing harvest and the European Common Market's closing its doors to imported beef, a move that temporarily paralyzed the Argentine beef trade. In 1975 the value of the country's exports declined by 24.7 percent while imports rose by 8.6 percent. (See Table No. 8.5.) Economic authorities tried desperately to revive rural confidence by raising support prices for the 1976 crop, but after three years of depressed beef prices, followed by Rodrigo's shock treatment and the wage-price spiral it reignited, rural confidence descended to a new low.[43]

TABLE 8.4
Industrial Production in 1974 and 1975
(percent change)

	1974	1975
Cement (tons)	+ 0.08	+ 1.67
Steel (tons)	+ 8.90	+ 1.67
Autos (units)	− 2.78	− 13.55

Source: Argentina, Instituto Nacional de Estadística y Censos. *Boletín estadístico trimestral* (julio-setiembre 1975; octubre 1975–marzo 1976; abril-junio 1976).

TABLE 8.5
Exports and Imports in 1974 and 1975
(Percent change in US$ Value)

	1974	1975
Exports	+ 20.4	− 24.7
Imports	+ 62.6	+ 8.6

Source: Argentina, Instituto Nacional de Estadística y Censos. *Boletín estadístico trimestral* (julio-setiembre 1975; octubre 1975–marzo 1976; abril-junio 1976).

Finally, in what must have marked Peronism's lowest point since the movement's creation three decades before, the government of Isabel Perón, in early March 1976, agreed, in exchange for stand-by loan assistance, to an International-Monetary-Fund-designed stabilization program in the hope of imposing some order on the collapsing Argentine economy. The IMF program, much like that adopted by Frondizi in 1958, proposed a massive devaluation of the peso to stimulate exports and foreign investments, an end to price controls, and a 12-percent ceiling on wage increases in 1976. But in contrast Juan Perón, who in 1952 could draw on labor loyalty to secure working-class cooperation with his stabilization effort, the best that Isabel Perón could do was warn CGT leaders that if they did not cooperate with the plan proposed by the government they had helped elect, they would soon face a more severe one imposed by a military that stood ready to overthrow the government if the IMF plan failed.

A Return to Authoritarian Austerity

The Peronists' change of course came too late to save a government already torn apart by internal conflict, corruption, and public disaffection. The final blow was struck in one of the most anticipated coups in Argentine history when, under the leadership of General Jorge Rafael Videla, the armed forces swiftly and quietly deposed Isabel Perón on March 24, 1976. After being sworn in, Videla announced that he was prepared to do everything necessary to eradicate domestic insurgency and political corruption and to put an end to the country's economic decline and demoralization. If it required the brutal repression of those who defied his authority and the imposition of harsh economic measures, then that was what he was prepared to do.

The economic course followed by Videla was a familiar one. Most of the conditions present in 1976 had been experienced several times before: record inflation, the collapse of business confidence, a rising foreign debt, and labor unrest. And once again Argentine authorities had an International Monetary Fund proposal to guide them, since an agreement had been signed between the Argentine government and the Fund just before the coup. To direct the economic recovery campaign, Videla chose José Alfredo Martínez de Hoz, a well-known and successful businessman whose family holdings included industrial as well as agricultural enterprises and whose previous government service included brief involvement in the administration of stabilization measures in 1962 and 1966.[44] Like most conservative entrepreneurs in Argentina, Martínez de Hoz believed that the country's economic crisis required action on two fronts: first, an improvement of the trade balance through the expansion of agricultural exports and the reduction of imports; and second, a drastic cut in the rate of inflation through the imposition of fiscal austerity and the freezing of wages. While he recognized that these remedies were not new, he maintained that they deserved another chance since they had never received a fair testing when they had been tried in various forms by Aramburu, Frondizi, and Onganía. This time, he promised, the government had the power and the will to see them through to their conclusion.

He began by outlawing strikes, controlling wages, raising agricultural support prices, increasing taxes, and reducing public expenditures in the areas of social welfare, education, and transfers to provincial governments. The fiscal measures conformed to International Monetary Fund demands for a reduction of the budget deficit from its 1975 level of 11 percent to a more tolerable 5 percent of the gross national product. In return the IMF made available a $1.3 billion loan package from private banks and its own resources to help meet the country's foreign debt obligations.[45]

Martínez de Hoz also introduced several measures aimed at restoring entrepreneurial confidence. Typical of them was the banking reorganization scheme he announced in June 1977. Its purpose was to increase the total financial resources available to investors by bringing the banking system under the control of the country's larger banks and financial houses at the expense of small savings and loan associations and government banks. A similar program had been launched by Krieger Vasena in 1967, only to be abandoned by his successors in 1969. The problem of inflation-induced capital flight and financial erosion had plagued the country for almost three decades. Bank deposits as a percentage of the gross domestic product had declined from 41 percent in 1945 to only 7 percent in 1976. This compared quite unfavorably with countries like Mexico where it was 45 percent. In addition to the freeing of interest rates and the liberation of the exchange market, Martínez de Hoz's bank reform included restrictions on the activites of fringe mortgage banks and savings and loan cooperatives. It was hoped that such measures would streamline Argentine banking and increase the influence of market forces on the cost of money and the exchange rate of the dollar. The fact that they would also increase the domination of the ten public and private banks which already controlled 50 percent of the nation's savings as well as reduce the availability of credit to low-income citizens did not deter officials from making a decision which they believed was justified on grounds of economic efficiency.[46]

The government's program was helped at the outset by a sudden rise in the production of exportable agricultural commodities. Beef exports, which had declined nearly 50 percent between 1973 and 1975 (due in part to the suspension of beef imports by the European Common Market), rose by 100 percent in 1976, eventually causing shortages in the domestic market that forced the government to suspend exports briefly in early 1977 in order to meet local consumer demand. It was also a good year for grain; as a result of excellent weather and increased plantings, the grain harvest grew by 35 percent in 1977, which put it 37 percent higher than the average for the 1969–77 period. With total exports up by 23 percent and imports down by 20 percent, the balance-of-payments deficit of $962 million in 1975 was transformed into a $650 million surplus in 1976.[47]

The new government also reduced the rate of inflation from an unprecedented 444 percent in 1976 to 150 percent in 1977. It did so, however, at the expense of industrial growth, for the real industrial product dropped by 1.5 percent in 1977, which left it 8 percent below the 1974 level. The price paid by industrialists for economic stabilization was not meager, but it caused far less hardship than the sacrifices forced upon the country's workers by the government's wage freeze. By mid 1977 the real minimum industrial wage had fallen 48 percent below what it had been twenty months before; moreover, the wage earners' share of the national income, which Perón had hoped to raise to 50 percent, had descended to only 31 percent during the same period, its lowest level since 1935.[48]

After some initial hesitation in the face of renewed government repression, the labor movement fought back. It began in October 1976 with a strike led by the light and power employees to protest the dismissal of 208 workers from government-owned utilities. The protest picked up momentum in January 1977 when Videla decreed a new labor law that increased the work week from 35 to 42 hours, eliminated union participation in the management of state enterprises, and limited the terms served by union leaders. This time the light and power workers were joined by nine other public employee unions in a direct confrontation with the government aimed at forcing it to rescind the new law. In the end a compromise was achieved, with the unions accepting a longer work week and public authorities agreeing to call off massive dismissals of public employees.[49] Though the government claimed a victory, it was clear that once again a military government had been stopped short in its attempt to conquer the labor movement. It could weaken it and impose its will on it temporarily, but it still could not totally subjugate it.

On the political front General Videla and his colleagues, like

Onganía before them, had no plan for the reconstruction of the country's political system. Videla, too, was preoccupied primarily with the suppression of those who opposed his rule rather than the design of new political processes. Political parties were closed, the CGT intervened and, in July 1977, the General Economic Confederation closed and its assets confiscated in order to deprive businessmen of a means of organized protest.[50] Nothing was offered to replace them, however. Instead a simple autocracy was again created to impose order on Argentine society by dealing with the nation's economic problems and the citizens responsible for them without reliance on traditional intermediaries.

What is most striking about the government created by the Argentine military in 1976 is its familiarity. Once again an autocratic government had been organized to bring order to Argentine society, and again the country's leaders had turned to the International Monetary Fund and the producers of commodity exports to rescue the country from an economic crisis. And as before, Argentine workers, small businessmen, and public employees were asked to pay for their past sins with renewed economic sacrifices. There was little reason to believe that this campaign would be any more effective economically or politically than its ill-fated predecessors. In 1978 Argentines were still deeply divided over the desirability of military rule, the nation's economy remained the prisoner of the producers of commodity exports, who refused to produce up to their capacity, most of the working class continued to distrust political authorities and its own leadership, and entrepreneurs still doubted the capacity of the Argentine government to sustain a consistent plan of attack long enough to eradicate the nation's economic woes.

The Politics of Reconciliation: Lessons and Legacies

It was the Peronists' good fortune that they had been accompanied in their return to power by CGE economists who offered an innovative approach to the management of the Argentine economy through a consensus-generating social contract. José Gelbard and his colleagues proved more sophisticated and educable than their many detractors had assumed. They had learned from the Illia experience that narrow partisanship was self-defeating, and from the failures of previous stabilization programs that any sudden redistribution of income, no matter how compelling in theory, contained the seeds of its own destruction. Yet, like Krieger Vasena, they also recognized that a balanced global attack on inflation was needed in order to set the stage for long-term development. Where they differed from Krieger Vasena was not over the immediate goal of stable prices, but in their ultimate objective of a more nationalistic, consumer-oriented industrial economy. Onganía's authoritarian regime had been designed to impose stability by force in order to attract foreign investors who would finance the country's industrialization and tie it more closely to the international economy. The Peronists, in contrast, believed that they could develop the economy without significant foreign assistance if they could persuade Argentine investors to finance the last stage of its industrial revolution. But since the latter were reluctant to invest as long as high rates of inflation and labor unrest plagued the country, they too had to be placated by a program aimed at economic stabilization. But where Krieger Vasena's attempt to attract foreign investors had relied on the harsh methods of authoritarian rule, Gelbard turned to voluntary working-class compliance through the use of a social contract that promised progressive income redistribution after price stability had been achieved.

The idea of the social contract was not new to western economists, nor was it unknown to Argentines, yet few had given it a chance of success in a country where labor had been so resistant to public authority and producer groups so suspicious of it. The social contract had been advocated by the CGE as a means of increasing its own influence over economic policy, but the country's presidents had persistently rejected the idea. Not until 1973, when it was clear that all other attempts to manage the economy had failed, was the idea of the social contract taken seriously. Its appeal to the Peronists rested in its conformity with their new conciliatory approach to the resolution of domestic conflicts. For non-Peronist groups, on the other hand, it offered a way of tying the government to a mutually agreed upon set of policy objectives. In sum, it seemed a solution whose time had come.

One is tempted to conclude that the adoption of the social

contract marked the conclusion of a long learning process that had taught Argentine leaders the futility of presidential retreats from the difficult but essential task of creating general agreements on development policy objectives in advance of their implementation. It did indeed appear that Argentina's leaders had at last discovered that neither the harsh methods of the authoritarians nor the partisan tactics of elected governments could succeed because of their inability to generate private-sector cooperation with the economy's managers. But unfortunately, what the Peronists had learned about mobilizing political support through formal agreements during the design of their policies was not matched by similar insights into the administration and renewal of such agreements. Consequently, the personalistic and capricious rule of Perón himself, as well as the power struggles of his successors, were allowed to undermine the country's most creative postwar experiment in economic policy making.

We have learned that the success of an incomes policy is determined in large part by the means used to enforce it and the confidence of the participants in the equity of its outcome. The designers of Argentina's Social Contract had been convinced that they possessed the instruments needed to implement it. Organized labor had finally become part of the ruling coalition; converging industrial, rural, and commercial groups appeared ready at last to join with labor to form a grand alliance; and Perón himself had returned to lend his personal authority to the enterprise.

On closer inspection we find that none of these conditions was as well-established as the optimistic designers of the Contract had assumed. The newly allied producer groups gathered within the CGE could be relied upon to support the regime only so long as they were not seriously threatened by its policies. Their commitment to the CGE and through it to the government's economic program was as much the product of political necessity as of a strong belief in the redistributive justice sought by the new government. More important, the CGT's agreement to the accord did not guarantee the support of the rank and file; it had been obvious since the late 1960s that labor leaders could not completely control their members, especially in hard times. Moreover, Argentine workers were not as content with the existing distribution of income in 1973 as they had been in the early

1950s, when Perón had once before asked them to accept a two-year wage freeze. They had seen their income rise and fall repeatedly under non-Peronist governments and were now anxious to use their leader's return to improve their condition. Thus, while most unions were willing to go along with Perón during the first year of the wage freeze, they had no tolerance left for its continuation by the political opportunists and CGT bureaucrats who tried to postpone income redistribution after his death.

Finally, the Peronists also failed to create the kind of quasi-governmental institutions needed to involve all participants in policy implementation. Despite the presence of Gelbard in the Ministry of Economy and of the CGT and CGE on the Price and Wage Council, it was really the personality of Perón, and the Contract's initial successes in holding down prices, that sustained it. But like the Peronist movement itself, government policy was also victimized by the personalistic leader, who paid little attention to the institutionalization of the processes of consensus maintenance. Perón was the juggler of competing political forces and not the manager of shared decision making. With each violation of wage freeze in 1974, he withdrew further from the conflict, relying more on futile exhortations and palace intrigues than on open negotiations with those who had signed the Contract. After his death, the sealing off of the presidency from critical economic groups was completed as López Rega and Isabel Perón retreated into the familiar role of leadership under siege, lashing out at the country's economic problems with ill-conceived, unilateral measures that only exacerbated social conflicts.

The failure to institutionalize participation in the Contract's implementation increased the problem of sustaining public confidence in its outcome. What had been conceived as a sensitive instrument became a blunt and inflexible one in the hands of its increasingly defensive managers. This was apparent as early as the beginning of 1974, when economic authorities failed to adapt their stabilization measures to changing economic conditions. Instead of using a favorable trade balance to cover the rising costs of essential raw-product imports, they further tightened controls, creating shortages and contributing to a thriving black market. Even more tragic was the crisis of confidence provoked by the heavy-handed tactics employed by Perón's successors. Their conspiracies and intrigues led labor leaders to fear the worst from them and, therefore, to drive a hard bargain during wage negotiations before the end of the two-year agreement. The government's response, which resembled the harsh measures of an Alsogaray or a Pinedo rather then the kind of bargains struck by Gelbard's original agreement, destroyed all illusions about the ability of the Peronists to maintain the new economic consensus. Sadly, it seemed in 1976 that the lessons they had learned from their predecessors had come to naught.

PART FIVE

Conclusions

9

Politics and Economic Policy Making in a Divided Society

One of the primary objectives of this study has been the analysis of the performance of contrasting political regimes and their policy-making processes. In separate sections we have examined the ways Peronist, democratic, and military authoritarian governments tried to deal with Argentina's postwar economic difficulties. We can now draw on those findings in order to develop some conclusions about the requirements of development policy making in an industrializing country.

The Policy Solutions to Argentina's Problems

After depression and war had shattered the illusion that Argentina could survive on the export of agricultural commodities alone, the country's leaders were forced to search anew for a strategy to guide the nation's development. Their goal was to reduce the country's vulnerability to the vicissitudes of the international economy; the means they selected to achieve it was industrialization. But what seemed so obvious and necessary at the time proved immensely difficult to accomplish because of the enormous financial and technological requirements of industrialization, the opposition of those who had vested interests in the export economy, and the high costs of satisfying the welfare demands of industrial workers.

Industrialization was also hindered by a fundamental difference of opinion over how it should be achieved. One approach,
championed by reform-oriented nationalists in the military, labor
leaders, and some sectors of the urban bourgeoisie, assumed that
only through the rapid transfer of resources from the rural to the
industrial sector could the economy be freed from its dependence on foreign trade. The other view, held primarily by conservative industrialists, foreign investors, and farmers not totally
opposed to industrialization, argued in favor of proceeding slowly
with industrialization, while at the same time encouraging exports and holding down the appetites of urban workers. Despite
the intense efforts of their proponents, neither of these views
nor their many variants came to prevail in the postwar years;
instead the debate over how to reduce the country's export dependency still rages in Argentina.

The first strategy saw the development problem as one of insufficient demand and capital shortage. What was needed, its
proponents argued, was a transfer of resources from rural producers and foreign investors to members of the national bourgeoisie and urban consumers, in order to promote the production of consumer goods. The transfer was to be achieved through
a redirection of conventional policy instruments and increased
state regulation and investment. Thus, by making creative use of
monetary and fiscal policies, overvalued and controlled exchange
rates, selective price controls, and the regulation of commodity
exports, the government would raise the income and encourage
the spending of Argentine consumers and foster industrial investment. If anyone suffered from the strategy in the short run,
it would be foreign investors and traders, who were displaced by
nationals, along with the producers of commodity exports, who
were being asked to finance economic growth. The strategy received its most thorough testing during the first three years of
Perón's first regime. Illia and the UCRP also followed it, though
much less closely, responding more to the need to boost production after the 1962 recession than to a well-designed strategy of
industrialization. The policies designed by José Gelbard for the
Peronists in 1973 incorporated nationalistic elements of the
strategy but postponed its redistributive, expansionary measures
until after an emergency stabilization plan had been implemented.

In none of its three applications, however, were the strategy's objectives fully achieved. During the first Peronist regime, and under Illia, adverse external events, as well as an overheating of demand, led to strategic retreats from economic expansion. Under the second Peronist regime, the government's program degenerated soon after Perón's death due to inattention to detail and mismanagement. In addition, its attempts to transfer income from farmers and cattlemen to industrialists and urban consumers proved counterproductive. Not only did they fail to terminate the country's dependence on commodity exports but they also demoralized rural entrepreneurs. In so doing they helped reinforce a tradition of rural apathy and inefficiency at a time when it could least be afforded.

Although it was only one of several factors that influenced the level of rural production, the government's policies were one of the most critical because of their long-term effects on rural confidence in the economy and those who managed its growth. In 1946 farmers and cattlemen had witnessed the state, which had in the past promoted their interests, suddenly transformed by the Peronists into a means of exploiting small and large farmers alike through a host of punitive measures. Not surprisingly, rural producers quickly lost confidence in authorities who, it seemed, cared more about the aggrandizement of the public sector and its urban supporters than the welfare of their rural constituents. Unfortunately, the cynicism and distrust spawned by the Peronists did not end with the fall of the Peronist government, but continued even in the face of later government efforts, like those of Aramburu and Frondizi, to promote rural production. Rather than take encouragement from occasional devaluations and higher prices, rural producers remained captives of their deep suspicions of economic authorities and reacted cautiously and often lethargically to policies aimed at increasing their output. Such conduct in turn served to reinforce the belief of many officials that farmers and cattlemen were indeed slackers who could not be relied upon to do their part in the country's economic development. Consequently, the barrier between the countryside and the capital, which the Peronists had erected, continued to grow throughout the postwar period until it became virtually impossible for government officials to gain the confidence of their rural constituents no matter what they offered them.

Those who took the nationalist-welfare route to Argentine development eventually discovered that while increasing the country's industrial product they also unleashed damaging inflationary and payments problems, demoralized a generation of cattlemen and farmers, and frightened off foreigners who were willing to finance the country's economic growth. And it was the misfortune of those whom they had tried to serve that their efforts led not to lasting prosperity but to harsh stabilization programs promulgated by their successors to compensate for the excesses of their campaigns to transform the country into a modern, industrialized welfare state.

The other development strategy that was followed in postwar Argentina was in many ways the opposite of the one just described. Rather than emphasizing nationalism and consumption, it stressed internationalism and investment. Its proponents agreed that Argentina lacked the financial resources needed to stimulate industrial growth, but instead of using state investments and inflationary financing to fill the gap, they concluded that Argentina should look abroad for the capital needed to pay for its economic development. In addition, because they were often faced with foreign-exchange crises when they initiated their programs, those who followed this strategy were also forced to commit themselves in the short run to the stimulation of the production of agricultural exports. The encouragement of agriculture has generated much confusion over their real intent and has led some to argue that this second strategy was in practice nothing more than a disguised attempt to return to the export economy of the 1930s. Such perceptions, however, have tended to mistake means for ends by overemphasizing the incentives given to agriculture and underemphasizing those going to long-term industrialization.

This strategy came in many different variations, but those who adhered to it shared a desire to generate high levels of commodity exports and attract substantial foreign investment, while containing domestic consumption and cutting back in public services until a process of industrial growth could be generated. At the same time, they often differed in the particular economic policy instruments they used to achieve these objectives. For example, Aramburu and Onganía froze wages but Frondizi did not; moreover, Frondizi relied more on the price mechanism and the free market than did the other two and also implemented a more drastic shift in income than either Aramburu or Onganía. In the end, all three succeeded in attracting foreign capital and temporarily limiting domestic consumption; but they also grossly overestimated their ability to stimulate a rapid increase in the production of agricultural commodities and to contain the political effects of labor protests.

The feeble response of farmers to their policies was a major disappointment for Aramburu, Frondizi, and Onganía. By increasing the income of farmers and removing the price and marketing controls they abhorred, they had hoped to spark rapid rural recoveries. But farmers responded cautiously to such measures, suspicious of the motives of economic authorities and critical of their failure to eliminate exchange retentions and land taxes. A major campaign was required to convince farmers who had been abused by the Peronists for a decade that the Argentine government did indeed want to serve their interests. But policy makers seldom made the effort to convince them, and instead relied on their farm policies to do the job for them. It was their misfortune that farmers remained skeptical of their promises and were plagued by a fear that at any moment they would be sacrificed in favor of more popular urban causes.

Also critical to the strategy's execution was the successful implementation of an incomes policy. It was essential both to the attack on inflation and the reallocation of resources to investors. Aramburu and Onganía froze wages while Frondizi relied primarily on state regulation of collective bargaining. In the short run each achieved some success in his fight against inflation at the expense of the country's workers. Yet, what they gained economically, they lost politically. Their antilabor measures served to reinforce labor hostility toward their rule and increase the determination of labor leaders to secure the military overthrow of their governments.

Learning From Mistakes

It was suggested in Chapter 1 that policy makers seek solutions to their economic problems from a variety of sources, each with its own advantages and disadvantages. In the case of Argentina we wanted to know which of these sources of policy learning were used and how they contributed to policy management.

Clearly, Argentine leaders have increased their understanding of the country's economic condition during the past three decades, even though their low rate of success in dealing with it might lead one to conclude otherwise. They drew knowledge from a variety of sources, including economic theory in the form of neoclassical, Keynesian, and structuralist doctrines, foreign example, and foreign advisors from the Economic Commission for Latin America and the International Monetary Fund. They also learned from their past mistakes, as evidenced in the more cautious and balanced approach of Perón's 1973 administration in contrast to his first one and the much more sophisticated and global effort launched by Onganía in comparison with the cruder shock treatment attempted by Frondizi.

The most impressive learning experience of the period came from the careful assessment of the costs of the IMF stabilization program executed by Frondizi in 1959. In different ways both Krieger Vasena in 1967 and Gelbard in 1973 applied lessons learned from the Frondizi-Alsogaray shock treatment. Their review of the IMF program and its effects taught them that the sledge-hammer approach used in late 1958 reallocated resources too swiftly, curtailed demand too suddenly, and called for too drastic a change in old economic habits. Instead of purging the system of its inefficiencies and restoring the free market, as intended, it had given rise to new distortions and behaviors that equally constrained long-term stability and growth. In order to avoid these errors, they concluded, the heavy hand of sudden liberalization would have to give way to a more balanced approach that mixed some controls with market incentives.

The contrast between the approaches taken by Krieger Vasena and Alsogaray is quite striking. Where Alsogaray was doctrinaire and blindly dedicated to the restoration of the free market, Krieger Vasena was pragmatic and willing to combine market and nonmarket instruments, as well as monetary expansion with fiscal restraint. To be sure, their ultimate objectives of a foreign-financed, capitalistic, industrial society were much the same, but through his study of Alsogaray's excesses as well as the successes of countries like Mexico, Spain, and Brazil, Krieger Vasena was able to design a much more sophisticated and well-integrated technical solution to his country's economic problems.

Gelbard also sought to design a more balanced approach to stabilization in 1973 by combining monetary restraint with price and wage controls through the use of an innovative social contract. Unfortunately, as occurred with Krieger Vasena's effort, the skill that went into the design of his economic policy was not matched by the political and administrative measures used to implement it. As a result, neither program could sustain its initial successes.

It would be satisfying to conclude that because of their sophistication and technical skill, Argentine leaders have put behind them the heavy-handed economic shock treatments of the 1950s and 1960s. Unfortunately, more than policy learning is required to avoid such drastic remedies, as we saw in early 1976 when officials, faced with record inflation and a near economic collapse brought on by the political chaos and economic indecision that followed Perón's death, looked to the IMF for emergency assistance and accepted its harsh prescriptions once again. Clearly, knowledge alone does not prevent officials from returning to old stabilization formulas when they are suddenly engulfed in a crisis, especially if they believe that harsh measures are needed to convince foreign creditors that they can put their economic house in order.

Policy Implementation: The Missing Links

Authorities in industrializing societies require institutions and processes that facilitate the resolution of policy conflicts and the mobilization of citizens into a cooperative effort to deal with the nation's economic difficulties. Critical to the creation and operation of such institutions is the development of linkages between policy makers, administrators, and the owners of land, labor, and capital that will enable the first two to lead the last in the pursuit of societal goals.

There are several ways in which authorities can develop the kinds of relationships between themselves and private interests that will facilitate economic management. In industrializing, capitalist societies there are two that stand out. One is competitive pluralism; it gives private interests and the organizations that represent them relatively free reign to use their resources to influence policy decisions. The other is corporatism; it involves the turning of private groups into instruments that the state can use to achieve its goals.

Competitive pluralism encourages the formulation and execution of public policy through a process of bargaining among diverse interests and public authorities in which the latter, by skillfully mediating policy conflicts, can foster exchanges among competitors which will lead to the attainment of government policy objectives. Two conditions are essential for the operation of this system. First, competitors must trust each other and public officials, and be willing to accept policy solutions that are achieved through a process of mutual accommodation. Second, the policy process must be open enough to allow competitors multiple points of access to policy makers and opportunities to influence policy decisions.[1] Competitive pluralism has never existed in a pure form anywhere in Latin America since the region's rigid class structures have limited competition and given privileged access to those with the largest amount of political resources; nevertheless, it has been approximated in several countries, including Chile and Uruguay before 1973, and Venezuela, Colombia, and Costa Rica in the 1960s and 1970s.

The second approach involves the use of corporatist institutions to establish state control over relevant private groups. This can be done in many different ways. One is for the state to foster the creation of sectoral associations that represent functional interests in the policy-making process. This allows authorities to determine the form that such groups will take as well as to determine the terms of their admission to government councils. If private interests are already organized, authorities may coopt them into the policy-making process by absorbing them into the ruling coalition or assigning them posts on government boards and commissions. Obviously, several arrangements are possible, ranging from loose ties to the state to complete subordination to authorities. Central to all corporatist systems, however, is the deliberate use of private organizations by the state to achieve its economic objectives.[2]

Latin American leaders long have appreciated the advantages of corporatist rule and several have tried to create corporatist organizations in one form or another. The results of their efforts have usually been crude and of short duration, seldom fulfilling the organizational requirements of the corporatist model they

seek to emulate. Frequently they have been resisted by powerful private interests who realize they have more to gain from
open competition or privileged access to authorities than subjugation through corporatist rule. Nevertheless, the appeal of
corporatist rule to Latin American leaders, especially military officers and technocrats, remains strong since it offers them a
well-known means for increasing state control over society.

Although they differ in fundamental ways, competitive pluralism and corporatism have one thing in common: they both
establish and maintain rules that govern relations between authorities and those whom they seek to regulate. The form that
they will take varies, but in both systems an essential connection
between the state and its constituents is developed and sustained. Most important, from such rules and the relationships
they create, authorities gain the political instruments they need
for managing a nation's public affairs, and private interests ac-
quire an understanding of the limits of permissible conduct and
the channels available to them for the exercise of influence over
authorities.

Once the importance of policy-making rules and established
links between the regulators and the regulated is recognized, the
Argentine experience can be more readily understood. The continual failure of Argentine leaders to secure the cooperation of
private interests in the implementation of their economic programs was not due to their excessive reliance on competitive
pluralism or corporatism, but their failure to develop either, or
any other system that linked policy makers with their constituents.

We saw, for example, how the country's constitutional democracies proved inhospitable to the development of the kind of
competitive pluralism that one might have expected under such
systems. Interest-group disputes over economic policy matters
that might have been resolved through the mediation of political
parties in other countries were frequently not resolved in Argentina because economic groups had little confidence in the
nation's parties and their leaders. Moreover, access to policy makers was neither open nor direct. Instead, the military often
blocked contacts between authorities and some groups while
narrow partisanship limited dealing with others. In addition, the
high level of societal conflict that surrounded economic policy

frequently caused presidents to fear that they would be the principal losers if they allowed others to bargain with them over the content of their programs. Yet, by refusing to deal directly with private interests, they only reinforced public distrust of them and encouraged their opponents to declare open warfare on their policy-making processes.

We also saw how the Peronist regimes, whose creators sought increased central direction of the economy, flirted with various corporatist devices. Essential to the operation of corporatist institutions is the existence of a multisector, state-dominated coalition that allows central coordination of the capitalist economy. Though he tried to create and lead such a coalition, Perón never consolidated his control over it. Instead, he relied disproportionately on labor, and in doing so alienated many of the nation's entrepreneurs. He also refused to accept the kind of contraints on his own conduct that came with the transformation of a social contract into a durable cooperative arrangement. In 1973 expedience prevailed once again, depriving the Peronists of another opportunity to end the conflicts they had helped create.

Military presidents were even less ambitious than democratic and Peronist leaders. They had no plan for the integration of private interests into the policy-making process. In fact, with the exception of Aramburu's brief use of an economic council to ratify his programs, they rejected all proposals for the involvement of producers and laborers in the management of the state's economic programs. They were convinced that it was precisely such "political" arrangements or attempts to create them that had made it impossible to mount a rational attack on the country's economic problems in the past. What they wanted was control, and they tried to secure it using the simplist means available, the organization of a crude dictatorship advised by technocrats who sought the conformity of citizens with their programs.

In the absence of institutions that are capable of securing public cooperation with government policy, policy makers are forced to deal with potential opponents in an ad hoc manner. In Argentina this has meant heavy reliance on indirect instruments like economic incentives and direct ones like coercion. Nowhere was this more apparent than in the ways each president dealt with the country's militant and well-organized labor movement.

The problem of securing the cooperation of organized labor

was especially acute for democratically elected non-Peronist presidents who gained office through elections that excluded the Peronists from the competition. Regardless of the economic policy they chose, they faced a labor movement that did not recognize the legitimacy of their rule. To some extent the same was true of the military authoritarian regimes since labor, along with most other groups, had no voice in their creation. Only the Peronists enjoyed the support of labor at the outset because of the direct ties between Perón and the masses. It is hard to overemphasize the policy-making advantage enjoyed by the government of an industrializing nation when it includes the labor movement within its governing coalition. Not only can it expect relative labor peace during good times, but it usually can count on labor's cooperation during hard times as well, such as when some kind of incomes policy is required. Perón, for example, could successfully demand income sacrifices from labor in 1952 and again in 1973, demonstrating repeatedly that labor will accept policies from the party it supports that it would never tolerate from an illegitimate opposition government. This fact was not lost on Argentina's military leaders when they were searching for a political solution in 1971 and 1972. Although they had hoped to create a non-Peronist government in the 1973 elections, they were willing to accept a Peronist one because at the time it seemed to be the only political regime that could hold labor in check.

For governments that did not enjoy labor-union support there were two ways of dealing with labor opponents: they could persecute them, keeping them disorganized and on the defensive, or they could tolerate them, while at the same time trying to win the rank and file away from the labor leadership. The first was the method of the military authoritarians and the second was followed by elected presidents.

The military authoritarian regimes had been created in part to mobilize the power of the state against the labor movement and its political organizations. They suspended collective bargaining, closed militant unions, and jailed union leaders. Clearly, if the authoritarian regime had any advantage over democratic ones, it was its ability to repress labor unions and other social groups. It is therefore not hard to understand why local entrepreneurs, foreign investors, and conservative party leaders, who had grown weary of labor militancy, welcomed the harsh antilabor measures of military regimes. But, as we saw repeatedly, the military authoritarians did not eliminate the labor movement as an important force in Argentine politics; they only repressed it temporarily and postponed its effects on policy. The labor movement could not be held down indefinitely, even by governments as strong as Onganía's. Sooner or later it retaliated, and when it did, it undermined not only the government's policy but also its claim to legitimacy on the basis of its ability to maintain public order. What the military authoritarian government failed to do was create alternative ways of integrating the labor movement into the policy-making process. By persecuting labor leaders without offering alternative channels for rank-and-file participation in the governing of the nation, they merely reinforced the hold of Peronist leaders on the Argentine working class.

Democratic presidents, in contrast, believed that the Peronists' control over the working class could be broken if the rank and file were encouraged to support other political parties. To some extent they had no other choice, for if they were going to make democracy work, they had to play by its libertarian and elective rules. Frondizi and Illia tried to make the best of a difficult situation by restoring labor's rights in the hope that the new freedom would induce it to support non-Peronist democratic parties. What they failed to appreciate, however, was the ability of Perón and his lieutenants to retain control over the rank and file despite their enticement by the government. They had assumed that they could treat laborers like unorganized voters who could be won over through favorable policies and conventional election rhetoric. But labor support could be delivered only with the collaboration of labor leaders and their organizations, as democratic presidents later learned to their regret.

Labor support may be a necessary condition for successful policy implementation, but it is not a sufficient one. Equally important in a capitalistic system is the cooperation of the nation's entrepreneurs. Argentine entrepreneurs have been more approachable than the country's labor leaders, yet their collaboration is still difficult to obtain. They are more approachable because they are less tied to political movements than labor and, therefore, are not as much concerned about which party governs as they are the government's openness to their influence. At the same time, they are difficult to control because they are quite diverse and frequently disagree with each other on policy matters. Even more than organized labor, entrepreneurs are represented by multiple organizations which claim to speak for different constituencies whom authorities can seldom satisfy simultaneously.

As they did with labor, democratic leaders tended to ignore the pleas of entrepreneurs for greater access to their deliberations and relied instead on their ability to use exhortation and economic incentives to win their cooperation. As a result, the leaders of entrepreneurial groups regarded democratic leaders with great suspicion, convinced that their decisions were guided by personal political ambition and determined through a process of intrigue and conspiracy rather than an open, cooperative effort. Thus, ironically, at a time that labor leaders viewed democratic presidents who were trying to win the rank and file away from them as instruments of the nation's bourgeoisie, entrepreneurs saw them as politicians whose pursuit of urban votes prevented them from sustaining probusiness policies.

While it appeared that Argentina's military authoritarians collaborated closely with the country's entrepreneurs, there actually existed substantial tension and distance between the two. To be sure, military authoritarians adopted probusiness policies aimed at increasing exports and foreign investment and were roundly praised by many entrepreneurs for their efforts. But the latter were also disappointed with the military authoritarians because they refused to deal directly with business spokesmen and their organizations on most policy matters. Entrepreneurs never completely trusted their military rulers and were always haunted by the knowledge that military presidents could turn against them just as they had against labor. Argentina's national bourgeoisie wanted something more than policies which encouraged foreign investors and sustained a kind of artificial political order; they also wanted to dominate the policy-making process. But that was exactly what the military refused to let them do.

If anyone learned the costs of excluding entrepreneurs from the policy-making process, it was the Peronists. During his first administration, Perón had abused many of the country's rural and industrial leaders while favoring those emerging entrepreneurs who supported his policies. In attacking the economic

elite he was motivated by the need to prove himself to his working-class followers and the conviction that he could bend the
private sector to his will. But what he learned to his misfortune
was how easy it was to undermine the entrepreneur's very
fragile confidence in public authorities and provoke their obstruction of government policies. In 1973, chastened by the
shortcomings of his first administration, Perón returned to
Argentina with an offer of collaboration through the instrument
of the Social Contract. This time he sought to achieve what the
democrats had been afraid to try and the military authoritarians
incapable of doing: the unity of labor, industry, commerce and
agriculture. But the Peronists had for too long lived by the rules
of combative politics. When they had to direct the collaborative
effort, they proved incapable of the subtle management and institutional reform that it required.

None of Argentina's postwar regimes proved very adept at
winning and sustaining entrepreneurial confidence in public policy. Instead, they fostered the growth of a deep distrust between
the country's entrepreneurs and its public officials. Democratic
politicians came to appear unreliable and unresponsive, authoritarian leaders, though regarded with greater favor by many,
as too autonomous, and Peronist leaders as combative and incapable of sustaining a probusiness policy. Though much of the
problem may have been due to the exaggerated expectations of
Argentina's entrepreneurs, it was also fostered by the lack of
communication between government policy makers and the
leaders of the organizations that represented the agricultural and
business communities.

The Roots of Conflict

Having demonstrated how Argentine presidents failed to gain
the confidence and cooperation of the country's entrepreneurs
and labor leaders, and how this failure limited their capacity to
achieve their development policy objectives, we must turn now
to one remaining question: namely, why was it so hard for them
to accomplish this fundamental task? More specifically, what was
it about the process of industrialization and responses to it that
made its orderly political management by the state so illusive?

It remains popular in Argentina to blame the country's malaise on one of the groups involved in the nation's persistent social and political conflicts. Some fault the clumsy but powerful Peronists, others blame selfish rural or urban entrepreneurs, and still others point to highly partisan political parties or ambitious but inept military officers. But as with most complex social processes, no single force or group is totally responsible. It was not one actor or a single decision that made political life so frustrating but a series of actions and reactions that have reinforced rather than lessened mutual distrust and social conflict during the past half century.

One can trace the origins of social and political conflict in Argentina as far back as the nineteenth century when disagreements over the form of the new republic was to take divided political activists. But if it is the relationship between the state and the groups which represent the primary participants in the industrializing, capitalist economy that interest us, then it is to the 1930s and the management of Argentine development after the depression that we again must turn. What distinguished Argentine politics during this period was not only the insistence of a conservative elite on tight control over emerging industrial and labor interests, but the very provocative way in which its control was reasserted. To understand the importance of this fact, a brief comparison with Argentina's neighbor Brazil is instructive.

Brazil, which also underwent a process of postdepression industrialization during the 1930s, had a tradition of state paternalism upon which to draw to manage the process of societal change. During the nineteenth century the Brazilian monarchy had established a strong, paternalistic state. When adapted to the requirements of industrialization by President Getulio Vargas between 1930 and 1945, it yielded a semicorporatist system of governance that involved the state in the creation and supervision of entrepreneurial and working-class organizations. Though not devoid of tension or dispute, the system made it possible for Vargas to guide Brazil through the initial phase of industrialization without an escalation of disruptive social conflict.[3] Argentina, in contrast, had no tradition of state paternalism to draw upon. The Argentine state had always been viewed as an instrument employed by narrow, partisan interests to gain advantages for themselves. First conservative rural and exporter interests in the late nineteenth and early twentieth centuries, and then the urban, middle-class Radicals captured the government and used its authority to satisfy their own needs.

When conservatives returned in 1930, they resurrected the partisan practices of the past. Rather than try to direct a process of industrialization by arbitrating the disputes of competing interests or by coopting and manipulating entrepreneurs and labor leaders as Vargas had done, they ruled defensively, determined to contain industrialization and repress the working class that grew with it. The state became the last line of defense for the farmers and cattlemen of the Rural Society and CARBAP and not an instrument of leaders intent on forging a broad ruling coalition.

The practice of using state authority for narrow partisan ends was extended by Perón in 1946. He merely turned the tables so that organized labor and an emerging corps of nationalistic entrepreneurs were served by the state rather than the rural and financial interests whom it had served before 1943. In so doing, Perón accomplished two things. First, he increased the number of groups who believed that they had a right to use state authority for their own ends. And, second, he reinforced the notion that the state was the prize which, when captured by one group, was to be used against the others.

The partisan character of the Argentine state and the problems it raised for the management of the nation's economy were no mystery to the politicians and military officers who tried to govern the country after 1955. Most of them were determined to end this tradition either by building coalitions large enough to generate cooperation among competing interests or by elevating the government above the conflict so that it could arbitrate disputes in an independent way. As we saw, Frondizi tried to build a multisector, multiparty coalition at the outset, Illia sought to encourage the resolution of disputes privately, Onganía attempted to detach the state from the competitive process, and, in 1973, Perón used a social contract to forge a new consensus. In the end, of course, each of their attempts failed. There were many reasons for this, but none was more important than the persistent conflict between their political strategies and economic policies.

Argentina's presidents were plagued after 1955 by an apparent contradiction between their desire to create an independent state capable of arbitrating economic conflicts, on the one hand, and a need to dictate economic policies with highly partisan effects, on the other. The victims of government policy varied with the particular content of each program, but sooner or later each saw itself affected adversely. No promise of future reimbursement for current sacrifices could reduce the effect such deprivations had in reinforcing perceptions of the state as a partisan instrument. Nor was it enough to argue that such policies were dictated by indisputable economic realities, since interpretations of those realities differed from sector to sector and from class to class. No president escaped the conflict. Whatever their claims of detachment, they still appeared to be partisans in a highly competitive political system. And once they recognized this harsh reality, they quickly abdicated their role as arbitrator in favor of that of dedicated enforcer of unpopular policies.

The Dynamics of Conflict

Argentina's political conflicts may have been more severe than those of other industrializing nations, but they certainly are not unique to this South American country. It is not unusual for groups whose interrelationships were clearly defined and relatively harmonious prior to industrialization to find a new divergence as economic growth and social change occur. Quite frequently they will come to disagree on the nature of growth, what causes it and what retards it, and the rules by which its increments should be divided. And because of the vulnerability of their economies to international conditions as well as natural disasters at home, they may also find themselves facing frequent economic crises. As a result, political issues that might have been manageable under conditions of prosperity and growth often become intractable when they become entangled with economic crisis. At the same time, economic problems whose solution might be within the grasp of governments that rule through a consensus on economic matters frequently elude insecure political leaders plagued by society conflicts over fundamental development issues.

If the structure of industrializing societies were relatively sim-

ple, and the number of organized interests few, the policy problems faced by their leaders would not be especially tough. But
simple societies are becoming increasingly rare. Those who govern most noncommunist industrializing societies face large
bureaucracies which regulate a wide range of economic activities, a diverse private sector whose members include traditional as well as modern producers, ambitious and powerful
foreign investors, and increasingly well-organized interests representing many different economic activities. To secure the
cooperation of the owners of land, labor, and capital in the development effort, authorities must offer incentives that are conducive to cooperative behavior, as well as disincentives to
uncooperative conduct. This might be managed with little strain
through the design of policies that benefited most groups and
fostered the creation of large, multisector coalitions. Economic
authorities are, however, seldom free to design policies that
satisfy all of the expectations of the suppliers of land, labor, and
capital. Indeed, they are frequently forced to take drastic actions
to alleviate foreign-exchange, price, and investment crises that
exact large sacrifices from several economic groups.

The dynamics of economic policy making in conflict-ridden,
industrializing societies like Argentina can be better understood
if we view them as an example of the kinds of conflict situations
described by game theorists. From the game perspective, the
major aspects of interest conflict that surround economic policy
decisions are not hard to characterize: an individual (the principal economic policy maker) finds himself in a situation from
which one of several possible outcomes will result and with respect to which he has certain personal preferences. Though he
may have some control over variables which determine the outcome, he does not have full control. Frequently, this control is
in the hands of several individuals or groups of individuals who,
like him, have preferences among the possible outcomes but
who in general do not agree in their preferences. Within this
context, the policy maker might seem to be playing a game
against nature where success depends very largely on correct
guesses of likely conflicts and probable outcomes, which, in
turn, depend on his own actions and on other circumstances that
he does not control but whose probabilities he roughly estimates. Yet, he will quickly learn that this one-person game

paradigm of decision making is not an adequate framework in which to formulate his problems; he is really involved in a kind of multiple-person game situation and to maximize his ends he must take the preferences of others into account.[4]

Elementary game theory not only offers interesting prescriptions about how rational actors should behave in order to maximize their objectives, ie., questions of strategy, but can also serve as a descriptive tool for the classification and analysis of social conflicts. It is the latter to which labor economists Richard Walton and Robert McKersie addressed themselves in their very instructive study of bargaining behaviors. Their approach is also useful to our analysis of policy conflicts in industrializing societies. They argue that economic bargaining usually can be separated into two types of negotiations. The first involves bargaining over "issues" involving a fixed total value, which can be allocated between parties in various shares or proportions, or, in other words, a zero-sum situation where what one party gains the other must lose. This they title the "distributive" process. The other type involves "problems," which contain possibilities for greater or lesser amounts of value that can be made available to the contending parties, or a variable-sum game, which they term the "integrative" or problem-solving process.

The outcomes of the distributive process are associated with such conditions and tactics as threats, credibility, and the degree of firmness and commitment demonstrated and perceived. The objective is to maximize one's gain at the expense of one's opponent or, at worst, to minimize one's losses. The integrative process, in contrast, seeks to improve the position of all parties through cooperation directed at solving common problems. Rather than maximizing threats and commitments and minimizing the exchange of information as was done in distributive bargaining, the solution of problems requires the maximum exchange of information and the utmost flexibility. In fact, only if the parties are motivated to cooperate by sharing all relevant information, and trust each other throughout, can they reach common solutions to their problems. Moreover, once success is achieved on one issue, the likelihood of success on others increases, as satisfaction with the outcomes of the first effort build more trust and reinforce problem-solving motives.[5]

Returning to the development policy maker's dilemma, we can

interpret presidential behavior within the context of the conflict situations they face when dealing with economic crises. They will begin by accepting the contention of their economic advisors that in order to open the way for steady economic growth they must redistribute resources to certain growth-inducing activities. This will require that they call on some citizens to sacrifice in favor of others in order to create the conditions that would produce the kind of sustained economic growth that would eventually benefit all and thereby compensate those who had made the temporary sacrifices.

Another way of interpreting this situation is to view economic authorities as leaders in a kind of two-part, policy-management game. The first and most critical part is the situation created by the government's economic program during its first few years. Because of its redistributive character, it will be perceived by citizens as a kind of zero-sum game in which the government's policy decisions dictate the game's initial winners and losers. The second part comes after the government has achieved its initial redistributions. This phase will approximate the variable-sum or integrative-type game, in which those who suffered in the first part will be compensated, at least in part, for their earlier losses. In other words, in the first phase income has to be redistributed in order to stimulate a particular form of economic growth, while in the second the increased payoffs made possible by sustained economic growth would yield some gains for all citizens. The critical policy management problem, of course, is moving successfully through the first game in such a way that the chances of realizing the benefits of the second are not jeopardized.

To survive both parts of the game with their program intact, policy makers need a set of policy measures that will lead to sustained economic growth and the means to execute the redistributive measures contained in their initial program. But, if they have no procedures for securing the consent of those who are affected by their policies, they will have to depend entirely on their ability to convince potential nonconformists that their compliance now will yield rewards later on. But if trust in government is already low, and political leaders have no means for increasing it, their chances of convincing constituents of their wisdom and sincerity are not high.

Their problem is further complicated by the separate strategies pursued by the other players in the game. Each player recognizes, for example, that if he complies with the government's demands but other players do not, the program could be subverted and the promised payoffs never realized. Thus, unless he can be reassured by past practice, or some kind of formalized and enforceable agreement, that others will comply, it is not in his interest to do so. But if policy makers believe that the creation of such an agreement is beyond their grasp or might endanger their program at the outset, they will refuse to try to create one. By refusing to consult with their potential adversaries, they will only antagonize them and provoke the kind of disobedience that will threaten policy implementation. And that, it appears, is exactly what happens in many industrializing countries plagued by economic conflict: economic authorities reject the consensus-building task as impossible and thereby reinforce the distrust of their constituents and provoke their defiance of the terms of the redistributive phase of the game.

Instead of building support for the zero-sum phase of their program, authorities frequently transform their policy management task from one of persuasion to one of forcing recalcitrant players to accept temporary income losses. They execute their development programs by retreating into the role of the stern leader whom destiny, in the form of elections or military coups, had called upon to administer bitter medicine to a resistant and often unappreciative patient. In meeting this challenge, they are frequently encouraged by the foreign and local economic advisors who argue that their complacent and selfish countrymen need a leader who will force them to live within their means. With such encouragement, policy makers can cloak themselves in self-righteousness and justify ignoring critics whose complaints merely confirm their view of a short-sighted people who do not understand what must be done to ignite economic growth.

In removing themselves from the bargaining arena, economic authorities cannot help but encourage those displeased with their policies to seek alternative remedies—ranging from the use of economic resources to undermine the execution of policies to securing the government's demise through military intervention. In Latin America, Africa, and Asia the military coup has become a political instrument of last resort for most political and economic groups; it is therefore not unusual to find aggrieved producers or laborers encouraging the military overthrow of a government in the hope that its successor will restructure the payoffs of the economic policy game more to their advantage. Even if not involved in actual plotting, they can assume that their obstruction of government policy will sooner or later undermine military confidence in the government and therefore secure its demise. And when it does, the ambitious leader will be deprived not only of his policies but of his regime as well.

By now it should be obvious that there is no easy escape from the vicious circle of economic crisis, political conflict, and policy failure in which export-dependént, industrializing nations like Argentina find themselves. Of course, some will be fortunate enough to discover that they possess a strategic commodity whose high value in world markets might by itself propel a sudden expansion of national income, which, if used wisely, might reduce conflict and help sustain economic growth. Others may find themselves with leaders who are strong and wise enough to impose a manageable economic and political order without being undermined by their opponents. Still others may give up entirely on the capitalistic mode of production and transform themselves into centrally directed, socialized economies. For many, none of these options will be possible and they will be left to limp along from crisis to crisis and government to government. But if their leaders have learned anything from their past failures, let us hope that it is the utter futility of trying to solve economic problems without complementary efforts to deal with political ones. Economic policy and political strategy cannot be separated in practice, especially in societies whose citizens refuse to stand by idly and watch as others try to impose their narrow-minded solutions on them. Recognition of this fact will not by itself end the vicious circle, but it may at least provide a more positive point of departure for those bold leaders who are willing to risk the involvement of their fellow citizens in their campaigns for economic development and national self-esteem.

Notes

Chapter 1

1. The concept "public problem-solver" used here is adapted from that of Albert Hirschman. See his *Journeys Toward Progress: Studies of Economic Policy-Making in Latin America* (New York: Anchor Books, 1963), and "Policymaking and Policy Analysis in Latin America—A Return Journey," *Policy Sciences* 6 (1975): 385–402.

2. Anderson's study sought to assess how well the institutions and processes of Spanish authoritarianism provided an "environment of choice" in which economic problems could be identified, alternative courses of action evaluated, and appropriate measures selected and implemented. Similarly, I want to know to what degree the institutions and processes of Peronist rule, quasi-democratic government, and military authoritarianism facilitated or hindered the solution of Argentina's postwar economic problems. See his *The Political Economy of Modern Spain: Policy-Making in an Authoritarian System* (Madison: University of Wisconsin Press, 1970).

3. For a brief summary of the region's development policy failures and a provocative discussion of their implications see: Robert Ayres, "Development Policy and the Possibility of a 'Livable' Future for Latin America," *American Political Science Review* 69 (1975): 507–25.

4. Hugh Heclo, *Modern Social Politics in Britain and Sweden: From Relief to Income Maintenance* (New Haven: Yale University Press, 1974), p. 305.

5. The concept of policy learning used here is adapted from the discussion of "political learning" by Heclo, ibid., Chapter 6.

6. The relationship of economic development to social conflict is explored to good effect in John Powelson, *Institutions of Economic Growth: A Theory of Conflict Management in Developing Countries* (Princeton: Princeton University Press, 1972).

7. Andrew Shonfield, *Modern Capitalism: The Changing Balance of Public and Private Power* (New York: Oxford University Press, 1965), p. 121.

8. For an extensive discussion of the problem of authority and political order in developing countries see: Samuel P. Huntington, *Political Order in Changing Societies* (New Haven: Yale University Press, 1968).

9. These economic problems are best summarized in Carlos F. Díaz Alejandro, *Essays on the Economic History of the Argentine Republic* (New Haven: Yale University Press, 1970), and *Exchange Rate Devaluation in a Semi-Industrialized Country* (Cambridge, Mass.: MIT Press, 1964), and in R. D. Mallon and J. V. Sourrouille, *Economic Policymaking in a Conflict Society: The Argentine Case* (Cambridge, Mass.: Harvard University Press, 1975).

10. The most articulate presentation of this interpretation is that of Argentine political scientist Guillermo O'Donnell in his *Modernization and Bureaucratic Authoritarianism: Studies in South American Politics* University of California Institute of International Studies, Politics of Modernization Series, no. 9 (Berkeley, 1973), Chapters 2, 3.

11. Their many different forms are described and compared in Juan Linz, "Totalitarian and Authoritarian Regimes," in *Handbook of Political Science*, vol. 3, eds. Fred Greenstein and Nelson Polsby (Reading, Mass.: Addison-Wesley, 1975), pp. 175–412.

12. My identification of economic policy objectives and instruments will follow the typology developed by E. S. Kirschen, et al., *Economic Policy in Our Time*, vol. 1 (Chicago: Rand McNally, 1967).

13. The analytical division of policy-making processes into such phases is discussed and defended in Anderson, *Political Economy of Modern Spain*, pp. 17–21.

Chapter 2

1. See Peter H. Smith, *Politics and Beef in Argentina* (New York: Columbia University Press, 1969), and *Argentina and the Failure of Democracy: Conflict Among Political Elites 1904-1955* (Madison: University of Wisconsin Press, 1974); Rodolfo Puiggros, *La democracia fraudulenta* (Buenos Aires: Editorial Jorge Alvarez, 1968); and Mark Falcoff and Ronald Dolkart, eds. *Prelude to Perón* (Berkeley: University of California Press, 1975).

2. Smith, *Politics and Beef*, pp. 47–48.

3. James R. Scobie, *Argentina: A City and A Nation*, 2d ed. (New York: Oxford University Press, 1971), p. 305. It should be pointed out that mixed farming has always been common in Argentina and became increasingly so after World War II. Until the 1930s, however, the immigrant farmer, both tenant and property owner, tended to specialize in the production of grains, while cattlemen, both large and small, concentrated their efforts on livestock, cultivating grains irregularly when prices and weather conditions encouraged it.

4. See Federación Agraria Argentina, *Un grito, una historia, una realidad* (Rosario: FAA, 1971). On the origin and growth of tenant farming in Argentina also see James Scobie, *Revolution on the Pampas: A Social History of Argentine Wheat 1860-1910* (Austin: University of Texas Press, 1964).

5. The best account of CARBAP's origins is that by its founder: Nemesio de Olariaga, *El ruralismo argentino: economia ganadera* (Buenos Aires: Editorial El Ateneo, 1943); also see Carl C. Taylor, *Rural Life in Argentina* (Baton Rouge: Louisana State University Press, 1948), pp. 401–20.

6. Roger Gravil, "State Intervention in Argentina's Export Trade Between the Wars," *Journal of Latin American Studies* 2 (1970): 160–61.

7. The composition of the Meat Board represented a substantial conquest for cattlemen because it included four cattlemen among its nine directors; the other five were divided among three from the government and two from the meat packers.

8. Gravil, "State Intervention," pp. 156–57.

9. Dardo Cuneo, *Comportamiento y crisis de la clase empresaria* (Buenos Aires: Editorial Pleamar, 1967), pp. 80–92.

10. On the fiscal and monetary reforms of the period see Rafael Olarra Jiménez, *Evolución monetaria argentina* (Buenos Aires: EUDEBA, 1971), pp. 83–95.

11. See Alejandro E. Bunge, *Una nueva Argentina* (Buenos Aires: Editorial Guillermo Kraft, Ltd., 1940); beginning in 1918 Bunge published articles on Argentine social and economic development in the periodical *Revista de Economia Argentina* in which he advocated a much stronger government effort to stimulate industrialization and improve urban welfare.

12. Unión Industrial Argentina, *Seis leyes económicas*, 3d ed. (Buenos Aires: UIA, 1943, originally published in 1935).

13. Unión Industrial Argentina, *Memoria y balance* (Buenos Aires: UIA), p. 4

14. Computed from Organización Techint, *Boletín Informativo no. 188* (octubre-noviembre 1972), Cuadro No. 2, p. 20.

15. República Argentina, Congreso Nacional, *Diario de Sessiones de la Cámara de Senadores,* 41 Reunión, 3ª sesion extraordinaria, 26 de noviembre de 1940, and 43ᵈ Reunión, 4ª sesion extraordinaria, 17 y 18 de diciembre de 1940.

16. Federico Pinedo, *En tiempos de la república y después,* (Buenos Aires: Editorial Mundo Forense, 1949), pp. 243–324.

17. Miguel Murmis and Juan Carlos Portantiero, *Estudios sobre los origenes del peronismo* (Buenos Aires: Siglo Vientiuno Editores, 1971), pp. 33–42. On the Radicals during the 1920s also see David Rock, *Politics in Argentina 1890–1930* (Cambridge: Cambridge University Press, 1975).

18. Felix Luna, *El 45* (Buenos Aires: Editorial Sudamericana, 1971), pp. 22–30.

19. Rubén Rotondaro, *Realidad y cambio en el sindicalismo* (Buenos Aires: Editorial Pleamar, 1971), pp. 19–20.

20. Ibid., pp. 39–40.

21. Dirección Nacional de Investigación Estadística y Censos, *Síntesis Estadística Mensual de la República,* Año I, no. 1, enero 1947, p. 7.

22. Rotondaro, *Realidad y cambio,* pp. 104–5.

23. Murmis and Portantiero, *Origenes del peronismo,* p. 87; despite their general hostility toward organized labor, the conservative governments of the 1930s did add some minor reforms to Argentina's labor laws, such as guaranteeing the Sunday holiday and incorporating bank employees and the merchant marine into the state-sponsored retirement system.

24. Rotondaro, *Realidad y cambio,* pp. 145, 157–58.

25. Another indicator of public expenditure growth is the difference between the 696 million pesos spent in 1928 and the 1.6 billion spent in 1942, a period in which prices rose by less than 5 percent. See Marcelo Ramón Lascano, *Presupuestos y dinero* (Buenos Aires: EUDEBA, 1972), pp. 92–95.

26. Smith, *Politics and Beef,* p. 138. For several assessments of the political economy of the Concordancia see: Falcoff and Dolkart, eds., *Prelude to Perón.*

Chapter 3

1. See, for example, Luna, *El 45;* Robert Potash, *The Army and Politics in Argentina 1928–1945* (Stanford: Stanford University Press, 1969); George Blanksten, *Peron's Argentina* (Chicago: University of Chicago Press, 1953); and Robert Alexander, *The Peron Era* (New York: Columbia University Press, 1951).

2. Robert Carri, *Sindicatos y poder en la Argentina* (Buenos Aires: Editorial Sudestada, 1967), pp. 28–31. Although there are very few reliable data on union growth between 1943 and 1946, and much debate over whether it was due to the transformation of old unions into new ones or the enlisting of new members, there are a few cases which clearly illustrate the phenomenal increase in membership that resulted from Perón's efforts; for example, the Unión Obrera Metalúrgica of 2,000 members in 1943 was transformed into the Asociación Metalúrgica with 100,000 members in 1945; the Unión Obrera Textil, which claimed 10,000 workers in 1943, became the Asociación Obrera Textil with 85,000 members in 1946.

3. See Luna, *El 45,* for a detailed account.

4. Though there was no single document that contained the full outline of the Peronist strategy in 1945, Alfredo Gómez Morales later published *Política económica peronista* (Buenos Aires: Escuela Superior Peronista, 1951); also see Antonio Cafiero, *Cinco años después* (Buenos Aires: edición del autor, 1961), and Ramón Antonio Cereijo, *Hacía un mayor y mejor conocimiento de la verdadera situación económica argentina* (Buenos Aires: n.p., 1951).

5. On the nationalization of the Central Bank see Decreto-Ley 8,503, Decreto-Ley 11,554, and Decreto-Ley 14,957; on the creation of the Argentine Institute for Trade Promotion see Decreto-Ley 15,344 and Decreto-Ley 15,350, all in 1946.

6. The debt-ridden British were anxious to sell the railways at the war's end but the Argentine government initially balked at the idea, preferring instead a mixed company, which it formed with the British on September 17, 1946. Under the arrangement, the Argentine government agreed to contribute 500 million pesos within five years and guaranteed British stockholders a minimum return of 5 percent, as well as the continuation of their tax-free status, which had been scheduled to end the following year. Soon thereafter, however, British authorities convinced the Argentine government to use the British currency that it had accumulated during the war to purchase the railways outright, and in mid February 1947 the sale was completed, at a cost to Argentina of an estimated 375 million dollars. The International Telephone and Telegraph Company–owned telephone company was also purchased at similar high prices. See: Julio Irazusta, *Perón y la crisis argentina* (Buenos Aires: La Voz del Plata, 1956), pp. 47–54.

7. Interview with Gómez Morales, May 27, 1971.

8. José Alfredo Martínez de Hoz (h), *La agricultura y la ganaderia argentina en el periodo 1930-1966* (Buenos Aires: Editorial Sudamericana, 1967), pp. 48–60.

9. Hugo Gambini, *El primer gobierno peronista* (Buenos Aires: Editor de América Latina, 1971), pp. 77–81.

10. República Argentina, Ministerio de Agricultura y Ganadería, *Arrendamientos y aparcerias rurales: leyes y decretos anteriores a la ley No. 13.246* (Buenos Aires, 1949); *Arrendamientos y aparcerias rurales—ley No. 13.246 y reglamentación general* (Buenos Aires, 1949); and *Arrendamientos rurales y aparcerias (anexo)* (Buenos Aires, 1954).

11. Díaz Alejandro, *Economic History*, pp. 256–62.

12. United Nations, Economic Commission for Latin America, *Economic Development and Income Distribution in Argentina* (New York, 1969), p. 245.

13. Ibid., pp. 246–47.

14. Computed from Organización Techint, *Boletín Informativo no. 188* (octubre-diciembre 1972), Cuadro No. 2, p. 20.

15. See for example, Seymour Martin Lipset, *Political Man: The Social Bases of Politics* (New York: Anchor Books, 1963), Chapter 5; also Blanksten, *Peron's Argentina*, and Alexander, *The Peron Era*. More recently scholars have questioned such simplistic labelling of the Peronist phenomenon and have begun to reformulate descriptions based on a reanalysis of the 1946–55 period. It is my hope that the present study contributes to the effort begun by such scholars as Eldon Kenworthy, "The Function of the Little Known Case in Theory Formation or What Peronism Wasn't," *Comparative Politics* 6 (1973): 17–46.

16. This was especially true of Perón and several of his military colleagues who were associated with the G.O.U. lodge. See: Robert Potash, *Army and Politics*, and Luna, *El 45*.

17. This definition of corporatism is adapted from J. T. Winkler, "Corporatism," *European Journal of Sociology* 17 (1976): 100–136, and Philippe Schmitter, "Still the Century of Corporatism?" *Review of Politics* 36 (1974): 84–131.

18. Figurola, who became one of Perón's closest but least-known advisors between 1943 and 1946, was born in Spain in 1897 and became a nationalized Argentine in 1930. His corporatist views, drawn largely from Spanish political thought and law, were published in his book *La colaboración social en Hispanoamerica* (Buenos Aires: Editorial Sudamericana, 1943).

19. Gambini, *El primer gobierno*, pp. 11–14.

20. *Review of the River Plate*, March 28, 1947, p. 17.

21. Ibid., August 5, 1949, pp. 12–13.

22. *La Prensa*, February 8, 1950, pp. 5–6.

23. This view was expressed by Dr. Gómez Morales in a conversation with the author on May 27, 1971.

24. Cuneo, *Comportamiento y crisis*, pp. 178–79.

25. Ibid., pp. 158–60.

26. Ibid., pp. 184–86.

27. José B. Gelbard, *Las organizaciones empresarias en la evolución argentina* (Buenos Aires: Confederación General Económica, 1971), pp. 21–24.

28. The congress's only accomplishment was the ratification of a government proposal setting very general economic policy objectives. *La Prensa*, March 27, 1955, p. 1 and March 30, 1955, p. 5. Six months after the congress, the Peronist government was overthrown by the *Revolución Libertadora*.

29. On the initial proposal for an agricultural products control board see *Review of the River Plate*, May 11, 1945, pp. 9–10; on the ill-fated margin fund see Ibid., June 1, 1945, pp. 28–29; on the government's rescinding of the program in response to criticism see Ibid., August 3, 1945, p. 13; and on its final application see Ibid., November 23, 1945, pp. 6–7; also see CARBAP, *XXI Congreso Rural, Tandil, noviembre 20–22, 1946*, p. 35.

30. Perón's abandonment of agrarian reform was a bitter disappointment to some of his associates, most notably Antonio Manuel Molinari and Mauricio Birabent, who worked through the Consejo Agrario Nacional, the newly created agrarian reform agency, between 1943 and 1946 to develop an agrarian reform scheme. But with the Consejo's expropriation of two estancias in April and May 1946, just after Perón's election, came increased opposition within his inner circle to agrarian reform, especially from his principal economic advisor, businessman Miguel Miranda. Just before Perón's inauguration, the Consejo Agrario was reduced from its semiautonomous status to a dependency of the Banco de la Nación; soon thereafter Molinari and Birabent resigned. Gambini, *El primer gobierno*, pp. 47–48, 73–77.

31. These measures did have some agrarian reform implications; Peronists and tenant farmers hoped that the added burden of frozen rents, rising costs, maximum prices, and declining profits would encourage landowners to sell plots to the tenants who farmed them. See República Argentina, Ministerio de Agricultura de la Nación, *Arrendamientos y aparcerias rurales: Ley No. 13,246 y reglamentación general*, 1949. On the role of the 33rd Congress of the Federación Agraria and its representatives working through congressional committees to secure this legislation see: FAA, *Los problemas actuales del agro, September 1956*, Part II.

32. Copies of the SRA's petitions to the government can be found in Sociedad Rural Argentina, *Memoria de la Sociedad Rural Argentina 1945–1946* and *Memoria de la Sociedad Rural Argentina 1946–1947*. Also see *Review of the River Plate*, May 30, 1946, p. 6 and April 11, 1947, p. 6. For Palermo speeches see *Review of the River Plate*, August 22, 1947, pp. 16–18 and August 20, 1948, pp. 18–22.

33. See *Review of the River Plate*, September 30, 1952, pp. 3–5.

34. United Nations, Economic Commission for Latin America, *Economic Bulletin for Latin America*, Vol. 1, no. 1 (January 1956), Tables 7 and 10. Corn also declined 30 percent in 1949, 113 percent in 1950, and then rose by 108.9 percent in 1951 and 15 percent in 1952.

35. Edward L. Chambers, "Some Factors in the Deterioration of Argentina's External Position 1946–1951," *Inter-American Economic Affairs* 8 (1954):29.

36. The cost-of-living index rose by 13 percent in 1948 and 32.7 percent in 1949; Centro Internacional de Información Econónmica, *La economia argentina: treinta años en cifras* (Buenos Aires: CIDIE, 1971), p. 12.

37. República Argentina, Consejo Económico Nacional, *Situación económico financiera del pais: examen de la situación económica del país al 31 enero de 1949*, pp. 1–20.

38. *Review of the River Plate,* May 6, 1949, pp. 3–4.

39. See República Argentina, Banco Central de la República Argentina, *Memoria 1948.*

40. See *Review of the River Plate,* February 17, 1949, pp. 4–5, April 18, 1950, pp. 6–8.

41. República Argentina, Consejo Económico Nacional, *El panorama económico del país en el segundo semestre de 1951 y perspectivas para 1952,* (junio 1951), pp. 1–33; and *Situación económica actual y perspectivas para 1952* (noviembre 1951), pp. 1–18. In these two confidential reports, Perón's economists placed most of the blame for the country's deteriorating payments situation and the failure of the measures adopted in 1949 on two unanticipated conditions: the rising cost of Argentina's imports due to the Korean War and the decline in rural production as a result of the drought. They went on to conclude that domestic austerity in both public and private consumption was absolutely necessary if the country was to survive the crisis. Needless to say, these very realistic assessments by the government economists stood out in marked contrast to the official rhetoric of the government up to Perón's February speech.

42. A copy of the speech can be found in *El Economista,* February 23, 1952, p. 3. For a more detailed summary of the policy measures proposed see the Peronist journal *Hechos e Ideas,* nos. 98–105 (May–December, 1952).

43. Centro Internacional de Información Económica, *La economia argentina,* pp. 5, 12, 54.

44. These conditions are described in some detail in United Nations Economic Commission for Latin America, *Economic Bulletin for Latin America,* vol. 1, no. 1 (1956), p. 26.

Chapter 4

1. Hirschman, *Journeys Toward Progress* and "Policymaking and Policy Analysis," pp. 385–402.

2. Rogelio Frigerio, a prolific writer and propagandist, has presented this development strategy in several works, the most notable of which are: *Las condiciones de la victoria* (Buenos Aires: Monteverde, 1959); *Crecimiento económico y democracia* (Buenos Aires: Losada, 1963); and *Estatuto del subdesarrollo* (Buenos Aires: Editorial Jorge Alvarez, 1967).

3. The confidential IMF report is summarized in *Economic Survey,* September 30, 1958, p. 8.

4. On the very controversial electoral alliance between Perón and Frondizi in 1958, which haunted the latter throughout his presidency, see Ramón Prieto, *El Pacto: ocho años de la política argentina* (Buenos Aires: Editorial En Marcha, 1963).

5. The December 29 speech is available in Arturo Frondizi, *Política económica nacional* (Buenos Aires: Ediciones Arayu, 1963), pp. 127–48.

6. The crisis, which was precipitated by military opposition to "Peronist influence" within Frondizi's government, as represented especially by the presence of Rogelio Frigerio, lasted from mid May until late June. Under the constant threat of a military coup, Frondizi first secured Frigerio's resignation and then turned his economic program over to Alvaro Alsogaray who demanded and received the right to appoint his own economic team as well as personal control over both the ministry of economy and the ministry of labor and social welfare. In return, Frondizi gained the forbearance, if not the support, of the military.

7. Organización Techint, *Boletín Informativo no. 170* (marzo-abril 1969), Cuadro no. 11 and Cuadro no. 20.

8. Ley No. 14,733/58.

9. The hearings are reproduced in Rogelio Frigerio, *Petroleo* (Buenos Aires: Editorial Desarrollo, 1964).

10. Organización Techint, *Boletín Informativo no. 173* (setiembre-octubre 1969), p. 29.

11. Martínez de Hoz (h), *Agricultura y ganadería*, pp. 85–90.

12. See *La Prensa*, November 12, 1956, p. 1; and Carlos R. Melo, *Los partidos políticos argentinos* (Córdoba: Universidad Nacional de Córdoba, 1964), pp. 76–98.

13. *Review of the River Plate*, July 10, 1959, pp. 11–12.

14. Ibid., April 29, 1961, p. 5. After concluding the toughest phase of stabilization, Frondizi decided to pave the way for the 1962 electoral campaign and his own political resurgence by replacing Alsogaray with Roberto Alemann in April 1961.

15. Rotondaro, *Realidad y cambio*, pp. 287–88.

16. Confederación General Económica, *Memoria y Balance 1970*, Cuadros 4–7; and Unión Industrial Argentina, *Guia de socios, 1970*, p. 4.

17. Because each of ACIEL's constituent organizations continued their influence efforts separately, this new organization concentrated most of its resources on publicity campaigns attacking elements of government policy which threatened "free enterprise." *Review of the River Plate*, June 10, 1958, p. 18 and June 30, 1958, p. 13.

18. "Debate sobre el plan de estabilización y desarrollo económico" Camara de Diputados, 34ª a 38ª reuniones, 12ª sesion ordinaria, 13 a 18 agosto de 1959, pp. 2050–506.

19. Carri, *Sindicatos*, p. 93; and Rotondaro, *Realidad y cambio*, p. 288. The *Plan Conintes* was a brief but concerted effort on the part of the national police and the military to break the will of labor unions to protest by jailing and harassing their leaders as well as some of the rank and file.

20. Santiago Senen González, *El sindicalismo después de Perón* (Buenos Aires: Editorial Galerna, 1971), Documento No. 3A, pp. 28-30. This "Declaration of Principles" also included for the first time a CGT demand for land reform measures directed at breaking up large holdings by giving land to those who worked it.

21. Ibid., p. 24.

22. Rotondaro, *Realidad y cambio*, p. 290.

23. Organización Techint, *Boletín Informativo no. 188*, and Centro de Información Economica, *La economía argentina*, p. 12.

24. UIA, *Memoria y Balance* 1958, p. 24.

25. CGE, *Memoria y Balance* 1960, p. 13.

26. Centro Internacional de Información Económica, *Boletin no. 188*, p. 54.

27. Lascano, *Presupuestos*, p. 189.

28. Díaz Alejandro, *Exchange Rate Devaluation*, p. 188.

29. See, for example, Clarence Zuvekas, "Argentine Economic Policy 1958–1962: The Frondizi Government's Development Plan," *Inter-American Economic Affairs* 22(1968): 45–74.

30. Martínez de Hoz (h), *Agricultura y ganaderia*, pp. 91–96.

31. See CARBAP, *Memoria y Balance* 1959–1960, p. 17.

32. Martinez de Hoz (h), *Agricultura y ganaderia*, pp. 96–102; on January 12, 1960, the Rural Society issued a declaration in which it claimed that "it is impossible to sit by with indifference as the economic situation deteriorates nor hide the alarm of the rural sector upon discovering that the effort put forth over the last two years has proved fruitless." SRA, *Memoria de la Sociedad Rural Argentina 1960–1961*, p. 25.

Chapter 5

1. For the hostile reactions of the nation's conservative financial press to Illia's unexpected victory and the policy indecision that followed, see *Review of the River Plate*, *Analisis*, *Economic Survey*, and *El Economista* during the last half of 1963.

2. The disastrous economic events of 1962 are summarized in Consejo Técnico de Inversiones, S.A., *La economía argentina—1962* (Buenos Aires, 1963).

3. This debate is discussed in Banco de Boston, *The Situation in Argentina—Supplement,* March 30, 1964, pp. 1–2.

4. Commentaries on the economic policy assumptions that guided the design of intital UCRP policies can be found in such publications as *Analisis* and *Economic Survey* between August and December 1963.

5. Consejo Técnico de Inversiones, S.A., *La economía argentina—1964* (Buenos Aires, 1965). Minister of Economy Eugenio Blanco died in August 1964 and was replaced by Radical party lawyer Juan Carlos Pugliese, who served in that post until the Illia government fell in June 1966.

6. On the Radical party see Gabriel de Mazo, *El radicalismo: notas sobre su historia y doctrina* (Buenos Aires: n.p., 1955), and *El radicalismo: el movimiento de intransigencia y renovación* (Buenos Aires: n.p., 1957); also Peter Snow, *Argentine Radicalism: The History and Doctrine of the Radical Civic Union* (Iowa City: University of Iowa Press, 1965). One critic of the Radical party described the costs of its partisan style well when he wrote: "The Radicals—democratic and genuinely concerned for individual freedoms and justice, but encased in a bureaucratic structure and addicted to petty fogging legalism—could have been at home in nineteenth century Italy. Their principal weakness is an inability to change with the times." Clive Peterson in the *Buenos Aires Herald,* July 27, 1973, p. 15.

7. *Review of the River Plate,* November 30, 1965, pp. 333–37.

8. See *Economic Survey, Review of the River Plate,* and *Analisis* for January through June 1964.

9. Illia is quoted to this effect in *Review of the River Plate,* Februrary 6, 1965, p. 167.

10. SRA, *Memoria de la Sociedad Rural Argentina 1964–1965,* pp. 55–63, and CARBAP, *Memoria y Balance 1964–1965,* pp. 13–27. Both groups accused the government of sacrificing "sound" economic development to its partisan economic philosophy.

11. These included: Ley No. 16,455/63; Ley No. 16/655/64; Leyes 16,676, 16,735, and 16,864 of 1965.

12. SRA, *Memoria de la Sociedad Rural Argentina, 1963–1964,* pp. 26–33, and *Memoria de la Sociedad Rural Argentina, 1964–1965,* pp. 47–70. In particular the SRA denounced the government's creation of price controls on consumer goods, its land tax proposal, its minimum wage bill, exchange controls, and expansion of the budget deficit.

13. On the beef crisis see Banco de Boston, *The Situation in Argentina,* June 29, 1964, p. 2; and on the reaction of cattlemen to the government's measures see CARBAP, *Memoria y Balance 1964–1965,* pp. 3–14, and SRA, *Memoria . . . 1963–1964,* p. 40.

14. In its review of the past two decades at its 1973 convention, the CGE even went so far as to claim that Illia's presidency had been "the most progressive of all postwar governments;" see quote in monthly newsletter *Interpretación,* vol. 1, no. 11, septiembre 1973, p. 2.

15. The UIA testified vigorously but unsuccessfully against it; see UIA, *Memoria y Balance 1964–1965,* pp. 23–48.

16. UIA, *Memoria y Balance 1965–1966,* p. 24.

17. A copy of the *Plan de Lucha,* which called for, among other things, an end to the persecution of labor leaders, the release of political prisoners, wage levels that reflected the rising cost of living, price controls, the annulment of Frondizi's contracts with foreign petroleum companies, and worker participation in the management of all enterprises, can be found in Senen Gonzales, *El sindicalismo,* Documento No. 6, pp. 52–57.

18. Ibid., pp. 63–65.

19. Banco Interamericano de Desarrollo y Deltec Panamericana, S.A., *El mercado de capitales en Argentina* (Mexico: CEMLA, 1968), Chapters 3–6.

20. Banco de Boston, *The Situation in Argentina*, May 31, 1965, p. 1, and August 31, 1965, p. 1.

21. Consejo Técnico de Inversiones, S.A., *La economía argentina 1966*, pp. 55, 295. The state deficit grew from 71.2 billion pesos in 1963 to 168.3 billion pesos in 1964, and state enterprises, the principal consumer being the railways, accounted for 46 percent of the total deficit.

22. *Review of the River Plate*, June 11, 1966, p. 365; also see British journal *The Economist*, September 25, 1965, p. xii, in which the magazine's correspondent concluded from conversations with financial and business leaders that both expected the military to intervene and overthrow the Illia government sometime in 1966 and establish a government of technocrats similar to that created by the military in Brazil in 1964.

23. Reglamento 969 de la Ley de Asociaciones Profesionales; in an effort to placate some of its industrialist and military critics as well as to weaken the Peronist labor movement that had defeated it in the March 1965 congressional elections, the government ended the requirement that there be only one union in each industry, thereby permitting the kind of competition for local control that the Peronists had long opposed. It is also significant that at the end of May 1966 Illia vetoed a bill strongly supported by the CGT which provided increased compensation for workers dismissed from their jobs; the CGT, though divided at the time, managed to pull off a twenty-four-hour general strike to protest the veto on June 7, 1966, an action which could not help but encourage the military officers who at the time were contemplating the coup they carried out three weeks later.

24. Consejo Técnico de Inversiones . . . *1966*, p. 295.

Chapter 6

1. While many agrarian and financial leaders expressed this point of view, its most articulate and prolific defender was Federico Pinedo, the former Treasury minister who had served Concordancia governments in the 1930s. See his *En tiempos de la república* and *Trabajoso resurgimiento argentino*, 2 vols. (Buenos Aires: Ediciones Fundación Banco de Galicia y Buenos Aires, 1968).

2. Summaries of this neoclassical approach to inflation are in Carlos García Martínez, *La inflación argentina* (Buenos Aires: Editorial Guillermo Kraft, 1965); and Alvaro Alsogaray, *Política y economía en Latinoamerica* (Buenos Aires: Editorial Atlantido, 1969) and *Bases para la acción política futura* (Buenos Aires: Editorial Atlantida, 1968).

3. The preliminary and final Prebisch reports are printed in *Review of the River Plate*, October 31, 1955, pp. 2–35; November 11, 1955, pp. 19–30; and January 20, 1956, pp. 18–47. For Prebisch's personal defense of the measures he proposed see Agrupación Reformista de Graduados en Ciencias Económicas, *Mesa redonda del informe Prebisch* (versión taquigráfica), 19 de diciembre de 1955, pp. 5–29 (hereafter *Mesa Redonda*).

4. United Nations, Economic Commission for Latin America, *Economic Bulletin for Latin America*, Vol. I. no. 1 (1956), p. 26 (hereafter ECLA *Bulletin*).

5. From an estimated 1,682 million in 1946. Banco de Boston, *The Situation in Argentina, October 31, 1955*, p. 1.

6. As, for example, in his famous pamphlet, *The Economic Development of Latin America and Its Principal Problems* (United Nations, 1950).

7. As he stated in *Mesa redonda* pp. 6–7. "I have referred in my report to the necessity of dismantling an absurd system of state intervention, but I do not in any way recommend a return to past formulas. I have sustained for some time that the rapid

economic development of Latin American countries requires a deliberate government effort. I cannot accept the assumption that the free market alone will solve the problem of economic growth faced by our countries." (translation mine)

8. Junta Nacional de Granos—Decreto-Ley 19.697/56; Junta Nacional de Carnes—Decreto-Ley 8509/56; also the Corporación Argentina de Productores de Carne (CAP), the producers' cooperative, was returned to joint public-private control by Decreto-Ley 7227/56.

9. Central Bank—Decreto-Ley 14,570/56. The decree also included the return of all bank deposits to the private banks.

10. One of Prebisch's most outspoken neoclassical critics was former Treasury minister Federico Pinedo; see, for example, *Review of the River Plate*, July 20, 1956, pp. 11–13, and September 29, 1956, p. 11.

11. ECLA *Bulletin*, pp. 35–38.

12. *Review of the River Plate*, December 30, 1955, pp. 5–7 and May 10, 1957, p. 16. Actually the government used several decree laws to impose the price controls it had temporarily removed in late December 1955. It continually revised its lists of controlled items and maximum prices during 1956 and 1957.

13. ECLA *Bulletin*, pp. 41–43.

14. *Review of the River Plate*, October 11, 1955, p. 13, and October 31, 1955, p. 18.

15. *Review of the River Plate*, January 10, 1956, p. 15.

16. On the Council's ratification of economic policy during the first half of 1956 see República Argentina, *Dictamen de la Comisión Asesora Honararia de Economia y Finanzas sobre el "Plan de Restablecimiento Economico,"* febrero de 1956; *Dictamen de la Comisión Asesora Honoraria de Economia y Finanzas sobre Control de Precios*, 28 de junio de 1956.

17. Before freezing wages in early 1956, Aramburu decreed a 10-percent, across-the-board increase, see decreto 2739/56. On the office holding prohibition, see decreto 7101/56.

18. On the abortive August 1957 CGT convention see Rotondaro, *Realidad y cambio*, p. 286. Also Rubén Zorrilla, *Estructura y dinámica del sindicalismo argentino* (Buenos Aires: La Pleyade, 1974), pp. 72–73.

19. According to one estimate, 281 labor contracts were signed during 1956 and 1957 despite the ban. Aramburu's failure to enforce his wage freeze convinced many industrial and rural sector leaders, erroneously it would appear, that he had sacrificed his hardline redistributive program to the working-class wolves. Carri, *Sindicatos*, p. 71.

20. See, for example, SRA, *Memoria de la Sociedad Rural Argentina 1957–1958*, pp. 21–22; CARBAP, *Memoria y Balance 1959–1960*, p. 17; and FAA, *Conclusiones del 55 Congreso Ordinario Anual 1967*, p. 10.

21. Decreto 2,187/57.

22. FAA, *Conclusiones del 54 Congreso ordinario anual 1966*, p. 9.

23. *Review of the River Plate* May 22, 1956, p. 15.

24. They also complained that the rural sector was inadequately represented on the governing boards of the Central Bank and the National Bank, the latter being the principal government lender to rural producers; see CARBAP, *Memoria. . . . 1956-1957*, pp. 40–42.

25. UIA, *Memoria y Balance 1958*, p. 15.

26. *El Economista*, February 2, 1957, p. 1; also *Review of the River Plate*, January 29, 1957, p. 5.

27. Verrier's ill-fated ministry is chronicled in: *El Economista*, Februrary 9, 1957, p. 1; March 2, 1957, p. 1; March 16, 1957, p. 1; March 30, 1957, p. 1. In an interview with the author on July 22, 1971, Verrier claimed that he was summoned to the government by Aramburu in early 1957 after deteriorating economic conditions, caused in part by the

rising cost of oil imports due to the Suez crisis, had convinced the president that austerity measures were required. Aramburu's views were not shared by many of his military colleagues, however, and he was forced to withdraw his support for Verrier's program when it leaked out. His military opponents, Verrier argued, feared labor discontent as a result of his measures and were unwilling to follow any economic policy that would undermine their holding peaceful elections in early 1958.

Chapter 7

1. On the conditions that led to the coup see O'Donnell, *Modernization*, Chapters 2-3; and "Reflexiones sobre las tendencias generales de cambio en el estado burocrático-autoritario," (Buenos Aires: Centro de Estudios de Estado y Sociedad, 1975).

2. Krieger Vasena's recognition of these problems is evidenced in his speech of March 13, 1967, announcing his economic program; see República Argentina, Ministerio de Economía y Trabajo, *Política económica argentina: discursos del Ministro de Economía y Trabajo,* febrero 1967–enero 1968, pp. 23–36.

3. Krieger Vasena's use of postwar European, as well as Brazilian and Mexican, economic programs as guides to his own effort is discussed in an article he wrote for the magazine *Progreso,* and reprinted in the Argentine financial newsletter *Economic Survey,* September 22, 1970, pp. 17–20.

4. See speech cited in note 2 *supra.* Also see Juan Carlos de Pablo, *Política anti-inflacionaria en la Argentina 1967–1970* (Buenos Aires: Amorrortu Editores, 1971), pp. 23–97.

5. Decreto-Ley 17,224/67.

6. Public opinion polls as well as a perusal of economic group publications indicate widespread support for the new government, though this can be interpreted as pleasure at the fall of the Radicals and expectations of new advantages under the military rather than hard support for the new government and its very amorphous program. See Carlos S. Fayt, *El político armado: dinámica del proceso político argentino 1960-1971* (Buenos Aires: Ediciones Pannedille, 1971), pp. 39 and 167-168; also O'Donnell, *Modernization,* pp. 115–16, and Rotondaro, *Realidad y cambio,* pp. 318—19.

7. The so-called revolutionary acts included the *Acta de la Revolucion Argentina* and three annexes: 1) *Mensaje de la Junta Revolucionaria al Pueblo Argentina;* 2) *Estatuto de la Revolución Argentina;* and 3) *Objectivos Políticos (Fines de la Revolución).* The acts justified the coup as necessary to put an end to the bad management of the public sector, the division, synicism and apathy of the Argentine people, and Marxist penetration of all areas of Argentine life. The Estatuto allocated to a president, to be chosen by the junta, all powers that were previously exercised by the Congress.

8. *Review of the River Plate,* September 12, 1966, pp. 387-393.

9. Fayt, *El político armado,* p. 157.

10. Though Onganía made no reference to particular theorists, his stage theory view of development, whose assumptions went far beyond Rostow's, was apparent in most of his speeches on Argentina's future and his proposals for shaping it.

11. See O'Donnell, "Reflexiones," p. 26.

12. While Krieger's so-called liberal views were well known, Borda's "corportist" prescriptions did not receive much attention until a speech he made on April 24, 1968, to the Foreign Press Association in which he attacked liberalism as the cause of the country's divisions and conflicts and offered a view of the "sociedad organizada, que se opone a la idea individualista," to replace it.

13. O'Donnell, "Reflexiones," cuadro II.

14. UIA, *Memoria . . . 1966–1967,* p. 30 and *Memoria y Balance 1967–1968,* p. 27.

15. UIA, *Memoria . . . 1966–1967*, p. 32.

16. CGE, *Memoria y Balance 1969*, pp. 10–56.

17. Ley No. 20,557/74 "Radicaciones de capitales extranajeros."

18. Ley 18.003/68.

19. SRA, *Memoria de la Sociedad Rural Argentina 1968–1969*, pp. 14, 55; CARBAP, *Memoria y Balance 1968–1969*, pp. 11 p. 11–20; and FAA, *Memoria y Balance 1968–1969*, p. 11. Also see Nidia, Margenat, *Las organizaciones corporativas del sector agrario y su posición frente a la renta potencial* (Buenos Aires: Centro de Investigaciones en Ciencias Sociales, 1973), pp. 9–29.

20. CARBAP, *Memoria . . . 1968–1969*, pp. 11–17.

21. Ley 17,253/67 was also known as the "Ley Raggio" after the Secretary of Agriculture Lorenzo Raggio, a representative of the more production-oriented large cattlemen, who was responsible for its design.

22. Until the new Peronist government halted expulsions under Ley 17,253/67 in early 1973, the Federación Agraria never ceased complaining of it; see, for example, FAA, *Memoria y Balance 1967–1968*, pp. 9–10 and *Memoria y Balance 1971–1972*, p. 23.

23. Total public revenues as a percentage of the GNP increased from 15.4 percent in 1966 to 17.2 percent in 1968, and revenues as a percentage of total public expenditures rose from 80.8 percent in 1966 to 94.8 percent in 1968; see United States Agency for International Development, *Summary of Economic and Social Indicators*, June 1972, pp. 25–28.

24. In a remarkable aboutface from the Illia years, he easily placed $50 million in bonds on the German market, $25 million in the United States, $25 million in the Eurodollar market and $71 million domestically; see *Review of the River Plate*, April 11, 1969, p. 485 and April 29, 1969, p. 609.

25. After criticizing the fallen Illia government because it had contributed to "chaotic economic, social and political conditions as well as a decline in authority and representation," the CGT statement of June 29, 1966 expressed the organization's concern for the deteriorating economic condition of the country, its opposition to the repressive labor laws enacted during the last year of the Illia administration, and its hope that the new government would resolve all of these matters in labor's favor; Senen González, *El sindicalismo*, Documento No. 15, pp. 95–98.

26. Rotondaro, *Realidad y cambio*, pp. 325–29, and Carri, *Sindicatos*, pp. 162–64.

27. Before the convention the three competing factions were: those favoring collaboration with the government who were led by Rogelio Coria of the construction workers and called "la nueva corriente de opinion," those who were willing to accept an informal dialogue with public authorities, known as the "62 Organizaciones" and led by Augusto Vandor of the metalurgical workers, and those, most of whose unions had been intervened the year before, who favored total opposition to the government and called themselves "62 Organizaciones a pie" under the leadership of Raimundo Ongaro.

28. The victorious Ongaro faction called itself CGT Paseo Colon after the 1968 convention, while the vanquished, after walking out of the convention, organized themselves under the leadership of Vandor, calling themselves the CGT Azopardo thereafter. This split continued to divide the CGT until mid 1970. Vandor, however, did not live to see the reunification as he was assassinated in June 1969.

29. On the emergence of the Córdoba unions and their marginalization from the CGT see Zorrilla, *Estructura y dinámica*, pp. 116–21; and Daniel Villar, *El Cordobazo* (Buenos Aires: La Historia Popular, 1971), pp. 32–36.

30. When asked in a June 1971 interview in Buenos Aires what would have happened in Brazil had there been an uprising similar to Argentina's Cordobazo, Roberto de Oliveira Campos, one of the principal authors of the Brazilian "economic miricle," admitted that "an episode like that would have ruined everything." *Pulso*, 22 a 28 de

junio 1971, p. 20. On the Brazilian patrimonial state see Riordon Roett, *Brazil: Politics in a Patrimonial Society* (Boston: Allyn-Bacon, 1972); and Philippe Schmitter, *Interest Conflict and Political Change in Brazil* (Stanford: Stanford University Press, 1971).

31. See *La Nación*, June 9, 10, 11, 1970. In a statement justifying Onganía's removal, Navy Chief Admiral Pedro Gnavi praised Onganía for cutting inflation, but criticized his hardline wage policy and refusal to come up with a plan for the restoration of civilian rule.

32. The Ferrer program is described in Mariano Grondona, "El actual plan economico," *Mercado*, 5 de noviembre de 1970, pp. 13-14.

33. Juan Carlos de Pablo, "Politica anti-inflationaria, en perspectiva," unpublished paper, Buenos Aires, 1973.

34. Like Onganía, Levingston had also made the mistake of firing Lanusse as chief of staff just prior to the latter's coup.

35. This division is described in O'Donnell, "Reflexiones," pp. 37-38.

36. De Pablo, "La politica," p. 3.

37. *La Nación*, December 4, 1971, p. 1.

38. Lester A. Sobel, ed., *Argentina and Perón 1970–1975* (New York: Facts on File, Inc., 1975), p. 62.

39. For example, the UIA and CGE both objected to the representation of the public sector in the council and then disagreed among themselves over whether the representation of industrial interests should be determined by the number of firms (which would favor the CGE) or their economic importance (favoring the UIA). See *El Economista*, September 10, 1971, p. 10; *El Cronista Comercial*, September 13, 1971, and September 14, 1971; also *La Razón*, April 12, 1972, for a discussion of Ley 19.569, creating the council.

40. República Argentina, Comisión para el Estudio de la Reforma Institucional, *Dictamines y antecedentes*, Buenos Aires, 1971.

41. In fairness to Lanusse it should be pointed out that several pre-election polls also predicted only a 35 to 40% vote for Cámpora in the first round balloting. Most of the polls, however, were taken in the area of the Federal Capital, and even though their predictions proved correct for those districts, they could not predict the much higher vote for the Peronists in the provinces. See *Review of the River Plate*, March 21, 1973, p. 377.

Chapter 8

1. Computed from Organización Techint, *Boletín Informativo no. 188* (octubre-diciembre 1972), cuadro, 2, p. 20.

2. United States Department of Agriculture, *Argentina: Growth Potential of the Grain and Livestock Sectors.* (Washington, D.C., 1972), p. 2 (herafter USDA, *Argentina*).

3. Cited in *Buenos Aires Herald*, August 5, 1973, p. 10.

4. USDA, *Argentina*, p. 39.

5. Inter-American Committee for Agricultural Development, *Land Tenure Conditions and Socio-Economic Development of the Agricultural Sector: Argentina* (Washington: Pan American Union, 1965), p. 42 (hereafter IACAD, *Land Tenure*).

6. USDA, *Argentina*, pp. 42–44.

7. See Chapter 2 for a discussion of the "beef cycle."

8. USDA, *Argentina*, p. 68; in 1965 pesos beef prices fluctuated around a mean of 27 pesos per kilo between 1945 and 1958 and a mean of 42 pesos between 1959 and 1970, after which they rose again by about 100 percent.

9. One recent study indicates that the government's tax policies during the 1960s

actually increased the adverse effects of the beef cycle. See: Lic. Stella M. MacDonell and Dr. Marcelo R. Lascano, "Incentivos tributarios y ciclo ganadero 1962–1972," Banco Ganadero, *La producción rural Argentina en 1974*, Buenos Aires, 1975, pp. 65–74.

10. An unexpected consequence of the wildly fluctuating beef prices associated with the beef cycle that was most pleasing to Argentine nationalists was the bankruptcy of several of the once despised foreign meat packers; the latter's share of the export beef trade fell from 49 percent in 1967 to only 21 percent in 1971 as many small but more modern and efficient Argentine packing firms rose to replace them; for details see Cámara de Frigorífico Regionales, *Evolución económico-financiera de la industria frigorífica* (Buenos Aires, 1972).

11. Several regression analyses of the price-production relationship are reviewed in USDA, *Argentina*, pp. 61–62.

12. Ibid., Table 5, p. 11.

13. IACAD, *Land Tenure*, p. 67.

14. Ibid., p. 37.

15. For the first time since the early 1950s all rural groups came together in a mass meeting on November 17, 1970, to protest the persistent neglect of the rural sector by public authorities. In particular, they claimed that since 1955 profits had been wiped out by rising farm costs, and they criticized the state's absorption of one-third of the country's GNP, the excessive centralization of economic policy making, and dual exchange rates that discriminated against the rural producer. As remedies they demanded more producer representatives on the meat and grain boards, the elimination of retentions and export taxes, and the elimination of state interference in the domestic beef market. *La Nación*, November 18, 1970, p. 16.

16. A campaign against foreign investors and their takeovers of Argentine firms was waged by the CGT and CGE throughout 1971, 1972, and 1973. This upsurge of antiforeignism coincided with the growing popularity of "dependency theory" among Argentine intellectuals and yielded significant new research into foreign economic penetration of Argentina; see, for example, Guillermo O'Donnell and Delfina Linck, *Dependencia y autonomia* (Buenos Aires: Amorrortu Editores, 1973); and Jorge Abot, et al., *El poder económico en la Argentina* (Buenos Aires: Centro de Investigaciones en Ciencias Sociales, 1974).

17. International Bank for Reconstruction and Development, *Private Foreign Direct Investment in Developing Countries*, Bank Staff Working Paper No. 14, April 19, 1973, Table No. 6. For more details on United States private capital in Argentina see Fundación de Investigaciones Económicas Latinoamericanas, *Las inversiones extranjeras en la Argentina* (Buenos Aires: FIEL, 1974), Chapter 4.

18. These state enterprises were, by rank: 1) Yacimientos Petroleros Fiscales (oil); 3) Segba (electricity); 4) Somisa (iron and steel); 6) Ferrocarriles Argentinas (railway); 7) Entel (telephone); 10) Corporación Argentina de Productores de Carne (meat products); 14) Aerolineas Argentinas (airline); 17) Agua y Energía (water and electricity); 19) ELMA (maritime transport); *Mercado*, August 2, 1973, pp. 96–97; also see Salvador Treber, *La empresa estatal argentina* (Buenos Aires: Ediciones Macchi, 1969).

19. Pedro R. Skupch, *Concentración industrial en la Argentina 1956–1966* (Buenos Aires: Editorial El Coloquio, 1972), pp. 15–21. According to another recent study, the sales of the top 92 private industrial firms accounted for 23.81 percent of the country's total manufacturing product in 1970; of this it is estimated that two thirds came from 54 foreign firms and their subsidiaries and only one fourth from nationally owned firms. Cited in O'Donnell and Linck, *Dependencia*, pp. 117–18.

20. The nine foreign firms were by rank: 2) Fiat; 5) Shell; 8)Ford; 9) Esso; 13) General Motors; 15) Kaiser-Renault; 16) Swift; 18) Nobleza; and 20) Chrysler. *Mercado*, August 2, 1973, pp. 96–97.

21. Lorenzo Juan Sigaut, *Acerca de la distribución y niveles de ingreso en la argentina 1950–1972* (Buenos Aires: Ediciones Macchi, 1972), p. 34, cuadro 8 y p. 57, cuadro 16. These estimates are slightly higher than those made by the United Nations and cited in Chapter 6.

22. United Nations, Economic Commission for Latin America, *Economic Development and Income Distribution in Argentina* (New York, 1969), pp. 256–264.

23. For an excellent survey of the administration of postwar incomes policies in Europe see Lloyd Ulman and Robert J. Flanagan, *Wage Restraint: A Study of Incomes Polices in Western Europe* (Berkeley: University of California Press, 1971).

24. Ibid., pp. 222–25.

25. Ibid., p. 218.

26. For a copy of the Social Contract see *Review of the River Plate*, June 19, 1973.

27. *La Opinión*, September 9, 1973, p. 16. The hostility of CARBAP to the agreement stemmed from its opposition to the government's land tax reform proposal and its continued resentment of the fact that it had been the only rural group deprived of its legal status during the first Peronist administration. See *La Opinión*, August 19, 1973, p. 13.

28. Among the bills proposed by the Social Contract were: 1) Land tax reforms; 2) Increased penalties for tax avoidance; 3) Nationalization of the grain and beef export trade; 4) Nationalization of bank deposits; 5) Tighter controls over foreign investment; 6) Public housing; and 7) The creation of a holding corporation for state industries. FREJULI held 146 of 243 Chamber seats and 44 of 69 Senate seats in 1973. The Radicals, in contrast, had only 51 seats in the Chamber and 12 in the Senate.

29. On the background to this new alliance see Mariano Grondona, "La crisis de ACIEL," *Mercado*, December 13, 1970, pp. 13–14.

30. See Mariano Grondona, "La ideologia rural," *Mercado*, November 26, 1970, pp. 13–14.

31. International Monetary Fund, *International Financial Statistics*, December 1974, p. 46.

32. *Review of the River Plate*, May 31, 1974, p. 741.

33. Ibid., July 12, 1974, p. 50.

34. Inter-American Development Bank, *Latin America in the World Economy* (Washington, 1975), p. 41.

35. *Review of the River Plate*, January 11, 1974, p. 16.

36. Clive Peterson in the *Buenos Aires Herald*, July 27, 1973, p. 11.

37. José López Rega was one of the most bizarre characters in a cast that already included the unusual. A minor police official during the first Peronist regime, he later offered his services to the exiled president and became his personal secretary during his last years in Spain. Though he occupied the post of secretary of welfare, he was a close personal advisor to Perón and his wife during and after their return to Argentina and was relied upon heavily by the latter after her husband's death. He received much attention in the foreign press for his devotion to astrology and the occult, but it was his ruthless struggle for power within the Peronist movement that concerned Argentines. Though he had no coherent political philosophy, his personal ties to conservative bourgeois elements within the Peronist movement led him to attack the more leftist and moderate sectors of the movement in an attempt to build a conservative autocracy of his own.

38. *La Opinión*, December 20, 1975, p. 24.

39. An excellent summary of the confrontation can be found in *Review of the River Plate*, July 22, 1975, pp. 88–90.

40. *La Opinión*, January 11, 1976, p. 13.

41. A study done by the Argentine National Statistics and Census Institute maintained that one hour of labor by the average worker, which would have purchased 9 kilograms

of flour in December 1974, would purchase only 5 kilograms in December 1975. Similarly, 4 kilograms of potatoes became 1.8 kilograms; 1 kilogram of pasta dropped to 0.8 kilos; 1.2 kilograms of beef to 0.9 kilograms; and 5 liters of milk to 4 liters. See *La Opinión*, January 10, 1976, p. 9.

42. On the obstacles to collecting accurate data on wage differentials among professions see *La Opinión*, October 24, 1975, p. 14. The regulation of salaries was made difficult during the last half of 1975 by wide wage differences among unions, which fostered a "catch up" psychology among union leaders.

43. On growing rural discontent see *Review of the River Plate*, July 22, 1975, p. 91, and August 21, 1975, p. 267.

44. Martínez de Hoz was initially assisted by Guillermo Walter Klein who served as director of the national planning office and Alberto Fraquio, secretary of foreign trade, both of whom had served on Krieger Vasena's economic team in 1967 and 1968. He also appointed Marío Cárdenas Madariago, a leader in the Rural Society, as minister of agriculture.

45. *Latin America Economic Report*, July 23, 1976, p. 113.

46. Ibid., June 17, 1977, p. 89. In the new law's measures
    A) Banks were freed to set their own interest rates;
    B) Credit cooperatives and savings and loan associations were prohibited from taking sight and term deposits;
    C) Fringe mortgage banks were restricted to the provision of home loans and thereby prohibited from financing the purchase of automobiles.

47. Ibid., March 11, 1977, p. 39.

48. Ibid., October 14, 1977, p. 169.

49. *Latin America Political Report* January 28, 1977, p. 25, and February 18, 1977, p. 52.

50. *Latin America Economic Report*, July 22, 1977, p. 111.

Chapter 9

1. On competitive pluralism and its manifestations in Latin America see Charles W. Anderson, *Politics and Economic Change in Latin America: The Governing of Restless Nations* (New York: D. Van Nostrand, 1967), and Hirschman, *Journeys Toward Progress*.

2. Contemporary and historical examples of Latin American corporatism are described in James M. Malloy, ed. *Authoritarianism and Corporatism in Latin America* (Pittsburgh: University of Pittsburgh Press, 1977), and Frederick Pike and Thomas Stritch, eds. *The New Corporatism* (Notre Dame: University of Notre Dame Press, 1974).

3. On the Brazilian patrimonial state and its adaptation during the rise of industrialization see Roett, *Brazil;* Schmitter, *Interest Conflict;* and Kenneth Paul Erickson, *The Brazilian Corporative State and Working Class Politics* (Berkeley: University of California Press, 1977).

4. See Anatol Rapoport, *N-Persons Game Theory: Concepts and Applications* (Ann Arbor: University of Michigan Press, 1970), and R. Duncan Luce and Howard Raiffa, *Games and Decisions: Introduction and Critical Survey* (New York: John Wiley and Sons, 1957).

5. Richard E. Walton and Robert B. McKersie, *A Behavioral Theory of Labor Negotiations: An Analysis of a Social Interaction System* (New York: McGraw Hill, 1965).

Bibliography

Books: General

Anderson, Charles W. *The Political Economy of Modern Spain: Policy-Making in an Authoritarian System.* Madison: University of Wisconsin Press, 1970.

————. *Politics and Economic Change in Latin America: The Governing of Restless Nations.* New York: D. Van Nostrand, 1967.

Cardoso, Fernando Henrique. *Ideologías de la burguesía industrial en sociedades dependientes: Argentina y Brazil.* Buenos Aires: Siglo Veintiuno Argentino Editores, 1971.

Cardoso, Fernando Henrique and Faleto, Enzo. *Dependencia y desarrollo en America Latina.* Buenos Aires: Siglo Veintiuno Argentino Editores, 1969.

Dahl, Robert A. *Polyarchy: Participation and Opposition.* New Haven: Yale University Press, 1971.

Drucker, Peter. *Management: Tasks, Practices, Responsibilities.* New York: Harper & Row, 1974.

Edelman, Murry and Fleming, R. W. *The Politics of Wage-Price Decisions: A Four Country Analysis.* Urbana: Univeristy of Illinois Press, 1965.

Galbraith, John Kenneth. *The New Industrial State.* Boston: Houghton Mifflin, 1967.

Gamson, William. *Power and Discontent.* Homewood, Ill.: The Dorsey Press, 1968.

Heclo, Hugh. *Modern Social Politics in Britain and Sweden: From Relief to Income Maintenance.* New Haven: Yale University Press, 1974.

Hirschman, Albert. *Journeys Toward Progress: Studies of Economic Policy-Making in Latin America.* New York: Anchor Books, 1963.

Huntington, Samuel P. *Political Order in Changing Societies.* New Haven: Yale University Press, 1968.

Johnson, John. *Political Change in Latin America: The Emergence of the Middle Sectors.* Stanford: Stanford University Press, 1958.

Kirschen, E. S., et al. *Economic Policy in Our Time.* vol. 1. Chicago: Rand McNally, 1967.

Lipset, Seymour M. *Political Man: Essays on the Sociology of Democracy.* New York: Anchor Books, 1963.

Lipset, Seymour M. and Solari, Aldo, eds. *Elites in Latin America.* Oxford: Oxford University Press, 1967.

Luce, R. Duncan and Raiffa, Howard. *Games and Decisions: Introduction and Critical Survey.* New York: John Wiley & Sons, 1967.

Malloy, James, ed. *Authoritarianism and Corporatism in Latin America.* Pittsburgh: University of Pittsburgh Press, 1977.

Pike, Frederick, and Stritch, Thomas, eds. *The New Corporatism: Social-Political Structures in the Iberian World.* Notre Dame: University of Notre Dame Press, 1974.

Powelson, John. *Institutions of Economic Growth: A Theory of Conflict Management in Developing Countries.* Princeton: Princeton University Press, 1972.

Rapoport, Anatol. *N-Person Game Theory: Concepts and Applications.* Ann Arbor: University of Michigan Press, 1969.

Roett, Riordon. *Brazil: Politics in a Patrimonial Society.* Boston: Allyn-Bacon, 1972.

Schmitter, Philippe C. *Interest Conflict and Political Change in Brazil*. Stanford: Stanford University Press, 1971.

Shonfield, Andrew. *Modern Capitalism: The Changing Balance of Public and Private Power*. Oxford: Oxford University Press, 1967.

Ulman, Lloyd and Flanagan, Robert J. *Wage Restraint: A Study of Incomes Policies in Western Europe*. Berkeley: University of California Press, 1971.

Veliz, Claudio, ed. *Obstacles to Change in Latin America*. Oxford: Oxford University Press, 1965.

Waldman, Sidney. *Foundations of Political Action: An Exchange Theory of Politics*. Boston: Little, Brown & Co., 1972.

Walton, Richard E., and McKersie, Robert B. *A Behavioral Theory of Labor Negotiations: An Analysis of a Social Interaction System*. New York: McGraw Hill, 1965.

Books: Argentina

Abot, Jorge, et al. *El poder económico en la Argentina*. Buenos Aires: Centro de Investigaciones en Ciencias Sociales, 1974.

Alemann, Roberto. *Curso de política económica argentina*. Buenos Aires: EUDEBA, 1970.

Alexander, Robert. *The Peron Era*. New York: Columbia University Press, 1951.

Alsogaray, Alvaro. *Bases para la acción política futura*. Buenos Aires: Editorial Atlantida, 1968.

————. *Política y economía en Latinoamerica*. Buenos Aires: Editorial Atlantida, 1969.

Argentato, Nicolás. *La inflación en la Argentina*. Buenos Aires: Asociación de Economistas Argentinos, 1968.

Bailey, Samuel. *Labor and Nationalism in Argentina*. New Brunswick: Rutgers University Press, 1967.

Banco Ganadero Argentina. *Temas de economía argentina: mercados y precios del ganado vacumo*. Buenos Aires, 1965.

Beveraggi Allende, Walter. *El dilema económico de la revolución: estudio crítico del Plan Prebisch*. Buenos Aires: edición del autor, 1956.

Blanksten, George. *Peron's Argentina*. Chicago: University of Chicago Press, 1953.

Borda, Guillermo; Costa Mendez, Nicor; Roth, Roberto; Diaz Coldrero, Mario; Vareal, Almirante Begigno J. *Cinco discursos y una revolución*. Buenos Aires: Publicaciones Movimiento Humanista de Derecho, 1968.

Braun, Oscar, ed. *El capitalismo argentino en crisis*. Buenos Aires: Siglo Veintiuno Argentino Editores, 1973.

Broner, Julio and Larriqueta, Daniel *La revolución industrial argentina*. Buenos Aires: Editorial Sudamericana, 1969.

Bunge, Alejandro. *Una nueva Argentina*. Buenos Aires: Editorial Guillermo Kraft, Ltd., 1940.

Cafiero, Antonio. *Cinco años después*. Buenos Aires: edición del autor, 1961.

Carri, Roberto. *Sindicatos y poder en la Argentina*. Buenos Aires; Susdestada, 1967.

Centro de Estudios de la Realidad Argentina. *Claves para la interpretación de la realidad argentina*. Buenos Aires: CERA, 1973.

Centro Internacional de Información Económica. *La economía argentina: treinta años en cifras*, cuaderno no. 2. Buenos Aires: CIDIE, 1971.

Cereijo, Ramón Antonio. *El plan económico de 1952 y la consolidación de la prosperidad nacional*. Buenos Aires, 1952.

———. *Hacía un mayor y mejor conocimiento de la verdadera situación económica argentina.* Buenos Aires, 1951.

Cuneo, Dardo. *Comportamiento y crisis de la clase empresaria.* Buenos Aires: Editorial Pleamar, 1967.

de Imaz, José Luis. *Los que mandan.* Buenos Aires: EUDEBA, 1964.

de Olariaga, Nemesio. *El ruralismo argentino: economía ganadera.* Buenos Aires: Editorial El Ateneo, 1943.

Diamand, Marcelo. *Doctrinas económicas, desarrollo e independencia.* Buenos Aires: Paidos, 1973.

Díaz Alejandro, Carlos. *Essays on the Economic History of the Argentine Republic.* New Haven: Yale University Press, 1970.

———. *Exchange Rate Devaluation in a Semi-Industrial Country.* Cambridge, Mass.: MIT Press, 1964.

Di Tella, Guido and Zymelman, Manuel, *Las etapas del desarrollo económico argentino.* Buenos Aires: EUDEBA, 1967.

Di Tella, Torcuarto. *El sistema político argentino y la clase obrera.* Buenos Aires: EUDEBA, 1964.

Di Tella, Torcuarto; Germani Gino; and Graciarena Jorge *Argentina: sociedad de masas.* Buenos Aires: EUDEBA, 1965.

Dorfman, Aldolfo. *Historia de la industria argentina.* Buenos Aires: Solar/Hachette, 1970.

Falcoff, Mark, and Dolkart, Ronald, eds. *Prelude to Perón* Berkeley: University of California Press, 1975.

Fayt, Carlos. *El politico armado: dinámica del proceso político argentino: 1960-1971.* Buenos Aires: Ediciones Pannedille, 1971.

———, ed. *La naturaleza del peronismo.* Buenos Aires: Viracocha, 1967.

Ferrer, Aldo. *The Argentine Economy.* Berkeley: University of California Press, 1967.

Ferrer, Aldo; Brodeshon, Mario; Eshag, Eprime; and Thorp, Rosemary. *Los planes de estabilización en la Argentina.* Buenos Aires: Paidos, 1969.

Figurola, José. *La colaboración social en Hispanoamérica.* Buenos Aires: Editorial Sudamericana, 1943.

Freels, John William Jr. *Industrial Trade Associations in Argentine Politics.* Ph.D. diss., University of California at Riverside, 1968.

Frigerio, Rogelio. *Crecimiento económico y democracia.* Buenos Aires: Losada, 1963.

———. *Estatuto del subdesarrollo.* Buenos Aires: Editorial Jorge Alvarez, 1967.

———. *Las condiciones de la victoria.* Buenos Aires: Monteverde, 1959.

———. *Los cuatro años (1958–1962): política económica para argentinos.* Buenos Aires: Ediciones Concordia, 1962.

———. *Petroleo.* Buenos Aires: Editorial Desarrollo, 1964.

Frondizi, Arturo. *Petroleo y nación.* Buenos Aires: Transición, 1963.

———. *Política económica nacional.* Buenos Aires: Ediciones Arayu, 1963.

Fuchs, Jaime. *Argentina: su desarrollo capitalista.* Buenos Aires: Editorial Cartago, 1965.

Fundación de Investigaciónes Económicas Latinoamericanas. *Las inversiones extranjeras en la Argentina.* Buenos Aires: FIEL, 1973.

Gambini, Hugo. *El primer gobierno peronista.* Buenos Aires: Centro Editor de America Latina, 1971.

García Martínez, Carlos. *La inflación argentina.* Buenos Aires: Guillermo Kraft, 1965.

García Martínez, Luis. *La revolución y las contradicciones nacionales.* Buenos Aires: Ediciones Argentina Contemporanea, 1970.

Germani, Gino *Política y sociedad en una epoca de transición: de la sociedad tradicional a la sociedad de las masas.* Buenos Aires: Paidos, 1962.

Giberti, Horacio. *Historia económica de la ganaderia argentina.* Buenos Aires: Hachette, 1961.

Gómez Morales, Alfredo. *Función del estado en la vida económica del país.* Buenos Aires: Banco Hipotecario Nacional, 1949.

———. *Política económica peronista.* Buenos Aires: Escuela Superior Peronista, 1951.

Grondona, Mariano. *La argentina en el tiempo y el mundo.* Buenos Aires: Editorial Primera Plana, 1967.

Guglialmelli, Juan Enrique. *120 días en el gobierno.* Buenos Aires: edición del autor, 1971.

Irazusta, Julio. *Perón y la crisis argentina.* Buenos Aires: La Voz del Plata, 1956.

Lascano, Marcelo Ramón. *El crecimiento económico, condición de la estabilidad monetaria en la Argentina.* Buenos Aires: EUDEBA, 1970.

———. *Presupuestos y dinero.* Buenos Aires: EUDEBA, 1972.

Lebedinsky, Mauricio. *Estructura de la ganaderia: historia y actual.* Buenos Aires: Editorial Quipo, 1967.

Luna, Felix. *Diálogos con Frondizi.* Buenos Aires: Editorial Desarrollo, 1963.

———. *El 45.* Buenos Aires: Editorial Sudamericana, 1971.

Margenat, Nidia. *Las organizaciónes corporativas del sector agraria y su posición frente a la renta potencial.* Buenos Aires: Centro de Investigaciones en Ciencias Sociales, 1973.

Martínez de Hoz (h), José Alfredo. *La agricultura y la ganaderia argentina en el periodo 1930–1960.* Buenos Aires: Editorial Sudamericana, 1967.

Melo, Carlos R. *Los partidos políticos argentinos.* Cordoba: Universidad Nacional de Córdoba, 1964.

Mende, Raul A. *El justicialismo.* Buenos Aires: Guillermo Kraft, 1951.

Monti, Angel. *Proyecto nacional: razón y diseño.* Buenos Aires: Paidos, 1972.

Murmis, Miguel and Portantiero, Juan Carlos, *Estudios sobre los origenes del peronismo.* Buenos Aires: Siglo Veintiuno Editores, 1971.

O'Donnell, Guillermo A. *Modernization and Bureaucratic Authoritarianism: Studies in South American Politics.* University of California Institute of International Studies, Politics of Modernization Series, no. 9, Berkeley, 1973.

O'Donnell, Guillermo A. and Linck, Delfina. *Dependencia y autonomia.* Buenos Aires: Amorrortu, 1973.

Olarra Jimenez, Rafael. *Evolución monetaria argentina.* Buenos Aires: EUDEBA, 1971.

Pazos, Felipe. *Medidas para detener la inflación crónica en América Latina.* Mexico: CEMLA, 1969.

Peña, Miciades. *Masas, caudillos y elites.* Buenos Aires: Ediciones Fichas, 1971.

Peralta Ramos, Mónica. *Etapas de acumulación y alianzas de clases en la Argentina 1930–1960.* Buenos Aires: Siglo Veintiuno Argentina Editores, 1972.

Pereira Pinto, Juan Carlos. *Aspectos de la historia económica de la República Argentina durante los últimos setenta años 1900–1971.* Buenos Aires: Editorial El Coloquio, 1973.

Perón, Juan. *Doctrina peronista: filosofía política social.* Buenos Aires: Editorial Fidelius, 1947.

———. *Filosofía peronista.* Buenos Aires: Editorial Mundo Peronista, 1954.

———. *Los vendepatria.* Buenos Aires: Editorial Liberacion, 1958.

Petras, James, ed. *Latin America: From Dependence to Revolution.* New York: John Wiley & Sons, 1973.

Pinedo, Federico. *En tiempos de la república y después.* 5 vols. Buenos Aires: Editorial Mundo Forense, 1949.

———. *Siglo y medio de economía argentina.* Mexico City: CEMLA, 1961.

———. *Trabajoso resurgimiento argentino.* 2 vols. Buenos Aires: Ediciones Fundación Banco de Galicia y Buenos Aires, 1968.

Prieto, Ramón. *El pacto: ocho años de la política argentina.* Buenos Aires: Editorial en Marcha, 1963.

Potash, Robert. *The Army and Politics in Argentina 1928–1945*. Stanford: Stanford University Press, 1969.

Puiggrós, Rodolfo. *La democracia fraudulenta*. Buenos Aires: Editorial Jorge Alvarez, 1968.

———. *Libre empresa o nacionalización en la industria de la carne*. Buenos Aires: Editorial Argumentos, 1957.

Rotondaro, Rubén. *Realidad y cambio en el sindicalismo*. Buenos Aires: Editorial Pleamar, 1971.

Scobie, James. *Argentina: A City and a Nation*, 2d ed. New York: Oxford University Press, 1971.

———. *Revolution on the Pampas: A Social History of Argentine Wheat, 1860-1910*. Austin: University of Texas Press, 1964.

Senen Gonzalez, Santiago. *El sindicalismo después de Perón*. Buenos Aires: Editorial Galerna, 1971.

Sigaut, Lorenzo Juan. *Acerca de la distribución y niveles de ingreso en la argentina 1950-1972*. Buenos Aires: Ediciones Macchi, 1972.

Skupch, Pedro R. *Concentración industrial en la Argentina 1956–1966*. Buenos Aires: Editorial El Coloquio, 1972.

Sobel, Lester A., ed. *Argentina and Peron, 1970–1975*. New York: Facts on File, 1975.

Smith, Peter. *Argentina and the Failure of Democracy: Conflict Among Political Elites, 1904-1955*. Madison: University of Wisconsin Press, 1974.

———. *Politics and Beef in Argentina*. New York: Columbia University Press, 1969.

Taylor, Carl C. *Rural Life in Argentina*. Baton Rouge: Louisiana State University Press, 1948.

Truber, Salvador. *La empresa estatal argentina*. Buenos Aires: Ediciones Macchi, 1969.

Villanueva, Javier. *The Inflationary Process in Argentina 1943-1960*. Ph.D. dissertation, Columbia University, 1964.

Villar, Daniel. *El cordobazo*. Buenos Aires: Centro Editor de America, 1971.

Villegas, Osiris Guillermo. *Políticas y estrategias para el desarrollo y la seguridad*. Buenos Aires: Pleamar, 1969.

Weil, Felix J. *Argentine Riddle*. New York: The John Day Company, 1944.

Articles

Ayres, Robert. "Development Policy and the Possibility of a 'Livable' Future for Latin America," *American Political Science Review* 69(1975):507–23.

Aleman, Roberto, "Economic Development in Argentina." In *Economic Development Issues: Latin America*, edited by Ray Blough. New York: Praeger, 1967.

Chambers, Edward L., "Some Factors in the Deterioration of Argentina's External Position 1946-1951," *Inter-American Economic Affairs* 8(1954):27–62.

Di Tella, Torcuarto, "Stalemate or Coexistence in Argentina." In *Latin America: Reform or Revolution*, edited by James Petras and Maurice Zeitlin. New York: Fawcett, 1968.

Gravil, Roger, "State Intervention in Argentina's Export Trade Between the Wars," *Journal of Latin American Studies* 2(1970):147–73.

Herschel, Federico Julio and Itzcovich, Samuel, "Fiscal Policy in Argentina," *Public Finance* 12(1957):97–115.

Hirschman, Albert, "Policymaking and Policy Analysis in Latin America: A Return Journey," *Policy Sciences* 6(1975):385–402.

Lanning, Eldon, "A Typology of Latin American Political Systems," *Comparative Politics* 6(1974):367–94.

Kenworthy, Eldon, "The Function of the Little Known Case in Theory Formation or What Peronism Wasn't," *Comparative Politics* 6(1973):17–46.

MacDonell, Stella M. and Lascano, Marcelo R. "Incentivos triutarios y ciclo ganadero 1962–1972." In *La producción rural Argentina en 1974*. Buenos Aires: Banco Ganadero, 1975, 65-74.

Merkx, Gilbert W., "Sectoral Clashes and Political Change: The Argentine Experience," *Latin American Research Review* 4(1969):89–114.

Randall, Laura, "Economic Development Policies and Argentine Economic Growth." In *Economic Development: Evolution or Revolution*, edited by Laura Randall. Boston: D.C. Health, 1964.

Schmitter, Philippe, "Still the Century of Corporatism?" *Review of Politics* 36(1974):85–131.

Thompson, John, "Argentine Economic Policy Under the Onganía Regime," *Inter-American Economic Affairs* 24(1970):51–76.

Winkler, J. T., "Corporatism," *European Journal of Sociology* 17(1976):100–136.

Yordon, Wesley J, "Inflation in Argentina: The Monetary Consequences of Social Conflict," *Western Economic Journal* 4(1965):72–90.

Zuvekas, Clarence, "Argentine Economic Policy 1958-1962: The Frondizi Government's Development Plan," *Inter-American Economic Affairs* 22(1968):45–74.

Public Documents; International and Foreign

Banco Interamericano de Desarrollo y Deltec Panamerica, S.A. *El mercado de capitales en Argentina*. Mexico: CEMLA, 1968.

Inter-American Committee for Agricultural Development. *Land Tenure Conditions and Socio-Economic Development of the Agricultural Sector: Argentina*. Washington: Pan American Union, 1965.

International Bank for Reconstruction and Development. *Private Foreign Direct Investment in Developing Countries*, Bank Staff Working Paper No. 14, 1973.

United Nations. Economic Commission for Latin America. *Economic Bulletin for Latin America*, Vol. 1, no. 1 (January 1956).

———. ———. *Economic Development and Income Distribution in Argentina*. New York, 1969.

———. ———. *The Economic Development of Latin America and Its Principal Problems*. New York, 1950.

United States. Agency for International Development. *Summary of Economic and Social Indicators*. Washington, D.C., 1972.

United States. Department of Agriculture. *Argentina: Growth Potential of the Grain and Livestock Sectors*. Foreign Agricultural Economic Report No. 78. Washington, D.C., 1972.

Public Documents: Argentina

República Argentina . Banco Central de la República. *Memorias*, 1944–1973 (annual).

———. ———. *Origen del producto y distribución del ingreso: años 1950–1969*. enero de 1971.

———. Comisión Asesora de Economía y Finanzas. *Dictamen sobre el "Plan de Restablecimiento Economico*," febrero de 1956.

———. ———. *Dictamen sobre control de precios*, junio de 1956.

———. Congreso Nacional. Diario de Sesiones. Cámara de Diputados. 34ª Reunion, 4ª sesion extraordinaria, 13 de agosto de 1959. (debate sobre el Plan de Estabilización y Desarrollo Económico.).

——. ——. ——. Cámara de Senadores. *43ª Reunion, 4ª sesion extraordinaria, 17 y 18 de diciembre de 1940* (debate sobre el Plan Pinedo.)

——. Consejo Económico Nacional. *El panorama económico del país en el segundo semestre de 1951 y perspectivas para 1952.* junio de 1951.

——. ——. *Situación económica actual y perspectivas para 1952,* noviembre de 1951.

——. ——. *Situación económica del país: examen de la situación económica del país at 31 enero de 1949.*

——. *Dirección Nacional de Investigación Estadística y Censos. Síntesis estadística mensual de la Republica,* Año I, no. 1, enero de 1947.

——. Ministerio de Agricultura y Ganaderia. *Arrendamientos y aparcerias rurales: leyes y decretos anteriores a la ley No. 13,246,* 1949.

——. ——. *Arrendamientos y aparcerias rurales: Ley No. 13,246 y reglamentación general,* 1949.

——. Ministerio de Economía y Trabajo. *Política económica argentina: discursos del Minstro de Economía y Trabajo,* 1968.

——. Ministerio de Finanzas. *Memorias 1949–1954* (annual).

——. Ministerio de Hacienda. *El ordenamiento económico-finaciero en el plan de gobierno 1947-1951,* enero de 1947.

——. ——. *Informe sobre la situación económica argentina a principios de 1957,* preparado por Roberto Verrier, marzo de 1957.

——. ——. *Memorias 1947-1952* (annual).

——. Presidencia de la Nación. Consejo Nacional de Desarrollo. *Plan nacional de desarrollo 1965-1969.*

——. ——. ——. *Tenencia de la tierra,* 1964.

——. ——. ——. *Censo nacional agropecuario 1969: datos comparativos 1969 y 1960.*

——. ——. Consejo Nacional de Desarrollo y Consejo Nacional de Seguridad. *Plan nacional de desarrollo y seguridad 1971-1975.*

——. *Libro negro de la segunda tirania,* 1958.

Argentine Economic Interest Group Publications

Cámara Argentina de Comercio, *Memorias y Balances,* 1946–1969 (annual).

Cámara de Frigoríficas Regionales, *Evolución económico-financiera de la industria frigorifica,* 1972.

Confederación General Económica. *Memorias y Balances,* 1960–1973 (annual).

Confederaciónes Rurales Argentinas. *V Congreso Rural Argentino,* 1947.

Confederaciones Rurales de Buenos Aires y La Pampa. *XX Congreso Rural,* 1942, *XXI Congreso Rural,* 1946, *XXII Congreso Rural,* 1958.

——. *Memorias y Balances,* 1945–1973 (annual).

Federación Agraria Argentina. *Conclusiones de los congresos ordinarios anuales,* 1960–1972 (annual).

——. *Los problemas actuales del agro,* 1956.

——. *Memorias y Balances,* 1960–1972 (annual).

——. *Un grito, una historia, una realidad,* 1971.

Sociedad Rural Argentina. *Memorias de la Sociedad Rural Argentina,* 1943–1973 (annual).

Unión Industrial Argentina. *Guia de socios,* 1970.

——. *Memorias y Balances,* 1935–1945, 1957–1973 (annual).

——. *Seis leyes económicas,* tercera edicion, 1943.

Periodicals

Analisis, 1963–1973 (weekly).

Banco de Boston, *The Situation in Argentina,* 1943–1973 (monthly).

Consejo Técnico de Inversiones, *La economía argentina,* 1962–1973 (annual).

Economic Survey, 1945–1973 (weekly).

El Cronista Comercial Anuario, diciembre de 1972.

El Economista, 1950–1973 (weekly).

Hechos e Ideas, 1945–1955 (monthly).

Horizones Economicos, 1946–1955 (monthly).

La Nación, 1945–1973 (daily).

La Opinión 1971–1975 (daily).

Latin America Political Report, 1973–1977 (weekly).

Latin America Economic Report, 1976–1977 (weekly).

Organización Techint. *Boletines Informativos nos. 170–88,* 1969–1972 (bi-monthly).

Panorama de la Economia Argentina, 1959–1970 (quarterly).

Pulso, 1966–1973 (weekly).

Review of the River Plate, 1943–1973 (thrice monthly).

Veritas, 15 de diciembre de 1970.

Index

DATE DUE

NOV 2 7 1997

GAYLORD

PRINT